John Fiske

The Beginnings of New England

The Puritan Theocracy in its Relation to Civil and Religious Liberty

John Fiske

The Beginnings of New England
The Puritan Theocracy in its Relation to Civil and Religious Liberty

ISBN/EAN: 9783337128838

Printed in Europe, USA, Canada, Australia, Japan

Cover: Foto ©Lupo / pixelio.de

More available books at **www.hansebooks.com**

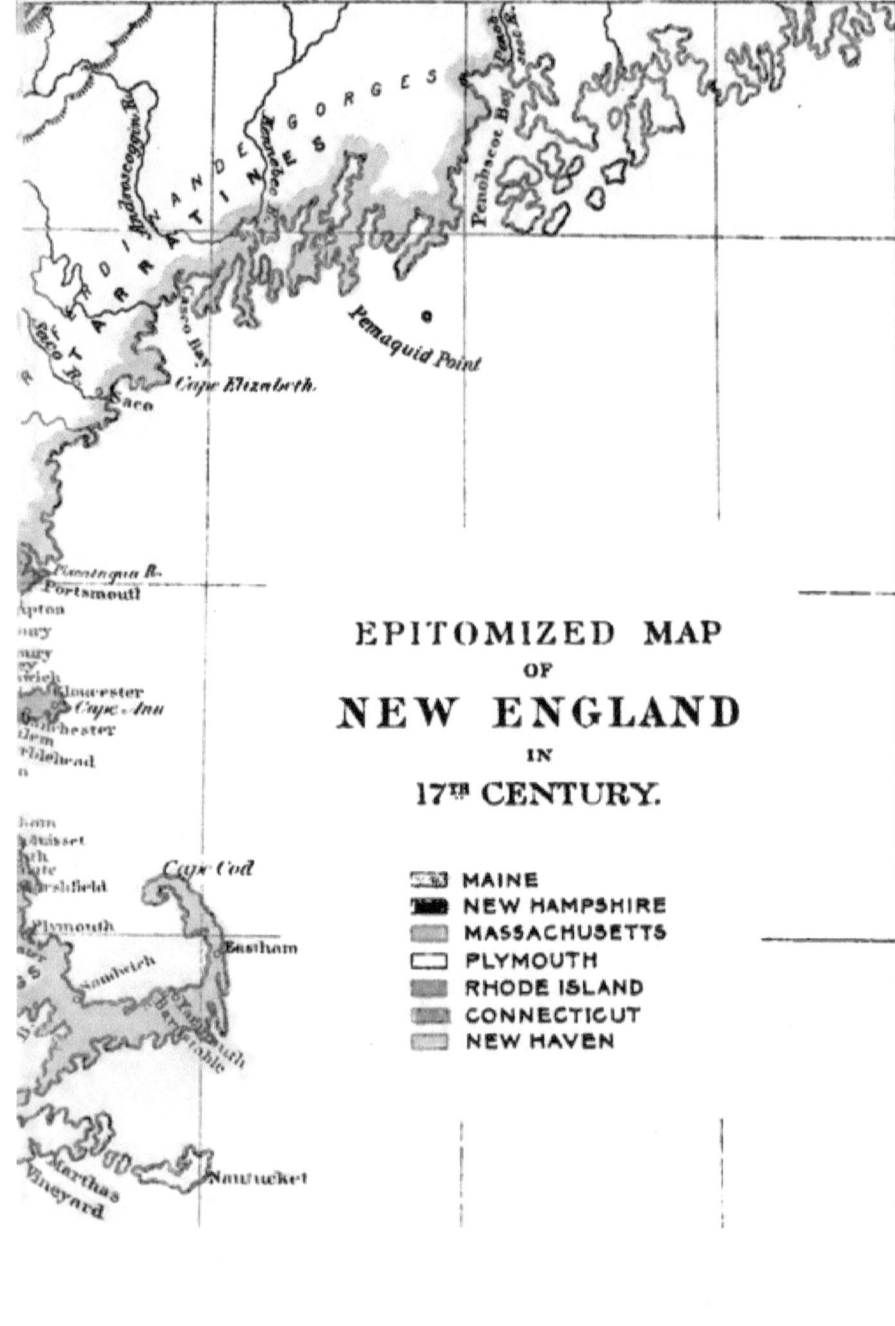

THE BEGINNINGS OF NEW ENGLAND
OR THE PURITAN THEOCRACY IN ITS RELATIONS TO CIVIL AND RELIGIOUS LIBERTY

BY

JOHN FISKE

"The Lord Christ intends to achieve greater matters by this little handful than the world is aware of." — EDWARD JOHNSON, *Wonder-Working Providence of Zion's Saviour in New England.* 1654.

BOSTON AND NEW YORK
HOUGHTON, MIFFLIN AND COMPANY
The Riverside Press, Cambridge
1899

To

MY DEAR CLASSMATES,

BENJAMIN THOMPSON FROTHINGHAM,

WILLIAM AUGUSTUS WHITE,

AND

FREDERIC CROMWELL,

I dedicate this Book.

PREFACE.

THIS book contains the substance of the lectures originally given at the Washington University, St. Louis, in May, 1887, in the course of my annual visit to that institution as University Professor of American History. The lectures were repeated in the following month of June at Portland, Oregon, and since then either the whole course, or one or more of the lectures, have been given in Boston, Newton, Milton, Chelsea, New Bedford, Lowell; Worcester, Springfield, and Pittsfield, Mass. Farmington, Middletown, and Stamford, Conn.; New York, Brooklyn, and Tarrytown, N. Y.; Philadelphia and Ogontz, Pa.; Wilmington, Del.; Chicago, Ill.; San Francisco and Oakland, Cal.

In this sketch of the circumstances which attended the settlement of New England, I have purposely omitted many details which in a formal history of that period would need to be included. It has been my aim to give the outline of such a narrative as to indicate the principles at work in the history of New England down to the Revolution of 1689. When I was writing the lectures I had just been reading, with much interest, the work of my former pupil, Mr. Brooks Adams, entitled "The Emancipation of Massachusetts." With the specific conclusions set forth in that book I found myself often agreeing, but it seemed to me that the general aspect of the case would be considerably modified and perhaps somewhat more adequately presented by enlarging the field of view. In forming historical judgments a great deal depends upon our perspective. Out of the very imperfect human nature which is so slowly and painfully casting off the original sin of its inheritance from primeval savagery, it is scarcely possible in any age to get a result which will look quite satisfactory to the men of a riper and more enlightened age. Fortunately we can learn something from the stumblings of our forefathers, and a good many things seem quite clear to us to-day which two centuries ago were only beginning to be dimly discerned by a few of the keenest and boldest spirits. The faults of the Puritan theocracy, which found its most complete development in Massachusetts, are so glaring that it is idle to seek to palliate them or to explain them away. But if we would really understand what was going on in the Puritan world of the seventeenth century, and how a better state of things has grown out of it, we must endeavour to distinguish and define the elements of wholesome strength in that theocracy no less than its elements of crudity and weakness.

The first chapter, on "The Roman Idea and the English Idea," contains a somewhat more developed statement of the points briefly indicated in the thirteenth section (pp. 85–95) of "The Destiny of Man." As all of the present book, except the first chapter, was written here under the shadow of the Washington University, I take pleasure in dating it from this charming and hospitable city where I have passed some of the most delightful hours of my life.

ST. LOUIS, *April* 15, 1889.

CONTENTS.

CHAPTER I.
THE ROMAN IDEA AND THE ENGLISH IDEA.

	PAGE
When did the Roman Empire come to an end?	1–3
Meaning of Odovakar's work	3
The Holy Roman Empire	4, 5
Gradual shifting of primacy from the men who spoke Latin, and their descendants, to the men who speak English	6–8
Political history is the history of nation-making	8, 9
The ORIENTAL method of nation-making; *conquest without incorporation*	9
Illustrations from eastern despotisms	10
And from the Moors in Spain	11
The ROMAN method of nation-making; *conquest with incorporation, but without representation*	12
Its slow development	13
Vices in the Roman system	14
Its fundamental defect	15
It knew nothing of political power delegated by the people to representatives	16
And therefore the expansion of its dominion ended in a centralized despotism	16
Which entailed the danger that human life might come to stagnate in Europe, as it had done in Asia	17
The danger was warded off by the Germanic invasions, which, however, threatened to undo the work which the Empire had done in organizing European society	17
But such disintegration was prevented by the sway which the Roman Church had come to exercise over the European mind	18
The wonderful thirteenth century	19
The ENGLISH method of nation-making; *incorporation with representation*	20

CONTENTS.

Pacific tendencies of federalism 21
Failure of Greek attempts at federation 22
Fallacy of the notion that republics must be small . . 23
"It is not the business of a government to support its people, but of the people to support their government" . 24
Teutonic March-meetings and representative assemblies . 25
Peculiarity of the Teutonic conquest of Britain . . 26, 27
Survival and development of the Teutonic representative assembly in England 28
Primitive Teutonic institutions less modified in England than in Germany 29
Some effects of the Norman conquest of England . . 30
The Barons' War and the first House of Commons . . 31
Eternal vigilance is the price of liberty 32
Conflict between Roman Idea and English Idea begins to become clearly visible in the thirteenth century . . 33
Decline of mediæval Empire and Church with the growth of modern nationalities 34
Overthrow of feudalism, and increasing power of the crown 35
Formidable strength of the Roman Idea . . . 36
Had it not been for the Puritans, political liberty would probably have disappeared from the world . . 37
Beginnings of Protestantism in the thirteenth century . . 38
The Cathari, or Puritans of the Eastern Empire . . 39
The Albigenses 40
Effects of persecution; its feebleness in England . . 41
Wyclif and the Lollards 42
Political character of Henry VIII.'s revolt against Rome . 43
The yeoman Hugh Latimer 44
The moment of Cromwell's triumph was the most critical moment in history 45
Contrast with France; fate of the Huguenots . . 46, 47
Victory of the English Idea 48
Significance of the Puritan Exodus 49

CHAPTER II.

THE PURITAN EXODUS.

Influence of Puritanism upon modern Europe . . 50, 51
Work of the Lollards 52
They made the Bible the first truly popular literature in England 53, 54
The English version of the Bible 54, 55

CONTENTS.

Secret of Henry VIII.'s swift success in his revolt against Rome 56
Effects of the persecution under Mary 57
Calvin's theology in its political bearings . . . 58, 59
Elizabeth's policy and its effects 60, 61
Puritan sea-rovers 61
Geographical distribution of Puritanism in England; it was strongest in the eastern counties 62
Preponderance of East Anglia in the Puritan exodus . . 63
Familiar features of East Anglia to the visitor from New England 64
Puritanism was not intentionally allied with liberalism . 65
Robert Brown and the Separatists 66
Persecution of the Separatists 67
Recantation of Brown; it was reserved for William Brewster to take the lead in the Puritan exodus 68
James Stuart, and his encounter with Andrew Melville . 69
What James intended to do when he became King of England 70
His view of the political situation, as declared in the conference at Hampton Court 71
The congregation of Separatists at Scrooby 72
The flight to Holland, and settlement at Leyden in 1609 . 73
Systematic legal toleration in Holland 74
Why the Pilgrims did not stay there; they wished to keep up their distinct organization and found a state . . 74
And to do this they must cross the ocean, because European territory was all preoccupied 75
The London and Plymouth companies 75
First explorations of the New England coast; Bartholomew Gosnold (1602), and George Weymouth (1605) . . . 76
The Popham colony (1607) 77
Captain John Smith gives to New England its name (1614) . 78
The Pilgrims at Leyden decide to make a settlement near the Delaware river 79
How King James regarded the enterprise 80
Voyage of the Mayflower; she goes astray and takes the Pilgrims to Cape Cod bay 81
Founding of the Plymouth colony (1620) . . . 82, 83
Why the Indians did not molest the settlers . . . 84, 85
The chief interest of this beginning of the Puritan exodus lies not so much in what it achieved as in what it suggested 86, 87

CHAPTER III.

THE PLANTING OF NEW ENGLAND.

Sir Ferdinando Gorges and the Council for New England	88, 89
Wessagusset and Merrymount	90, 91
The Dorchester adventurers	92
John White wishes to " raise a bulwark against the Kingdom of Antichrist	93
And John Endicott undertakes the work of building it	94
Conflicting grants sow seeds of trouble; the Gorges and Mason claims	94, 95
Endicott's arrival in New England, and the founding of Salem	95
The Company of Massachusetts Bay; Francis Higginson takes a powerful reinforcement to Salem	96
The development of John White's enterprise into the Company of Massachusetts Bay coincided with the first four years of the reign of Charles I.	97
Extraordinary scene in the House of Commons (June 5, 1628)	98, 99
The King turns Parliament out of doors (March 2, 1629)	100
Desperate nature of the crisis	100, 101
The meeting at Cambridge (Aug. 26, 1629), and decision to transfer the charter of the Massachusetts Bay Company, and the government established under it, to New England	102
Leaders of the great migration; John Winthrop	102
And Thomas Dudley	103
Founding of Massachusetts; the schemes of Gorges overwhelmed	104
Beginnings of American constitutional history; the question as to self-government raised at Watertown	105
Representative system established	106
Bicameral assembly; story of the stray pig	107
Ecclesiastical polity; the triumph of Separatism	108
Restriction of the suffrage to members of the Puritan congregational churches	109
Founding of Harvard College	110
Threefold danger to the New England settlers in 1636: —	
1. From the King, who prepares to attack the charter, but is foiled by dissensions at home	111–113
2. From religious dissensions; Roger Williams	114–116
Henry Vane and Anne Hutchinson	116–119
Beginnings of New Hampshire and Rhode Island	119–120

3. From the Indians; the Pequot supremacy 121
First movements into the Connecticut valley, and disputes
    with the Dutch settlers of New Amsterdam . . 122, 123
Restriction of the suffrage leads to disaffection in Massachu-
    setts; profoundly interesting opinions of Winthrop and
    Hooker 123, 124
Connecticut pioneers and their hardships 125
Thomas Hooker, and the founding of Connecticut . . 126
The Fundamental Orders of Connecticut (Jan. 14, 1639);
    the first written constitution that created a government . 127
Relations of Connecticut to the genesis of the Federal
    Union 128
Origin of the Pequot War; Sassacus tries to unite the Indian
    tribes in a crusade against the English . . . 129, 130
The schemes of Sassacus are foiled by Roger Williams . 130
The Pequots take the war path alone 131
And are exterminated 132–134
John Davenport, and the founding of New Haven . . 135
New Haven legislation, and legend of the "Blue Laws" . 136
With the meeting of the Long Parliament, in 1640, the
    Puritan exodus comes to its end 137
What might have been 138, 391

CHAPTER IV.

THE NEW ENGLAND CONFEDERACY.

The Puritan exodus was purely and exclusively English . 140
And the settlers were all thrifty and prosperous; chiefly
    country squires and yeomanry of the best and sturdiest
    type 141, 142
In all history there has been no other instance of colonization
    so exclusively effected by picked and chosen men . . 143
What, then, was the principle of selection? The migration
    was not intended to promote what we call religious
    liberty 144, 145
Theocratic ideal of the Puritans 146
The impulse which sought to realize itself in the Puritan
    ideal was an ethical impulse 147
In interpreting Scripture, the Puritan appealed to his
    reason 148, 149
Value of such perpetual theological discussion as was car-
    ried on in early New England 150, 151

CONTENTS.

Comparison with the history of Scotland 152
Bearing of these considerations upon the history of the New
  England confederacy 153
The existence of so many colonies (Plymouth, Massachu-
  setts, Connecticut, New Haven, Rhode Island, the Pis-
  cataqua towns, etc.) was due to differences of opinion on
  questions in which men's religious ideas were involved . 154
And this multiplication of colonies led to a notable and sig-
  nificant attempt at confederation 155
Turbulence of dissent in Rhode Island 156
The Earl of Warwick, and his Board of Commissioners . 157
Constitution of the Confederacy 158
It was only a league, not a federal union 159
Its formation involved a tacit assumption of sovereignty . 160
The fall of Charles I. brought up, for a moment, the ques-
  tion as to the supremacy of Parliament over the colonies . 161
Some interesting questions 162
Genesis of the persecuting spirit 163
Samuel Gorton and his opinions 163–165
He flees to Aquedneck and is banished thence . . . 166
Providence protests against him 167
He flees to Shawomet, where he buys land of the Indians . 168
Miantonomo and Uncas 169, 170
Death of Miantonomo 171
Edward Johnson leads an expedition against Shawomet . 172
Trial and sentence of the heretics 173
Winthrop declares himself in a prophetic opinion . . . 174
The Presbyterian cabal 175–177
The Cambridge Platform; deaths of Winthrop and Cotton . 177
Views of Winthrop and Cotton as to toleration in matters of
  religion 178
After their death, the leadership in Massachusetts was in the
  hands of Endicott and Norton 179
The Quakers; their opinions and behavior . . . 179–181
Violent manifestations of dissent 182
Anne Austin and Mary Fisher; how they were received in
  Boston 183
The confederated colonies seek to expel the Quakers; noble
  attitude of Rhode Island 184
Roger Williams appeals to his friend, Oliver Cromwell . 185
The "heavenly speech" of Sir Harry Vane 185
Laws passed against the Quakers 186
How the death penalty was regarded at that time in New
  England 187

CONTENTS.   XV

Executions of Quakers on Boston Common . . . 188, 189
Wenlock Christison's defiance and victory . . . 189, 190
The "King's Missive" 191
Why Charles II. interfered to protect the Quakers . . 191
His hostile feeling toward the New England governments . 192
The regicide judges, Goffe and Whalley . . . 193, 194
New Haven annexed to Connecticut 194, 195
Abraham Pierson, and the founding of Newark . . . 196
Breaking-down of the theocratic policy 197
Weakening of the Confederacy 198

CHAPTER V.

KING PHILIP'S WAR.

Relations between the Puritan settlers and the Indians . . 199
Trade with the Indians 200
Missionary work; Thomas Mayhew 201
John Eliot and his translation of the Bible . . . 202
His preaching to the Indians 203
His villages of Christian Indians 204
The Puritan's intention was to deal gently and honourably
    with the red men 205
Why Pennsylvania was so long unmolested by the Indians, 205, 206
Difficulty of the situation in New England 207
It is hard for the savage and the civilized man to understand
    one another 208
How Eliot's designs must inevitably have been misinter-
    preted by the Indians 209
It is remarkable that peace should have been so long pre-
    served 210
Deaths of Massasoit and his son Alexander 211
Very little is known about the nature of Philip's designs . 212
The meeting at Taunton 213
Sausamon informs against Philip 213
And is murdered 214
Massacres at Swanzey and Dartmouth 214
Murder of Captain Hutchinson 215
Attack on Brookfield, which is relieved by Simon Willard . 216
Fighting in the Connecticut valley; the mysterious stranger
    at Hadley 217, 218
Ambuscade at Bloody Brook 219
Popular excitement in Boston 220

The Narragansetts prepare to take the war-path . . . 221
And Governor Winslow leads an army against them . 222, 223
Storming of the great swamp fortress 224
Slaughter of the Indians 225
Effect of the blow 226
Growth of the humane sentiment in recent times, due to the fact that the horrors of war are seldom brought home to everybody's door 227, 228
Warfare with savages is likely to be truculent in character . 229
Attack upon Lancaster 230
Mrs. Rowlandson's narrative 231–233
Virtual extermination of the Indians (February to August, 1676) 233, 234
Death of Canonchet 234
Philip pursued by Captain Church 235
Death of Philip 236
Indians sold into slavery 237
Conduct of the Christian Indians 238
War with the Tarratines 239
Frightful destruction of life and property 240
Henceforth the red man figures no more in the history of New England, except in frontier raids under French guidance 241

CHAPTER VI.

THE TYRANNY OF ANDROS.

Romantic features in the early history of New England . 242
Captain Edward Johnson, of Woburn, and his book on "The Wonder-working Providence of Zion's Saviour in New England" 243, 244
Acts of the Puritans often judged by an unreal and impossible standard 245
Spirit of the "Wonder-working Providence" . . . 246
Merits and faults of the Puritan theocracy 247
Restriction of the suffrage to church members . . . 248
It was a source of political discontent 249
Inquisitorial administration of justice 250
The "Halfway Covenant" 251
Founding of the Old South church 252
Unfriendly relations between Charles II. and Massachusetts 253
Complaints against Massachusetts 254

CONTENTS. xvii

The Lords of Trade 255
Arrival of Edward Randolph in Boston 256
Joseph Dudley and the beginnings of Toryism in New England 257, 258
Charles II. erects the four Piscataqua towns into the royal province of New Hampshire 259
And quarrels with Massachusetts over the settlement of the Gorges claim to the Maine district 260
Simon Bradstreet and his verse-making wife 261
Massachusetts answers the king's peremptory message . . 262
Secret treaty between Charles II. and Louis XIV. . . 263
Shameful proceedings in England 264
Massachusetts refuses to surrender her charter; and accordingly it is annulled by decree of chancery, June 21, 1684 . 265
Effect of annulling the charter 266
Death of Charles II., accession of James II., and appointment of Sir Edmund Andros as viceroy over New England, with despotic powers 267
The charter oak 268
Episcopal services in Boston 268, 269
Founding of the King's Chapel 269
The tyranny 270
John Wise of Ipswich 271
Fall of James II. 271
Insurrection in Boston, and overthrow of Andros . . . 272
Effects of the Revolution of 1689 273
Need for union among all the northern colonies . . . 274
Plymouth, Maine, and Acadia annexed to Massachusetts . 275
Which becomes a royal province 276
And is thus brought into political sympathy with Virginia . 276
The seeds of the American Revolution were already sown, and the spirit of 1776 was foreshadowed in 1689 . 277, 278

THE BEGINNINGS OF NEW ENGLAND.

CHAPTER I.

THE ROMAN IDEA AND THE ENGLISH IDEA.

It used to be the fashion of historians, looking superficially at the facts presented in chronicles and tables of dates, without analyzing and comparing vast groups of facts distributed through centuries, or even suspecting the need for such analysis and comparison, to assign the date 476 A. D. as the moment at which the Roman Empire came to an end. It was in that year that the soldier of fortune, Odovakar, commander of the Herulian mercenaries in Italy, sent the handsome boy Romulus, son of Orestes, better known as "little Augustus," from his imperial throne to the splendid villa of Lucullus near Naples, and gave him a yearly pension of $35,000 [6,000 solidi] to console him for the loss of a world. As 324 years elapsed before another emperor was crowned at Rome, and as the political headship of Europe after that happy restoration remained upon the German soil to which the events of the eighth century had shifted it, nothing could seem

When did the Roman Empire come to an end?

more natural than the habit which historians once had, of saying that the mighty career of Rome had ended, as it had begun, with a Romulus. Sometimes the date 476 was even set up as a great landmark dividing modern from ancient history. For those, however, who took such a view, it was impossible to see the events of the Middle Ages in their true relations to what went before and what came after. It was impossible to understand what went on in Italy in the sixth century, or to explain the position of that great Roman power which had its centre on the Bosphorus, which in the code of Justinian left us our grandest monument of Roman law, and which for a thousand years was the staunch bulwark of Europe against the successive aggressions of Persian, Saracen, and Turk. It was equally impossible to understand the rise of the Papal power, the all-important politics of the great Saxon and Swabian emperors, the relations of mediæval England to the Continental powers, or the marvellously interesting growth of the modern European system of nationalities.

Since the middle of the nineteenth century the study of history has undergone changes no less sweeping than those which have in the same time affected the study of the physical sciences. Vast groups of facts distributed through various ages and countries have been subjected to comparison and analysis, with the result that they have not only thrown fresh light upon one another, but have in many cases enabled us to recover historic points of view that had long been buried in oblivion. Such an instance was furnished about twenty-five years ago by Dr. Bryce's epoch-making work on the Holy Roman Empire. Since then historians still recognize the importance of the date 476 as that which left the Bishop of Rome the dominant personage in Italy, and marked the shifting of the political centre of gravity from the Palatine to the Lateran. This was one of those subtle changes which escape notice until after some of their effects have attracted attention. The most important effect, in this instance, realized after three centuries, was not the overthrow of Roman power in the West, but its indefinite extension and expansion. The men of 476 not only had no idea that they were entering upon a new era, but least of all did they dream that the Roman Empire had come to an end, or was ever likely to. Its cities might be pillaged, its provinces overrun, but the supreme imperial power itself was something without which the men of those days could not imagine the world as existing. It must have its divinely ordained representative in one place if not in another. If the throne in Italy was vacant, it was no more than had happened before; there was still a throne at Constantinople, and to its occupant Zeno the Roman Senate sent a message, saying that one emperor was enough for both ends of the earth, and begging him to confer upon the gallant Odovakar the title of patrician, and entrust the affairs of Italy to his care. So when Sicambrian Chlodwig set up his Merovingian kingdom in northern Gaul, he was glad to array himself in the robe of a Roman consul, and obtain from the eastern emperor a formal ratification of his rule.

Meaning of Odovakar's work.

Countless examples show that the event of 476 was understood as the virtual reunion of West and East under a single head; whereas, on the other hand, the impressive scene in the basilica of St. Peter's on the Christmas of 800, when Pope Leo III. placed the diadem of the Cæsars upon the Frankish brow of Charles the Great, was regarded, not as the restoration of an empire once extinguished, but as a new separation between East and West, a re-transfer of the world's political centre from the Bosphorus to the Tiber. When after two centuries more the sceptre had passed from the line of Frankish Charles to the line of Saxon Otto, this Holy Roman Empire, shaped by the alliance of German king with Italian pontiff, acquired such consistency as to outlast the whole group of political conditions in which it originated. These conditions endured for five centuries after the coronation in 800; the empire preserved a continuous existence for yet five centuries more. Until after the downfall of the great Hohenstauffen emperors, late in the thirteenth century, soon followed by the Babylonish exile of the popes at Avignon, the men of western Europe felt themselves in a certain sense members of a political whole of which Rome was the centre. By the beginning of the sixteenth century this feeling had almost disappeared. Men's world had enlarged till Rome no longer seemed so great to them as it had seemed to their forefathers who had lived under its mighty spell, or as it seems to us who view it through the lenses of history. Within its own imperial domains powerful nations had

The Holy Roman Empire.

slowly grown up, whose speech would have sounded strange to Cicero; while beyond ocean were found new lands where the name of Cæsar had never been heard. By the side of Louis XII. or Ferdinand of Aragon, it was not easy to recognize a grander dignity in the Hapsburg successor of Augustus; and the mutterings of revolt against papal supremacy already heralded the storm which was soon to rend all Christendom in twain. After the Reformation, the conception of a universal Christian monarchy, as held whether by St. Augustine or by Dante, had ceased to have a meaning and faded from men's memories. Yet in its forms and titles the Holy Roman Empire continued to survive, until, as Voltaire said, it had come to be neither holy, nor Roman, nor an empire. So long did it remain upon the scene that in 1790 an illustrious American philosopher, Benjamin Thompson, a native of Woburn in Massachusetts and sometime dweller in Rumford, New Hampshire, was admitted to a share in its dignities as Count Rumford. When at length in 1806, among the sweeping changes wrought by the battle of Austerlitz, the Emperor Francis II. resigned his position as head of the Germanic body, there were perhaps few who could have told why that head should have been called emperor rather than king; fewer still, no doubt, who realized that the long succession of Cæsars had now first come to an end.

I cite this final date of 1806 as interesting, but not as important, in connection with a political system which had already quite ceased to exist, save in so far as one might say that the spirit of it still survives in political methods and habits of thought that will yet be long in dying out. With great political systems, as with typical forms of organic life, the processes of development and of extinction are exceedingly slow, and it is seldom that the stages can be sharply marked by dates. The processes which have gradually shifted the seat of empire until the prominent part played nineteen centuries ago by Rome and Alexandria, on opposite sides of the Mediterranean, has been at length assumed by London and New York, on opposite sides of the Atlantic, form a most interesting subject of study. But to understand them, one must do much more than merely catalogue the facts of political history; one must acquire a knowledge of the drifts and tendencies of human thought and feeling and action from the earliest ages to the times in which we live. In covering so wide a field we cannot of course expect to obtain anything like complete results. In order to make a statement simple enough to be generally intelligible, it is necessary to pass over many circumstances and many considerations that might in one way and another qualify what we have to say. Nevertheless it is quite possible for us to discern, in their bold general outlines, some historic truths of supreme importance. In contemplating the salient features of the change which has now for a long time been making the world more English and less Roman, we shall find not only intellectual pleasure and profit but practical guidance. For in order to understand this slow but mighty change, we must

Gradual shifting of primacy from the men who spoke Latin, and their descendants, to the men who speak English.

look a little into that process of nation-making which has been going on since prehistoric ages and is going on here among us to-day, and from the recorded experience of men in times long past we may gather lessons of infinite value for ourselves and for our children's children. As in all the achievements of mankind it is only after much weary experiment and many a heart-sickening failure that success is attained, so has it been especially with nation-making. Skill in the political art is the fruit of ages of intellectual and moral discipline; and just as picture-writing had to come before printing and canoes before steamboats, so the cruder political methods had to be tried and found wanting, amid the tears and groans of unnumbered generations, before methods less crude could be put into operation. In the historic survey upon which we are now to enter, we shall see that the Roman Empire represented a crude method of nation-making which began with a masterful career of triumph over earlier and cruder methods, but has now for several centuries been giving way before a more potent and satisfactory method. And just as the merest glance at the history of Europe shows us Germanic peoples wresting the supremacy from Rome, so in this deeper study we shall discover a grand and far-reaching Teutonic Idea of political life overthrowing and supplanting the Roman Idea. Our attention will be drawn toward England as the battle-ground and the seventeenth century as the critical moment of the struggle; we shall see in Puritanism the tremendous militant force that determined the issue;

and when our perspective has thus become properly adjusted, we shall begin to realize for the first time how truly wonderful was the age that witnessed the Beginnings of New England. We have long had before our minds the colossal figure of Roman Julius as "the foremost man of all this world," but as the seventeenth century recedes into the past the figure of English Oliver begins to loom up as perhaps even more colossal. In order to see these world-events in their true perspective, and to make perfectly clear the manner in which we are to estimate them, we must go a long distance away from them. We must even go back, as nearly as may be, to the beginning of things.

If we look back for a moment to the primitive stages of society, we may picture to ourselves the surface of the earth sparsely and scantily covered with wandering tribes of savages, rude in morals and manners, narrow and monotonous in experience, sustaining life very much as lower animals sustain it, by gathering wild fruits or slaying wild game, and waging chronic warfare alike with powerful beasts and with rival tribes of men. In the widest sense the subject of political history is the description of the processes by which, under favourable circumstances, innumerable such primitive tribes have become welded together into mighty nations, with elevated standards of morals and manners, with wide and varied experience, sustaining life and ministering to human happiness by elaborate arts and sciences, and putting a curb upon warfare by limiting its scope, diminishing its cruelty, and interrupt-

Political history is the history of nation-making.

ing it by intervals of peace. The story, as laid before us in the records of three thousand years, is fascinating and absorbing in its human interest for those who content themselves with the study of its countless personal incidents, and neglect its profound philosophical lessons. But for those who study it in the scientific spirit, the human interest of its details becomes still more intensely fascinating and absorbing. Battles and coronations, poems and inventions, migrations and martyrdoms, acquire new meanings and awaken new emotions as we begin to discern their bearings upon the solemn work of ages that is slowly winning for humanity a richer and more perfect life. By such meditation upon men's thoughts and deeds is the understanding purified, till we become better able to comprehend our relations to the world and the duty that lies upon each of us to shape his conduct rightly.

In the welding together of primitive shifting tribes into stable and powerful nations, we can seem to discern three different methods that have been followed at different times and places, with widely different results. In all cases the fusion has been effected by war, but it has gone on in three broadly contrasted ways. The first of these methods, which has been followed from time immemorial in the Oriental world, may be roughly described as *conquest without incorporation*. A tribe grows to national dimensions by conquering and annexing its neighbours, without admitting them to a share in its political life. Probably there is always at first some incorporation, or even perhaps some crude

<small>The Oriental method of nation-making.</small>

germ of federative alliance ; but this goes very little way, — only far enough to fuse together a few closely related tribes, agreeing in speech and habits, into a single great tribe that can overwhelm its neighbours. In early society this sort of incorporation cannot go far without being stopped by some impassable barrier of language or religion. After reaching that point, the conquering tribe simply annexes its neighbours and makes them its slaves. It becomes a superior caste, ruling over vanquished peoples, whom it oppresses with frightful cruelty, while living on the fruits of their toil in what has been aptly termed Oriental luxury. Such has been the origin of many eastern despotisms, in the valleys of the Nile and Euphrates, and elsewhere. Such a political structure admits of a very considerable development of material civilization, in which gorgeous palaces and artistic temples may be built, and perhaps even literature and scholarship rewarded, with money wrung from millions of toiling wretches. There is that sort of brutal strength in it, that it may endure for many long ages, until it comes into collision with some higher civilization. Then it is likely to end in sudden collapse, because the fighting quality of the people has been destroyed. Populations that have lived for centuries in fear of impalement or crucifixion, and have known no other destination for the products of their labour than the clutches of the omnipresent tax-gatherer, are not likely to furnish good soldiers. A handful of freemen will scatter them like sheep, as the Greeks did twenty-three centuries ago at Kynaxa, as the English did the other day at Tel el-Kebir. On the other hand, where the manliness of the vanquished people is not crushed, the sway of the conquerors who cannot enter into political union with them is likely to be cast off, as in the case of the Moors in Spain. There was a civilization in many respects admirable. It was eminent for industry, science, art, and poetry; its annals are full of romantic interest; it was in some respects superior to the Christian system which supplanted it; in many ways it contributed largely to the progress of the human race; and it was free from some of the worst vices of Oriental civilizations. Yet because of the fundamental defect that between the Christian Spaniard and his Mussulman conqueror there could be no political fusion, this brilliant civilization was doomed. During eight centuries of more or less extensive rule in the Spanish peninsula, the Moor was from first to last an alien, just as after four centuries the Turk is still an alien in the Balkan peninsula. The natural result was a struggle that lasted age after age till it ended in the utter extermination of one of the parties, and left behind it a legacy of hatred and persecution that has made the history of modern Spain a dismal record of shame and disaster.

In this first method of nation-making, then, which we may call the Oriental method, one now sees but little to commend. It was better than savagery, and for a long time no more efficient method was possible, but the leading peoples of the world have long since outgrown it; and although the resulting form of political government is the oldest we know and is not yet extinct, it nevertheless has not the elements of permanence. Sooner or later it will disappear, as savagery is disappearing, as the rudest types of inchoate human society have disappeared.

The second method by which nations have been made may be called the Roman method; and we may briefly describe it as *conquest with incorporation, but without representation*. The secret of Rome's wonderful strength lay in the fact that she incorporated the vanquished peoples into her own body politic. In the early time there was a fusion of tribes going on in Latium, which, if it had gone no further, would have been similar to the early fusion of Ionic tribes in Attika or of Iranian tribes in Media. But whereas everywhere else this political fusion soon stopped, in the Roman world it went on. One after another Italian tribes and Italian towns were not merely overcome but admitted to a share in the political rights and privileges of the victors. By the time this had gone on until the whole Italian peninsula was consolidated under the headship of Rome, the result was a power incomparably greater than any other that the world had yet seen. Never before had so many people been brought under one government without making slaves of most of them. Liberty had existed before, whether in barbaric tribes or in Greek cities. Union had existed before, in Assyrian or Persian despotisms. Now liberty and union were for the first time joined together, with consequences enduring and stupendous. The whole

<small>The Roman method of nation-making.</small>

Mediterranean world was brought under one government; ancient barriers of religion, speech, and custom were overthrown in every direction; and innumerable barbarian tribes, from the Alps to the wilds of northern Britain, from the Bay of Biscay to the Carpathian mountains, were more or less completely transformed into Roman citizens, protected by Roman law, and sharing in the material and spiritual benefits of Roman civilization. Gradually the whole vast structure became permeated by Hellenic and Jewish thought, and thus were laid the lasting foundations of modern society, of a common Christendom, furnished with a common stock of ideas concerning man's relation to God and the world, and acknowledging a common standard of right and wrong. This was a prodigious work, which raised human life to a much higher plane than that which it had formerly occupied, and endless gratitude is due to the thousands of steadfast men who in one way or another devoted their lives to its accomplishment.

This Roman method of nation-making had nevertheless its fatal shortcomings, and it was only very slowly, moreover, that it wrought out its own best results. It was but *Its slow development.* gradually that the rights and privileges of Roman citizenship were extended over the whole Roman world, and in the mean time there were numerous instances where conquered provinces seemed destined to no better fate than had awaited the victims of Egyptian or Assyrian conquest. The rapacity and cruelty of Caius Verres could hardly have been outdone by the worst of Persian satraps;

but there was a difference. A moral sense and political sense had been awakened which could see both the wickedness and the folly of such conduct. The voice of a Cicero sounded with trumpet tones against the oppressor, who was brought to trial and exiled for deeds which under the Oriental system, from the days of Artaxerxes to those of the Grand Turk, would scarcely have called forth a reproving word. It was by slow degrees that the Roman came to understand the virtues of his own method, and learned to apply it consistently until the people of all parts of the empire were, in theory at least, equal before the law.

In theory, I say, for in point of fact there was enough of viciousness in the Roman system to prevent it from achieving permanent success. Historians have been fond of showing how the vitality of the whole system was impaired by wholesale slave-labour, by the false political economy which taxes all for the benefit of a few, by the debauching view of civil office which regards it as private perquisite and not as public trust, and — worst of all, perhaps — by the communistic practice of feeding an idle proletariat out of the imperial treasury. The names of these deadly social evils are not unfamiliar to American ears. Even of the last we have heard ominous whispers in the shape of bills to promote mendicancy under the specious guise of fostering education or rewarding military services. And is it not a striking illustration of the slowness with which mankind learns the plainest rudiments of wisdom and of justice, that only in the full light of the nineteenth century, and at the cost of a terrible war, should the most intelligent people on earth have got rid of a system of labour devised in the crudest ages of antiquity and fraught with misery to the employed, degradation to the employers, and loss to everybody?

These evils, we see, in one shape or another, have existed almost everywhere; and the vice of the Roman system did not consist in the fact that under it they were fully developed, but in the fact that it had no adequate means of overcoming them. Unless helped by something supplied from outside the Roman world, civilization must have succumbed to these evils, the progress of mankind must have been stopped. What was needed was the introduction of a fierce spirit of personal liberty and local self-government. The essential vice of the Roman system was that it had been unable to avoid weakening the spirit of personal independence and crushing out local self-government among the peoples to whom it had been applied. It owed its wonderful success to joining Liberty with Union, but as it went on it found itself compelled gradually to sacrifice Liberty to Union, strengthening the hands of the central government and enlarging its functions more and more, until by and by the political life of the several parts had so far died away that, under the pressure of attack from without, the Union fell to pieces and the whole political system had to be slowly and painfully reconstructed.

<small>Its essential defect.</small>

Now if we ask why the Roman government found itself thus obliged to sacrifice personal liberty and local independence to the paramount necessity of holding the empire together, the answer will point us to the essential and fundamental vice of the Roman method of nation-making. It lacked the principle of representation. The old Roman world knew nothing of representative assemblies. Its senates were assemblies of notables, constituting in the main an aristocracy of men who had held high office; its popular assemblies were primary assemblies, — town-meetings. There was no notion of such a thing as political power delegated by the people to representatives who were to wield it away from home and out of sight of their constituents. The Roman's only notion of delegated power was that of authority delegated by the government to its generals and prefects who discharged at a distance its military and civil functions. When, therefore, the Roman popular government, originally adapted to a single city, had come to extend itself over a large part of the world, it lacked the one institution by means of which government could be carried on over so vast an area without degenerating into despotism. Even could the device of representation have occurred to the mind of some statesman trained in Roman methods, it would probably have made no difference. Nobody would have known how to use it. You cannot invent an institution as you would invent a plough. Such a notion as that of representative government must needs start from small beginnings and grow in men's minds until it should become part and parcel of their mental habits. For the want of it the home government at Rome

It knew nothing of representation.

And therefore ended in despotism.

became more and more unmanageable until it fell into the hands of the army, while at the same time the administration of the empire became more and more centralized; the people of its various provinces, even while their social condition was in some respects improved, had less and less voice in the management of their local affairs, and thus the spirit of personal independence was gradually weakened. This centralization was greatly intensified by the perpetual danger of invasion on the northern and eastern frontiers, all the way from the Rhine to the Euphrates. Do what it would, the government must become more and more a military despotism, must revert toward the Oriental type. The period extending from the third century before Christ to the third century after was a period of extraordinary intellectual expansion and moral awakening; but when we observe the governmental changes introduced under the emperor Diocletian at the very end of this period, we realize how serious had been the political retrogression, how grave the danger that the stream of human life might come to stagnate in Europe, as it had long since stagnated in Asia.

Two mighty agents, coöperating in their opposite ways to prevent any such disaster, were already entering upon the scene. The first was the colonization of the empire by Germanic tribes already far advanced beyond savagery, already somewhat tinctured with Roman civilization, yet at the same time endowed with an intense spirit of personal and local independence. With this wholesome spirit they were about to refresh and revivify the empire, but at the risk of undoing its work of political organization and reducing it to barbarism. The second was the establishment of the Roman church, an institution capable of holding European society together in spite of a political disintegration that was widespread and long-continued. While wave after wave of Germanic colonization poured over romanized Europe, breaking down old boundary-lines and working sudden and astonishing changes on the map, setting up in every quarter baronies, dukedoms, and kingdoms fermenting with vigorous political life; while for twenty generations this salutary but wild and dangerous work was going on, there was never a moment when the imperial sway of Rome was quite set aside and forgotten, there was never a time when union of some sort was not maintained through the dominion which the church had established over the European mind. When we duly consider this great fact in its relations to what went before and what came after, it is hard to find words fit to express the debt of gratitude which modern civilization owes to the Roman Catholic church. When we think of all the work, big with promise of the future, that went on in those centuries which modern writers in their ignorance used once to set apart and stigmatize as the "Dark Ages"; when we consider how the seeds of what is noblest in modern life were then painfully sown upon the soil which imperial Rome had prepared; when we think of the various work of a Gregory, a Benedict, a Boniface, an Alfred, a Charlemagne; we feel that there is a sense in which the most brilliant achievements of pagan antiquity are dwarfed in comparison with these. Until quite lately, indeed, the student of history has had his attention too narrowly confined to the ages that have been preëminent for literature and art — the so-called classical ages — and thus his sense of historical perspective has been impaired. When Mr. Freeman uses Gregory of Tours as a text-book, he shows that he realizes how an epoch may be none the less portentous though it has not had a Tacitus to describe it, and certainly no part of history is more full of human interest than the troubled period in which the powerful streams of Teutonic life pouring into Roman Europe were curbed in their destructiveness and guided to noble ends by the Catholic church. Out of the interaction between these two mighty agents has come the political system of the modern world. The moment when this interaction might have seemed on the point of reaching a complete and harmonious result was the glorious thirteenth century, the culminating moment of the Holy Roman Empire. Then, as in the times of Cæsar or Trajan, there might have seemed to be a union among civilized men, in which the separate life of individuals and localities was not submerged. In that golden age alike of feudal system, of empire, and of church, there were to be seen the greatest monarchs, in fullest sympathy with their peoples, that Christendom has known,— an Edward I., a St. Louis, a Frederick II. Then, when in the pontificates of Innocent III. and his successors the Roman church reached its apogee, the religious yearnings of men sought expression

The wonderful thirteenth century.

in the sublimest architecture the world has seen. Then Aquinas summed up in his profound speculations the substance of Catholic theology, and while the morning twilight of modern science might be discerned in the treatises of Roger Bacon, while wandering minstrelsy revealed the treasures of modern speech, soon to be wrought under the hands of Dante and Chaucer into forms of exquisite beauty, the sacred fervour of the apostolic ages found itself renewed in the tender and mystic piety of St. Francis of Assisi. It was a wonderful time, but after all less memorable as the culmination of mediæval empire and mediæval church than as the dawning of the new era in which we live to-day, and in which the development of human society proceeds in accordance with more potent methods than those devised by the genius of pagan or Christian Rome.

For the origin of these more potent methods we must look back to the early ages of the Teutonic people; for their development and application on a grand scale we must look chiefly to the history of that most Teutonic of peoples in its institutions, though perhaps not more than half-Teutonic in blood, the English, with their descendants in the New World. The third method of nation-making may be called the Teutonic or preëminently the English method. It differs from the Oriental and Roman methods which we have been considering in a feature of most profound significance; it contains the principle of representation. For this reason, though like all nation-making it was in its early stages attended with war and conquest, it nevertheless

The English method of nation-making.

does not necessarily require war and conquest in order to be put into operation. Of the other two methods war was an essential part. In the typical Oriental nation, such as Assyria or Persia, we see a conquering tribe holding down a number of vanquished peoples, and treating them like slaves: here the nation is very imperfectly made, and its government is subject to sudden and violent changes. In the Roman empire we see a conquering people hold sway over a number of vanquished peoples, but instead of treating them like slaves, it gradually makes them its equals before the law; here the resulting political body is much more nearly a nation, and its government is much more stable. A Lydian of the fifth century before Christ felt no sense of allegiance to the Persian master who simply robbed and abused him; but the Gaul of the fifth century after Christ was proud of the name of Roman and ready to fight for the empire of which he was a citizen. We have seen, nevertheless, that for want of representation the Roman method failed when applied to an immense territory, and the government tended to become more and more despotic, to revert toward the Oriental type. Now of the English or Teutonic method, I say, war is not an essential part; for where representative government is once established, it is possible for a great nation to be formed by the peaceful coalescence of neighbouring states, or by their union into a federal body. An instance of the former was the coalescence of England and Scotland effected early in the eighteenth century after ages of mutual hostility; for instances of the

Pacific tendencies of federalism.

latter we have Switzerland and the United States. Now federalism, though its rise and establishment may be incidentally accompanied by warfare, is nevertheless in spirit pacific. Conquest in the Oriental sense is quite incompatible with it; conquest in the Roman sense is hardly less so. At the close of our Civil War there were now and then zealous people to be found who thought that the southern states ought to be treated as conquered territory, governed by prefects sent from Washington, and held down by military force for a generation or so. Let us hope that there are few to-day who can fail to see that such a course would have been fraught with almost as much danger as the secession movement itself. At least it would have been a hasty confession, quite uncalled for and quite untrue, that American federalism had thus far proved itself incompetent, — that we had indeed preserved our national unity, but only at the frightful cost of sinking to a lower plane of national life.

But federalism, with its pacific implications, was not an invention of the Teutonic mind. The idea was familiar to the city communities of ancient Greece, which, along with their intense love of self-government, felt the need of combined action for warding off external attack. In their Achaian and Aitolian leagues the Greeks made brilliant attempts toward founding a nation upon some higher principle than that of mere conquest, and the history of these attempts is exceedingly interesting and instructive. They failed for lack of the principle of representation, which was practically unknown to the world until introduced by the Teutonic colonizers of the Roman empire. Until the idea of power delegated by the people had become familiar to men's minds in its practical bearings, it was impossible to create a great nation without crushing out the political life in some of its parts. Some centre of power was sure to absorb all the political life, and grow at the expense of the outlying parts, until the result was a centralized despotism. Hence it came to be one of the commonplace assumptions of political writers that republics must be small, that free government is practicable only in a confined area, and that the only strong and durable government, *Fallacy of the notion that republics must be small.* capable of maintaining order throughout a vast territory, is some form of absolute monarchy. It was quite natural that people should formerly have held this opinion, and it is indeed not yet quite obsolete, but its fallaciousness will become more and more apparent as American history is better understood. Our experience has now so far widened that we can see that despotism is not the strongest but wellnigh the weakest form of government; that centralized administrations, like that of the Roman empire, have fallen to pieces, not because of too much but because of too little freedom; and that the only perdurable government must be that which succeeds in achieving national unity on a grand scale, without weakening the sense of personal and local independence. For in the body politic this spirit of freedom is as the red corpuscles in the blood; it carries the life with it. It makes the difference between a society of self-respecting men and women and a society of puppets.

Your nation may have art, poetry, and science, all the refinements of civilized life, all the comforts and safeguards that human ingenuity can devise; but if it lose this spirit of personal and local independence, it is doomed and deserves its doom. As President Cleveland has well said, it is not the business of a government to support its people, but of the people to support their government; and once to lose sight of this vital truth is as dangerous as to trifle with some stealthy narcotic poison. Of the two opposite perils which have perpetually threatened the welfare of political society — anarchy on the one hand, loss of self-government on the other — Jefferson was right in maintaining that the latter is really the more to be dreaded because its beginnings are so terribly insidious. Many will understand what is meant by a threat of secession, where few take heed of the baneful principle involved in a Texas Seed-bill.

That the American people are still fairly alive to the importance of these considerations, is due to the weary ages of struggle in which our forefathers have manfully contended for the right of self-government. From the days of Arminius and Civilis in the wilds of lower Germany to the days of Franklin and Jefferson in Independence Hall, we have been engaged in this struggle, not without some toughening of our political fibre, not without some refining of our moral sense. Not among our English forefathers only, but among all the peoples of mediæval and modern Europe has the struggle gone on, with various and instructive results. In all parts of romanized Europe invaded and colonized by Teutonic tribes, self-government attempted to spring up. What may have been the origin of the idea of representation we do not know; like most origins, it seems lost in the prehistoric darkness. Wherever we find Teutonic tribes settling down over a wide area, we find them holding their primary assemblies, usually their annual March-meetings, like those in which Mr. Hosea Biglow and others like him have figured. Everywhere, too, we find some attempt at representative assemblies, based on the principle of the three estates, clergy, nobles, and commons. But nowhere save in England does the representative principle become firmly established, at first in county-meetings, afterward in a national parliament limiting the powers of the national monarch as the primary tribal assembly had limited the powers of the tribal chief. It is for this reason that we must call the method of nation-making by means of a representative assembly the English method. While the idea of representation was perhaps the common property of the Teutonic tribes, it was only in England that it was successfully put into practice and became the dominant political idea. We may therefore agree with Dr. Stubbs that in its political development England is the most Teutonic of all European countries, — the country which in becoming a great nation has most fully preserved the local independence so characteristic of the ancient Germans. The reasons for this are complicated, and to try to assign them all would needlessly encumber our exposition. But there is one that is apparent and

Teutonic March-meetings and representative assemblies.

extremely instructive. There is sometimes a great advantage in being able to plant political institutions in a virgin soil, where they run no risk of being modified or perhaps metamorphosed through contact with rival institutions. In America the Teutonic idea has been worked out even more completely than in Britain; and so far as institutions are concerned, our English forefathers settled here as in an empty country. They were not obliged to modify their political ideas so as to bring them into harmony with those of the Indians; the disparity in civilization was so great that the Indians were simply thrust aside, along with the wolves and buffaloes.

This illustration will help us to understand the peculiar features of the Teutonic settlement of Britain. Whether the English invaders really slew all the romanized Kelts who dwelt in the island, except those who found refuge in the mountains of Cumberland, Wales, and Cornwall, or fled across the channel to Brittany, we need not seek to decide. It is enough to point out one respect in

Peculiarity of the Teutonic conquest of Britain.

which the Teutonic conquest was immeasurably more complete in Britain than in any other part of the empire. Everywhere else the tribes who settled upon Roman soil — the Goths, Vandals, Suevi, and Burgundians — were christianized, and so to some extent romanized, before they came to take possession. Even the more distant Franks had been converted to Christianity before they had completed their conquest of Gaul. Everywhere except in Britain, therefore, the conquerors had already imbibed Roman ideas, and the authority of Rome was in a certain sense acknowledged. There was no break in the continuity of political events. In Britain, on the other hand, there was a complete break, so that while on the continent the fifth and sixth centuries are seen in the full midday light of history, in Britain they have lapsed into the twilight of half-legendary tradition. The Saxon and English tribes, coming from the remote wilds of northern Germany, whither Roman missionaries had not yet penetrated, still worshipped Thor and Wodan; and their conquest of Britain was effected with such deadly thoroughness that Christianity was destroyed there, or lingered only in sequestered nooks. A land once christianized thus actually fell back into paganism, so that the work of converting it to Christianity had to be done over again. From the landing of heathen Hengest on the isle of Thanet to the landing of Augustine and his monks on the same spot, one hundred and forty-eight years elapsed, during which English institutions found time to take deep root in British soil with scarcely more interference, as to essential points, than in American soil twelve centuries afterward.

The century and a half between 449 and 597 is therefore one of the most important epochs in the history of the people that speak the English language. Before settling in Britain our forefathers had been tribes in the upper stages of barbarism; now they began the process of coalescence into a nation in which the principle of self-government should be retained and developed. The township and its town-meeting we find there, as later in New England. The county-meeting we also find, while the county is a little state in itself and not a mere administrative district. And in this county-meeting we may observe a singular feature, something never seen before in the world, something destined to work out vaster political results than Cæsar ever dreamed of. This county-meeting is not a primary assembly; all the freemen from all the townships cannot leave their homes and their daily business to attend it. Nor is it merely an assembly of notables, attended by the most important men of the neighbourhood. It is a representative assembly, attended by select men from each township. We may see in it the germ of the British parliament and of the American congress, as indeed of all modern legislative bodies, for it is a most suggestive commentary upon what we are saying that in all other countries which have legislatures, they have been copied, within quite recent times, from English or American models. We can seldom if ever fix a date for the beginning of anything, and we can by no means fix a date for the beginning of representative assemblies in England. We can only say that where we first find traces of county organization, we find traces of representation. Clearly, if the English conquerors of Britain had left the framework of Roman institutions standing there, as it remained standing in Gaul, there would have been great danger of this principle of representation not surviving. It would most likely have been crushed in its callow infancy.

Survival and development of Teutonic representative assembly in England.

The conquerors would insensibly have fallen into the Roman way of doing things, as they did in Gaul.

From the start, then, we find the English nationality growing up under very different conditions from those which obtained in other parts of Europe. So far as institutions are concerned, Teutonism was less modified in England than in the German fatherland itself. For the gradual conquest and christianization of Germany which began with Charles the Great, and went on until in the thirteenth century the frontier had advanced eastward to the Vistula, entailed to a certain extent the romanization of Germany. For a thousand years after Charles the Great, the political head of Germany was also the political head of the Holy Roman Empire, and the civil and criminal code by which the daily life of the modern German citizen is regulated is based upon the jurisprudence of Rome. Nothing, perhaps, could illustrate more forcibly than this sheer contrast the peculiarly Teutonic character of English civilization. Between the eighth and the eleventh centuries, when the formation of English nationality was approaching completion, it received a fresh and powerful infusion of Teutonism in the swarms of heathen Northmen or Danes who occupied the eastern coasts, struggled long for the supremacy, and gradually becoming christianized, for a moment succeeded in seizing the crown. Of the invasion of partially romanized Northmen from Normandy which followed soon after, and which has so pro-

Primitive Teutonic institutions less modified in England than in Germany.

foundly affected English society and English speech, we need notice here but two conspicuous features. First, it increased the power of the crown and the clergy, brought all England more than ever under one law, and strengthened the feeling of nationality. It thus made England a formidable military power, while at the same time it brought her into closer relations with continental Europe than she had held since the fourth century. Secondly, by superposing a new feudal nobility as the upper stratum of society, it transformed the Old-English thanehood into the finest middle-class of rural gentry and yeomanry that has ever existed in any country; a point of especial interest to Americans, since it was in this stratum of society that the two most powerful streams of English migration to America — the Virginia stream and the New England stream — alike had their source.

By the thirteenth century the increasing power and pretensions of the crown, as the unification of English nationality went on, brought about a result unlike anything known on the continent of Europe; it brought about a resistless coalition between the great nobles, the rural gentry and yeomanry, and the burghers of the towns, for the purpose of curbing royalty, arresting the progress of centralization, and setting up representative government on a truly national scale. This grand result was partly due to peculiar circumstances which had their origin in the Norman conquest; but it was largely due to the political habits generated by long experience of local representative assemblies, — habits which made it comparatively easy for different classes of society to find their voice and use it for the attainment of ends in common. On the continent of Europe the encroaching sovereign had to contend with here and there an arrogant vassal, here and there a high-spirited and rebellious town; in England, in this first great crisis of popular government, he found himself confronted by a united people. The fruits of the grand combination were *first*, the wresting of Magna Charta from King John in 1215, and *secondly*, the meeting of the first House of Commons in 1265. Four years of civil war were required to secure these noble results. The Barons' War, of the years 1263 to 1267, was an event of the same order of importance as the Great Rebellion of the seventeenth century and the American Revolution; and among the founders of that political freedom which is enjoyed to-day by all English-speaking people, the name of Simon de Montfort, Earl of Leicester, deserves a place in our grateful remembrance beside the names of Cromwell and Washington. Simon's great victory at Lewes in 1264 must rank with Naseby and Yorktown. The work begun by his House of Commons was the same work that has continued to go on without essential interruption down to the days of Cleveland and Gladstone. The fundamental principle of political freedom is "no taxation without representation"; you must not take a farthing of my money without consulting my wishes as to the use that shall be made of it. Only when this principle of justice was first practically recognized, did

The Barons' War and the first House of Commons.

government begin to divorce itself from the primitive bestial barbaric system of tyranny and plunder, and to ally itself with the forces that in the fulness of time are to bring peace on earth and good will to men. Of all dates in history, therefore, there is none more fit to be commemorated than 1265; for in that year there was first asserted and applied at Westminster, on a national scale, that fundamental principle of "no taxation without representation," that innermost kernel of the English Idea, which the Stamp Act Congress defended at New York exactly five hundred years afterward. When we think of these dates, by the way, we realize the import of the saying that in the sight of the Lord a thousand years are but as a day, and we feel that the work of the Lord cannot be done by the listless or the slothful. So much time and so much strife by sea and land has it taken to secure beyond peradventure the boon to mankind for which Earl Simon gave up his noble life on the field of Evesham! Nor without unremitting watchfulness can we be sure that the day of peril is yet past.

Eternal vigilance is the price of liberty.

From kings, indeed, we have no more to fear; they have come to be as spooks and bogies of the nursery. But the gravest dangers are those which present themselves in new forms, against which people's minds have not yet been fortified with traditional sentiments and phrases. The inherited predatory tendency of men to seize upon the fruits of other people's labour is still very strong, and while we have nothing more to fear from kings, we may yet have trouble enough from commercial monopolies and favoured industries, marching to the polls their hordes of bribed retainers. Well indeed has it been said that eternal vigilance is the price of liberty. God never meant that in this fair but treacherous world in which He has placed us we should earn our salvation without steadfast labour.

To return to Earl Simon, we see that it was just in that wonderful thirteenth century, when the Roman idea of government might seem to have been attaining its richest and most fruitful development, that the richer and more fruitful English idea first became incarnate in the political constitution of a great and rapidly growing nation. It was not long before the struggle between the Roman Idea and the English Idea, clothed in various forms, became the dominating issue in European history. We have now to observe the rise of modern nationalities, as new centres of political life, out of the various provinces of the Roman world. *Conflict between Roman Idea and English Idea begins to become clearly visible in the thirteenth century.* In the course of this development the Teutonic representative assembly is at first everywhere discernible, in some form or other, as in the Spanish Cortes or the States-General of France, but on the continent it generally dies out. Only in such nooks as Switzerland and the Netherlands does it survive. In the great nations it succumbs before the encroachments of the crown. The comparatively novel Teutonic idea of power delegated by the people to their representatives had not become deeply enough rooted in the political soil of the continent; and accordingly we find it more and more disused and at length almost forgotten, while the old and deeply rooted Roman idea of power delegated by the governing body to its lieutenants and prefects usurps its place. Let us observe some of the most striking features of this growth of modern nationalities.

The reader of mediæval history cannot fail to be impressed with the suddenness with which the culmination of the Holy Roman Empire, in the thirteenth century, was followed by a swift decline. The imperial position of the Hapsburgs was far less splendid than that of the Hohenstauffen; it rapidly became more German and less European, until by and by people began to forget what the empire originally meant. The change which came over the papacy was even more remarkable. The grandchildren of the men who had witnessed the spectacle of a king of France and a king of England humbled at the feet of Innocent III., the children of the men who had found the gigantic powers of a Frederick II. unequal to the task of curbing the papacy, now beheld the successors of St. Peter carried away to Avignon, there to be kept for seventy years under the supervision of the kings of France. Henceforth the glory of the papacy in its political aspect was to be but the faint shadow of that with which it had shone before. This sudden change in its position showed that the mediæval dream of a world-empire was passing away, and that new powers were coming uppermost in the shape of modern nationalities with their national sovereigns. So long as these nationalities were in the weakness of their early formation, it was possible for pope and

Growth of modern nationalities.

emperor to assert, and sometimes to come near maintaining, universal supremacy. But the time was now at hand when kings could assert their independence of the pope, while the emperor was fast sinking to be merely one among kings.

As modern kingdoms thus grew at the expense of empire and papacy above, so they also grew at the expense of feudal dukedoms, earldoms, and baronies below. The fourteenth and fifteenth centuries were as fatal to feudalism as to world-empire and world-church. A series of wars occurring at this time were especially remarkable for the wholesale slaughter of the feudal nobility, whether on the field or under the headsman's axe. This was a conspicuous feature of the feuds of the Trastamare in Spain, of the English invasions of France, followed by the quarrel between Burgundians and Armagnacs, and of the great war of the Roses in England. So thorough-going was the butchery in England, for example, that only twenty-nine lay peers could be found to sit in the first parliament of Henry VII. in 1485. The old nobility was almost annihilated, both in person and in property; for along with the slaughter there went wholesale confiscation, and this added greatly to the disposable wealth of the crown. The case was essentially similar in France and Spain. In all three countries the beginning of the sixteenth century saw the power of the crown increased and increasing. Its vast accessions of wealth made it more independent of legislative assemblies, and at the same time enabled it to make the baronage more subservient in character by fill-

Increasing power of the crown.

ing up the vacant places with new creations of its own. Through the turbulent history of the next two centuries we see the royal power aiming at unchecked supremacy and in the principal instances attaining it except in England. Absolute despotism was reached first in Spain, under Philip II.; in France it was reached a century later, under Louis XIV.; and at about the same time in the hereditary estates of Austria; while over all the Italian and German soil of the disorganized empire, except among the glaciers of Switzerland and the dykes of the Netherlands, the play of political forces had set up a host of petty tyrannies which aped the morals and manners of the great autocrats at Paris and Madrid and Vienna.

As we look back over this growth of modern monarchy, we cannot but be struck with the immense practical difficulty of creating a strong nationality without sacrificing self-government. Powerful, indeed, is the tendency toward over-centralization, toward stagnation, toward political death. Powerful is the tendency to revert to the Roman, if not to the Oriental method. As often as we reflect upon the general state of things at the end of the seventeenth century — the dreadful ignorance and misery which prevailed among most of the people of continental Europe, and apparently without hope of remedy — so often must we be impressed anew with the stupendous significance of the part played by self-governing England in overcoming dangers which have threatened the very existence of modern civilization. It is not too much to say that in

Formidable strength of the Roman Idea.

the seventeenth century the entire political future of mankind was staked upon the questions that were at issue in England. To keep the sacred flame of liberty alive required such a rare and wonderful concurrence of conditions that, had our forefathers then succumbed in the strife, it is hard to imagine how or where the failure could have been repaired. Some of these conditions we have already considered; let us now observe one of the most important of all. Let us note the part played by that most tremendous of social forces, the religious sentiment, in its relation to the political circumstances which we have passed in review. If we ask why it was that among modern nations absolute despotism was soonest and most completely established in Spain, we find it instructive to observe that the circumstances under which the Spanish monarchy grew up, during centuries of deadly struggle with the Mussulman, were such as to enlist the religious sentiment on the side of despotic methods in church and state. It becomes interesting, then, to observe by contrast how it was that in England the dominant religious sentiment came to be enlisted on the side of political freedom.

Had it not been for the Puritans, political liberty would probably have disappeared from the world.

In such an inquiry we have nothing to do with the truth or falsity of any system of doctrines, whether Catholic or Protestant. The legitimate purposes of the historian do not require him to intrude upon the province of the theologian. Our business is to trace the sequence of political cause and effect. Nor shall we get much help from crude sweeping statements which set forth Catholicism as invariably the enemy and Protestantism as invariably the ally of human liberty. The Catholic has a right to be offended at statements which would involve a Hildebrand or a St. Francis in the same historical judgment with a Sigismund or a Torquemada. The character of ecclesiastical as of all other institutions has varied with the character of the men who have worked them and the varying needs of the times and places in which they have been worked; and our intense feeling of the gratitude we owe to English Puritanism need in nowise diminish the enthusiasm with which we praise the glorious work of the mediæval church. It is the duty of the historian to learn how to limit and qualify his words of blame or approval; for so curiously is human nature compounded of strength and weakness that the best of human institutions are likely to be infected with some germs of vice or folly.

Of no human institution is this more true than of the great mediæval church of Gregory and Innocent when viewed in the light of its claims to unlimited temporal and spiritual sovereignty. In striking down the headship of the emperors, it would have reduced Europe to a sort of Oriental caliphate, had it not been checked by the rising spirit of nationality already referred to. But there was another and even mightier agency coming in to curb its undue pretensions to absolute sovereignty. That same thirteenth century which witnessed the culmination of its power witnessed also the first bold

Beginnings of Protestantism in the thirteenth century.

and determined manifestation of the Protestant temper of revolt against spiritual despotism. It was long before this that the earliest Protestant heresy had percolated into Europe, having its source, like so many other heresies, in that eastern world where the stimulating thought of the Greeks busied itself with the ancient theologies of Asia. From Armenia in the eighth century came the Manichæan sect of Paulicians into Thrace, and for twenty generations played a considerable part in the history of the Eastern Empire. In the Bulgarian tongue they were known as Bogomilians, or men constant in prayer. In Greek they were called Cathari, or "Puritans." They accepted the New Testament, but set little store by the Old; they laughed at transubstantiation, denied any mystical efficiency to baptism, frowned upon image-worship as no better than idolatry, despised the intercession of saints, and condemned the worship of the Virgin Mary. As for the symbol of the cross, they scornfully asked, "If any man slew the son of a king with a bit of wood, how could this piece of wood be dear to the king?" Their ecclesiastical government was in the main presbyterian, and in politics they showed a decided leaning toward democracy. They wore long faces, looked askance at frivolous amusements, and were terribly in earnest. Of the more obscure pages of mediæval history, none are fuller of interest than those in which we decipher the westward progress of these sturdy heretics through the Balkan peninsula into Italy, and thence into southern France, where toward the end

The Cathari, or Puritans of the Eastern Empire.

of the twelfth century we find their ideas coming to full blossom in the great Albigensian heresy. It was no light affair to assault the church in the days of Innocent III. The terrible crusade against the Albigenses, beginning in 1207, was the joint work of the most powerful of popes and one of the most powerful of French kings. On the part of Innocent it was the stamping out of a revolt that threatened the very existence of the Catholic hierarchy; on the part of Philip Augustus it was the suppression of those too independent vassals the Counts of Toulouse, and the decisive subjection of the southern provinces to the government at Paris. Nowhere in European history do we read a more frightful story than that which tells of the blazing fires which consumed thousand after thousand of the most intelligent and thrifty people in France. It was now that the Holy Inquisition came into existence, and after forty years of slaughter these Albigensian Cathari or Puritans seemed exterminated. The practice of burning heretics, first enacted by statute in Aragon in 1197, was adopted in most parts of Europe during the thirteenth century, but in England not until the beginning of the fifteenth. The Inquisition was never established in England. Edward II. attempted to introduce it in 1311 for the purpose of suppressing the Templars, but his utter failure showed that the instinct of self-government was too strong in the English people to tolerate the entrusting of so much power over men's lives to agents of the papacy. Mediæval England was ignorant and bigoted enough, but un-

The Albigenses.

der a representative government which so strongly permeated society, it was impossible to set the machinery of repression to work with such deadly thoroughness as it worked under the guidance of Roman methods. When we read the history of persecution in England, the story in itself is dreadful enough; but when we compare it with the horrors enacted in other countries, we arrive at some startling results. During the two centuries of English persecution, from Henry IV. to James I., some 400 persons were burned at the stake, and three-fourths of these cases occurred in 1555-57, the last three years of Mary Tudor. Now in a single province of Spain, in the single year 1482, about 2000 persons were burned. The lowest estimates of the number slain for heresy in the Netherlands in the course of the sixteenth century place it at 75,000. Very likely such figures are in many cases grossly exaggerated. But after making due allowance for this, the contrast is sufficiently impressive. In England the persecution of heretics was feeble and spasmodic, and only at one moment rose to anything like the appalling vigour which ordinarily characterized it in countries where the Inquisition was firmly established. Now among the victims of religious persecution must necessarily be found an unusual proportion of men and women more independent than the average in their thinking, and more bold than the average in uttering their thoughts. The Inquisition was a diabolical winnowing machine for removing from society the most flexible minds and the stoutest hearts; and

Effects of persecution: its feebleness in England.

among every people in which it was established for a length of time it wrought serious damage to the national character. It ruined the fair promise of Spain, and inflicted incalculable detriment upon the fortunes of France. No nation could afford to deprive itself of such a valuable element in its political life as was furnished in the thirteenth century by the intelligent and sturdy Cathari of southern Gaul.

The spirit of revolt against the hierarchy, though broken and repressed thus terribly by the measures of Innocent III., continued to live on obscurely in sequestered spots, in the mountains of Savoy, and Bosnia, and Bohemia, ready on occasion to spring into fresh and vigorous life. In the following century Protestant ideas were rapidly germinating in England, alike in baron's castle, in yeoman's farmstead, in citizen's shop, in the cloistered walks of the monastery. Henry Knighton, writing in the time of Richard II., declares, with the exaggeration of impatience, that every second man you met was a Lollard, or "babbler," for such was the nickname given to these free-thinkers, of whom the most eminent was John Wyclif, professor at Oxford, and rector of Lutterworth, greatest scholar of the age.

Wyclif and the Lollards. The career of this man is a striking commentary upon the difference between England and continental Europe in the Middle Ages. Wyclif denied transubstantiation, disapproved of auricular confession, opposed the payment of Peter's pence, taught that kings should not be subject to prelates, translated the Bible into English and circulated it among the people, and even denounced the reigning pope as Antichrist; yet he was not put to death, because there was as yet no act of parliament for the burning of heretics, and in England things must be done according to the laws which the people had made.[1] Pope Gregory XI. issued five bulls against him, addressed to the king, the archbishop of Canterbury, and the university of Oxford; but their dictatorial tone offended the national feeling, and no heed was paid to them. Seventeen years after Wyclif's death, the statute for burning heretics was passed, and the persecution of Lollards began. It was feeble and ineffectual, however. Lollardism was never trampled out in England as Catharism was trampled out in France. Tracts of Wyclif and passages from his translation of the Bible were copied by hand and secretly passed about to be read on Sundays in the manor-house, or by the cottage fireside after the day's toil was over. The work went on quietly, but not the less effectively, until when the papal authority was defied by Henry VIII., it soon became apparent that England was half-Protestant already. It then appeared also that in this Reformation there were two forces coöperating, — the sentiment of national independence which would not brook dictation from Rome, and the Puritan sentiment of revolt against the hierarchy in general. The first sentiment had found expression again and again in refusals to pay tribute to Rome, in defiance of papal bulls, and in the famous statutes of *præmunire*, which made it a criminal offence to acknowledge any authority in England higher than the

[1] Milman, *Lat. Christ.* vii. 395.

crown. The revolt of Henry VIII. was simply the carrying out of these acts of Edward I. and Edward III. to their logical conclusion. It completed the detachment of England from the Holy Roman Empire, and made her free of all the world. Its intent was political rather than religious. Henry, who wrote against Martin Luther, was far from wishing to make England a Protestant country. Elizabeth, who differed from her father in not caring a straw for theology, was by temperament and policy conservative. Yet England could not cease to be Papist without ceasing in some measure to be Catholic; nor could she in that day carry on war against Spain without becoming a leading champion of Protestantism. The changes in creed and ritual wrought by the government during this period were cautious and skilful; and the resulting church of England, with its long line of learned and liberal divines, has played a noble part in history.

Political character of Henry VIII.'s revolt against Rome.

But along with this moderate Protestantism espoused by the English government, as consequent upon the assertion of English national independence, there grew up the fierce uncompromising democratic Protestantism of which the persecuted Lollards had sown the seeds. This was not the work of government. By the side of Henry VIII. stands the sublime figure of Hugh Latimer, most dauntless of preachers, the one man before whose stern rebuke the headstrong and masterful Tudor monarch quailed. It was Latimer that renewed the work of Wyclif, and in his life as well as in his martyrdom, — to use

The yeoman, Hugh Latimer.

his own words of good cheer uttered while the fagots were kindling around him, — lighted "such a candle in England as by God's grace shall never be put out." This indomitable man belonged to that middle-class of self-governing, self-respecting yeomanry that has been the glory of free England and free America. He was one of the sturdy race that overthrew French chivalry at Crecy and twice drove the soldiery of a tyrant down the slope of Bunker Hill. In boyhood he worked on his father's farm and helped his mother to milk the thirty kine; he practised archery on the village green, studied in the village school, went to Cambridge, and became the foremost preacher of Christendom. Now the most thorough and radical work of the English Reformation was done by this class of men of which Latimer was the type. It was work that was national in its scope, arousing to fervent heat the strong religious and moral sentiment of the people, and hence it soon quite outran the cautious and conservative policy of the government, and tended to introduce changes extremely distasteful to those who wished to keep England as nearly Catholic as was consistent with independence of the pope. Hence before the end of Elizabeth's reign, we find the crown set almost as strongly against Puritanism as against Romanism. Hence, too, when under Elizabeth's successors the great decisive struggle between despotism and liberty was inaugurated, we find all the tremendous force of this newly awakened religious enthusiasm coöperating with the English love of self-government and carrying it under Cromwell to victory. From this fortunate alliance of religious and political forces has come all the noble and fruitful work of the last two centuries in which men of English speech have been labouring for the political regeneration of mankind. But for this alliance of forces, it is quite possible that the fateful seventeenth century might have seen despotism triumphant in England as on the continent of Europe, and the progress of civilization indefinitely arrested.

<small>The moment of Cromwell's triumph was the most critical moment in history.</small>

In illustration of this possibility, observe what happened in France at the very time when the victorious English tendencies were shaping themselves in the reign of Elizabeth. In France there was a strong Protestant movement, but it had no such independent middle-class to support it as that which existed in England; nor had it been able to profit by such indispensable preliminary work as that which Wyclif had done; the horrible slaughter of the Albigenses had deprived France of the very people who might have played a part in some way analogous to that of the Lollards. Consequently the Protestant movement in France failed to become a national movement. Against the wretched Henry III. who would have temporized with it, and the gallant Henry IV. who honestly espoused it, the oppressed peasantry and townsmen made common cause by enlisting under the banner of the ultra-Catholic Guises. The mass of the people saw nothing in Protestantism but an idea favoured by the aristocracy and which they could not comprehend. Hence the great king who would have

<small>Contrast with France; fate of the Huguenots.</small>

been glad to make France a Protestant country could only obtain his crown by renouncing his religion, while seeking to protect it by his memorable Edict of Nantes. But what a generous despot could grant, a bigoted despot might revoke; and before another century had elapsed, the good work done by Henry IV. was undone by Louis XIV., the Edict of Nantes was set aside, the process of casting out the most valuable political element in the community was carried to completion, and seven per cent. of the population of France was driven away and added to the Protestant populations of northern Germany and England and America. The gain to these countries and the damage to France was far greater than the mere figures would imply; for in determining the character of a community a hundred selected men and women are more potent than a thousand men and women taken at random. Thus while the Reformation in France reinforced to some extent the noble army of freemen, its triumphs were not to be the triumphs of Frenchmen, but of the race which has known how to enlist under its banner the forces that fight for free thought, free speech, and self-government, and all that these phrases imply.

In view of these facts we may see how tremendous was the question at stake with the Puritans of the seventeenth century. Everywhere else the Roman idea seemed to have conquered or to be conquering, while they seemed to be left as the forlorn hope of the human race. But from the very day when Oliver Cromwell reached forth his mighty arm to stop the persecutions in Savoy, the victorious English idea began to change the face of things. The next century saw William Pitt allied with Frederick of Prussia to save the work of the Reformation in central Europe and set in motion the train of events that were at last to make the people of the Teutonic fatherland a nation. At that same moment the keenest minds in France were awaking to the fact that in their immediate neighbourhood, separated from them only by a few miles of salt water, was a country where people were equal in the eye of the law. It was the ideas of Locke and Milton, of Vane and Sidney, that, when transplanted into French soil, produced that violent but salutary Revolution which has given fresh life to the European world. And contemporaneously with all this, the American nation came upon the scene, equipped as no other nation had ever been, for the task of combining sovereignty with liberty, indestructible union of the whole with indestructible life in the parts. The English idea has thus come to be more than national, it has become imperial. It has come to rule, and it has come to stay.

Victory of the English Idea.

We are now in a position to answer the question when the Roman Empire came to an end, in so far as it can be answered at all. It did not come to its end at the hands of an Odovakar in the year 476, or of a Mahomet II. in 1453, or of a Napoleon in 1806. It has been coming to its end as the Roman idea of nation-making has been at length decisively overcome by the English idea. For such a fact it is impossible to assign a date, because it is not an event but a stage in the endless procession of events. But we can point to landmarks on the way. Of movements significant and prophetic there have been many. The whole course of the Protestant reformation, from the thirteenth century to the nineteenth, is coincident with the transfer of the world's political centre of gravity from the Tiber and the Rhine to the Thames and the Mississippi. The whole career of the men who speak English has within this period been the most potent agency in this transfer. In these gigantic processes of evolution we cannot mark beginnings or endings by years, hardly even by centuries. But among the significant events <small>Significance of the Puritan Exodus.</small> which prophesied the final triumph of the English over the Roman idea, perhaps the most significant — the one which marks most incisively the dawning of a new era — was the migration of English Puritans across the Atlantic Ocean, to repeat in a new environment and on a far grander scale the work which their forefathers had wrought in Britain. The voyage of the Mayflower was not in itself the greatest event in this migration; but it serves to mark the era, and it is only when we study it in the mood awakened by the general considerations here set forth that we can properly estimate the historic importance of the great Puritan Exodus.

CHAPTER II.

THE PURITAN EXODUS.

In the preceding chapter I endeavoured to set forth and illustrate some of the chief causes which have shifted the world's political centre of gravity from the Mediterranean and the Rhine to the Atlantic and the Mississippi; from the men who spoke Latin to the men who speak English. In the course of the exposition we began to catch glimpses of the wonderful significance of the fact that — among the people who had first suggested the true solution of the difficult problem of making a powerful nation without sacrificing local self-government — when the supreme day of trial came, the dominant religious sentiment was arrayed on the side of political freedom and against political despotism. If we consider merely the territorial area which it covered, or the numbers of men slain in its battles, the war of the English parliament against Charles I. seems a trivial affair when contrasted with the gigantic but comparatively insignificant work of barbarians like Jinghis or Tamerlane. But if we consider the moral and political issues involved, and the influence of the struggle upon the future welfare of mankind, we soon come to see that there never was a conflict of more world-wide importance than that from which Oliver

Cromwell came out victorious. It shattered the monarchical power in England at a time when monarchical power was bearing down all opposition in the other great countries of Europe. *Influence of Puritanism upon modern Europe.* It decided that government by the people and for the people should not then perish from the earth. It placed free England in a position of such moral advantage that within another century the English Idea of political life was able to react most powerfully upon continental Europe. It was the study of English institutions by such men as Montesquieu and Turgot, Voltaire and Rousseau, that gave shape and direction to the French Revolution. That violent but wholesome clearing of the air, that tremendous political and moral awakening, which ushered in the nineteenth century in Europe, had its sources in the spirit which animated the preaching of Latimer, the song of Milton, the solemn imagery of Bunyan, the political treatises of Locke and Sidney, the political measures of Hampden and Pym. The noblest type of modern European statesmanship, as represented by Mazzini and Stein, is the spiritual offspring of seventeenth-century Puritanism. To speak of Naseby and Marston Moor as merely English victories would be as absurd as to restrict the significance of Gettysburg to the state of Pennsylvania. If ever there were men who laid down their lives in the cause of all mankind, it was those grim old Ironsides whose watchwords were texts from Holy Writ, whose battle-cries were hymns of praise.

It was to this unwonted alliance of intense religious enthusiasm with the instinct of self-government and the spirit of personal independence that the preservation of English freedom was due. When James I. ascended the English throne, the forces which prepared the Puritan revolt had been slowly and quietly gathering strength among the people for at least two centuries. The work which Wyclif had begun in the fourteenth century had continued to go on in spite of occasional spasmodic attempts to destroy it with the aid of the statute passed in 1401 for the burning of heretics. The Lollards can hardly be said at any time to have constituted a sect, marked off from the established church by the possession of a system of doctrines held in common. The name by which they were known was a nickname which might cover almost any amount of diversity in opinion, like the modern epithets "free-thinker" and "agnostic." The feature which characterized the Lollards in common was a bold spirit of inquiry which led them, in spite of persecution, to read Wyclif's English Bible and call in question such dogmas and rites of the church as did not seem to find warrant in the sacred text. Clad in long robes of coarse red wool, barefoot, with pilgrim's staff in hand, the Lollard preachers fared to and fro among the quaint Gothic towns and shaded hamlets, setting forth the word of God wherever they could find listeners, now in the parish church or under the vaulted roof of the cathedral, now in the churchyard or market-place, or on some green hillside. During the fifteenth century persecution did much to check this open preaching, but pas-

<small>Work of the Lollards.</small>

sages from Wyclif's tracts and texts from the Bible were copied by hand and passed about among tradesmen and artisans, yeomen and plough-boys, to be pondered over and talked about and learned by heart. It was a new revelation to the English people, this discovery of the Bible. Christ and his disciples seemed to come very near when the beautiful story of the gospels was first read in the familiar speech of every-day life. Heretofore they might well have seemed remote and unreal, just as the school-boy hardly realizes that the Cato and Cassius over whom he puzzles in his Latin lessons were once living men like his father and neighbours, and not mere nominatives governing a verb, or ablatives of means or instrument. Now it became possible for the layman to contrast the pure teachings of Christ with the doctrines and demeanour of the priests and monks to whom the spiritual guidance of Englishmen had been entrusted. Strong and self-respecting men and women, accustomed to manage their own affairs, could not but be profoundly affected by the contrast.

While they were thus led more and more to appeal to the Bible as the divine standard of right living and right thinking, at the same time they found in the sacred volume the treasures of a most original and noble literature unrolled before them; stirring history and romantic legend, cosmical theories and priestly injunctions, profound metaphysics and pithy proverbs, psalms of unrivalled grandeur and pastorals of exquisite loveliness, parables fraught with solemn meaning, the mournful wisdom of the preacher, the exultant faith of the apostle, the matchless eloquence of Job and Isaiah, the apocalyptic ecstasy of St. John. At a time when there was as yet no English literature for the common people, this untold wealth of Hebrew literature was implanted in the English mind as in a virgin soil. Great consequences have flowed from the fact that the first truly popular literature in England — the first which stirred the hearts of all classes of people, and filled their minds with ideal pictures and their every-day speech with apt and telling phrases — was the literature comprised within the Bible.

The English version of the Bible. The superiority of the common English version of the Bible, made in the reign of James I., over all other versions, is a fact generally admitted by competent critics. The sonorous Latin of the Vulgate is very grand, but in sublimity of fervour as in the unconscious simplicity of strength it is surpassed by the English version, which is scarcely if at all inferior to the original, while it remains to-day, and will long remain, the noblest monument of English speech. The reason for this is obvious. The common English version of the Bible was made by men who were not aiming at literary effect, but simply gave natural expression to the feelings which for several generations had clustered around the sacred text. They spoke with the voice of a people, which is more than the voice of the most highly gifted man. They spoke with the voice of a people to whom the Bible had come to mean all that it meant to the men who wrote it. To the Englishmen who listened to Latimer, to the Scotchmen who listened to Knox, the Bible more than filled the place which in modern times is filled by poem and essay, by novel and newspaper and scientific treatise. To its pages they went for daily instruction and comfort, with its strange Semitic names they baptized their children, upon its precepts, too often misunderstood and misapplied, they sought to build up a rule of life that might raise them above the crude and unsatisfying world into which they were born.

It would be wrong to accredit all this awakening of spiritual life in England to Wyclif and the Lollards, for it was only after the Bible, in the translations of Tyndall and Coverdale, had been made free to the whole English people in the reign of Edward VI. that its significance began to be apparent; and it was only a century later, in the time of Cromwell and Milton, that its full fruition was reached. It was with the Lollards, however, that the spiritual awakening began and was continued until its effects, when they came, were marked by surprising maturity and suddenness. Because the Lollards were not a clearly defined sect, it was hard to trace the manifold ramifications of their work. During the terrible Wars of the Roses, contemporary chroniclers had little or nothing to say about the labours of these humble men, which seemed of less importance than now, when we read them in the light of their world-wide results. From this silence some modern historians have carelessly inferred that the nascent Protestantism of the Lollards had been extinguished by persecution under the Lancastrian kings, and was in nowise continuous with modern English Protestantism. Nothing could be more erroneous. The extent to which the Lollard leaven had permeated all classes of English society was first clearly revealed when Henry VIII. made his domestic affairs the occasion for a revolt against the Papacy. Despot and brute as he was in many ways, Henry had some characteristics which enabled him to get on well with his people. He not only represented the sentiment of national independence, but he had a truly English reverence for the forms of law. In his worst acts he relied upon the support of his Parliament, which he might in various ways cajole or pack, but could not really enslave. In his quarrel with Rome he could have achieved but little, had he not happened to strike a chord of feeling to which the English people, trained by this slow and subtle work of the Lollards, responded quickly and with a vehemence upon which he had not reckoned. As if by magic, the fabric of Romanism was broken to pieces in England, monasteries were suppressed and their abbots hanged, the authority of the Pope was swept away, and there was no powerful party, like that of the Guises in France, to make such sweeping measures the occasion for civil war. The whole secret of Henry's swift success lay in the fact that the English people were already more than half Protestant in temper, and needed only an occasion for declaring themselves. Hence, as soon as Catholic Henry died, his youthful son found himself seated on the throne of a Protestant

Secret of Henry VIII.'s swift success in his revolt against Rome.

nation. The terrible but feeble persecution which followed under Mary did much to strengthen the extreme Protestant sentiment by allying it with the outraged feeling of national independence. The bloody work of the grand-daughter of Ferdinand and Isabella, the doting wife of Philip II., was rightly felt to be Spanish work; and never, perhaps, did England feel such a sense of relief as on the auspicious day which welcomed to the throne the great Elizabeth, an Englishwoman in every fibre, and whose mother withal was the daughter of a plain country gentleman. But the Marian persecution not only increased the strength of the extreme Protestant sentiment; but indirectly it supplied it with that Calvinistic theology which was to make it indomitable. Of the hundreds of ministers and laymen who fled from England in 1555 and the two following years, a great part found their way to Geneva, and thus came under the immediate personal influence of that man of iron who taught the very doctrines for which their souls were craving, and who was then at the zenith of his power.

<small>Effects of the persecution under Mary.</small>

Among all the great benefactors of mankind the figure of Calvin is perhaps the least attractive. He was, so to speak, the constitutional lawyer of the Reformation, with vision as clear, with head as cool, with soul as dry, as any old solicitor in rusty black that ever dwelt in chambers in Lincoln's Inn. His sternness was that of the judge who dooms a criminal to the gallows. His theology had much in it that is in striking harmony with modern scientific philosophy, and much in it, too, that the descendants of his Puritan converts have learned to loathe as sheer diabolism. It is hard for us to forgive the man who burned Michael Servetus, even though it was the custom of the time to do such things and the tender-hearted Melanchthon found nothing to blame in it. It is not easy to speak of Calvin with enthusiasm, as it comes natural to speak of the genial, whole-souled, many-sided, mirth-and-song-loving Luther. Nevertheless it would be hard to overrate the debt which mankind owe to Calvin. The spiritual father of Coligny, of William the Silent, and of Cromwell must occupy a foremost rank among the champions of modern democracy. Perhaps not one of the mediæval popes was more despotic in temper than Calvin; but it is not the less true that the promulgation of his theology was one of the longest steps that mankind have taken toward personal freedom. Calvinism left the individual man alone in the presence of his God. His salvation could not be wrought by priestly ritual, but only by the grace of God abounding in his soul; and wretched creature that he felt himself to be, through the intense moral awakening of which this stern theology was in part the expression, his soul was nevertheless of infinite value, and the possession of it was the subject of an everlasting struggle between the powers of heaven and the powers of hell. In presence of the awful responsibility of life, all distinctions of rank and fortune vanished; prince and pauper were alike the helpless creatures of Jehovah and

<small>Calvin's theology in its political bearings.</small>

suppliants for his grace. Calvin did not originate these doctrines; in announcing them he was but setting forth, as he said, the Institutes of the Christian religion; but in emphasizing this aspect of Christianity, in engraving it upon men's minds with that keen-edged logic which he used with such unrivalled skill, Calvin made them feel, as it had perhaps never been felt before, the dignity and importance of the individual human soul. It was a religion fit to inspire men who were to be called upon to fight for freedom, whether in the marshes of the Netherlands or on the moors of Scotland. In a church, moreover, based upon such a theology there was no room for prelacy. Each single church tended to become an independent congregation of worshippers, constituting one of the most effective schools that has ever existed for training men in local self-government.

When, therefore, upon the news of Elizabeth's accession to the throne, the Protestant refugees made their way back to England, they came as Calvinistic Puritans. Their stay upon the Continent had been short, but it had been just enough to put the finishing touch upon the work that had been going on since the days of Wyclif. Upon such men and their theories Elizabeth could not look with favour. With all her father's despotic temper, Elizabeth possessed her mother's fine tact, and she represented so grandly the feeling of the nation in its life-and-death-struggle with Spain and the pope, that never perhaps in English history has the crown wielded so much real power as during the five-and-forty years of her wonderful reign.

One day Elizabeth asked a lady of the court how she contrived to retain her husband's affection. The lady replied that "she had confidence in her husband's understanding and courage, well founded on her own steadfastness not to offend or thwart, but to cherish and obey, whereby she did persuade her husband of her own affection, and in so doing did command his." "Go to, go to, mistress," cried the queen, "You are wisely bent, I find. After such sort do I keep the good will of all my husbands, my good people; for if they did not rest assured of some special love towards them, they would not readily yield me such good obedience." [1]

Elizabeth's policy, and its effects.

Such a theory of government might work well in the hands of an Elizabeth, and in the circumstances in which England was then placed; but it could hardly be worked by a successor. The seeds of revolt were already sown. The disposition to curb the sovereign was growing and would surely assert itself as soon as it should have some person less loved and respected than Elizabeth to deal with. The queen in some measure foresaw this, and in the dogged independence and uncompromising enthusiasm of the Puritans she recognized the rock on which monarchy might dash itself into pieces. She therefore hated the Puritans, and persecuted them zealously with one hand, while circumstances forced her in spite of herself to aid and abet them with the other. She could not maintain herself against Spain without helping the Dutch and the Huguenots; but every soldier she sent across the channel came back,

[1] Gardiner, *The Puritan Revolution*, p. 12.

if he came at all, with his head full of the doctrines of Calvin; and these stalwart converts were reinforced by the refugees from France and the Netherlands who came flocking into English towns to set up their thrifty shops and hold prayer-meetings in their humble chapels. To guard the kingdom against the intrigues of Philip and the Guises and the Queen of Scots, it was necessary to choose the most zealous Protestants for the most responsible positions, and such men were more than likely to be Calvinists and Puritans. Elizabeth's great ministers, Burleigh, Walsingham, and Nicholas Bacon, were inclined toward Puritanism; and so were the naval heroes who won the most fruitful victories of that century, by shattering the maritime power of Spain and thus opening the way for Englishmen to colonize North America. If we would realize the dangers that would have beset the Mayflower and her successors but for the preparatory work of these immortal sailors, we must remember the dreadful fate of Ribault and his Huguenot followers in Florida, twenty-three years before that most happy and glorious event, the destruction of the Spanish Armada. But not even the devoted men and women who held their prayer-meetings in the Mayflower's cabin were more constant in prayer or more assiduous in reading the Bible than the dauntless rovers, Drake and Hawkins, Gilbert and Cavendish. *Puritan sea-rovers.*

In the church itself, too, the Puritan spirit grew until in 1575-83 it seized upon Grindal, archbishop of Canterbury, who incurred the queen's disfavour by refusing to meddle with the troublesome reformers or to suppress their prophesyings. By the end of the century the majority of country gentlemen and of wealthy merchants in the towns had become Puritans, and the new views had made great headway in both universities, while at Cambridge they had become dominant.

This allusion to the universities may serve to introduce the very interesting topic of the geographical distribution of Puritanism in England. No one can study the history of the two universities without being impressed with the greater conservatism of Oxford, and the greater hospitality of Cambridge toward new ideas. Possibly the explanation may have some connection with the situation of Cambridge upon the East Anglian border. The eastern counties of England have often been remarked as rife in heresy and independency. For many generations the coast region between the Thames and the Humber was a veritable *litus hæreticum*. Longland, bishop of Lincoln in 1520, reported Lollardism as especially vigorous and obstinate in his diocese, where more than two hundred heretics were once brought before him in the course of a single visitation. It was in Lincolnshire, Norfolk, Suffolk, and Essex, and among the fens of Ely, Cambridge, and Huntingdon, that Puritanism was strongest at the end of the sixteenth century. It was as member and leading spirit of the Eastern Counties Association that Oliver Cromwell began his military career; and in so far as there was anything sectional in the struggle between Charles I. and the Long Parliament, it was a struggle which ended in the victory

Puritanism was strongest in the eastern counties.

of east over west. East Anglia was from first to last the one region in which the supremacy of Parliament was unquestionable and impregnable, even after the strength of its population had been diminished by sending some thousands of picked men and women to America. While every one of the forty counties of England was represented in the great Puritan exodus, the East Anglian counties contributed to it far more than all the rest. Perhaps it would not be far out of the way to say that two-thirds of the American people who can trace their ancestry to New England might follow it back to the East Anglian shires of the mother-country; one-sixth might follow it to those southwestern countries — Devonshire, Dorset, and Somerset — which so long were foremost in maritime enterprise; one-sixth to other parts of England. I would not insist upon the exactness of such figures, in a matter where only a rough approximation is possible; but I do not think they overstate the East Anglian preponderance. It was not by accident that the earliest counties of Massachusetts were called Norfolk, Suffolk, and Essex, or that Boston in Lincolnshire gave its name to the chief city of New England. The native of Connecticut or Massachusetts who wanders about rural England to-day finds no part of it so homelike as the cosy villages and smiling fields and quaint market towns as he fares leisurely and in not too straight a line from Ipswich toward Hull. Countless little unobtrusive features remind him of home. The very names on the sign-boards over the sleepy shops have an un-

Preponderance of East Anglia in the Puritan exodus.

wontedly familiar look. In many instances the homestead which his forefathers left, when they followed Winthrop or Hooker to America, is still to be found, well-kept and comfortable; the ancient manor-house built of massive unhewn stone, yet in other respects much like the New England farmhouse, with its long sloping roof and gable end toward the road, its staircase with twisted balusters running across the shallow entry-way, its low ceilings with their sturdy oaken beams, its spacious chimneys, and its narrow casements from which one might have looked out upon the anxious march of Edward IV. from Ravenspur to the field of victory at Barnet in days when America was unknown. Hard by, in the little parish church which has stood for perhaps a thousand years, plain enough and bleak enough to suit the taste of the sternest Puritan, one may read upon the cold pavement one's own name and the names of one's friends and neighbours in startling proximity, somewhat worn and effaced by the countless feet that have trodden there. And yonder on the village green one comes with bated breath upon the simple inscription which tells of some humble hero who on that spot in the evil reign of Mary suffered death by fire. Pursuing thus our interesting journey, we may come at last to the quiet villages of Austerfield and Scrooby, on opposite banks of the river Idle, and just at the corner of the three shires of Lincoln, York, and Nottingham. It was from this point that the Puritan exodus to America was begun.

It was not, however, in the main stream of Puritanism, but in one of its obscure rivulets that this world-famous movement originated. During the reign of Elizabeth it was not the purpose of the Puritans to separate themselves from the established church of which the sovereign was the head, but to remain within it and reform it according to their own notions. For a time they were partially successful in this work, especially in simplifying the ritual and in giving a Calvinistic tinge to the doctrines. In doing this they showed no conscious tendency toward freedom of thought, but rather a bigotry quite as intense as that which animated the system against which they were fighting. The most advanced liberalism of Elizabeth's time was not to be found among the Puritans, but in the magnificent treatise on "Ecclesiastical Polity" by the churchman Richard Hooker. *Puritanism was not intentionally allied with liberalism.* But the liberalism of this great writer, like that of Erasmus a century earlier, was not militant enough to meet the sterner demands of the time. It could not then ally itself with the democratic spirit, as Puritanism did. It has been well said that while Luther was the prophet of the Reformation that has been, Erasmus was the prophet of the Reformation that is to come, and so it was to some extent with the Puritans and Hooker. The Puritan fight against the hierarchy was a political necessity of the time, something without which no real and thorough reformation could then be effected. In her antipathy to this democratic movement, Elizabeth vexed and tormented the Puritans as far as she deemed it prudent; and in the conservative temper of the people she found enough support to prevent their transforming the church as they would have liked to do. Among the Puritans themselves, indeed, there was no definite agreement on this point. Some would have stopped short with Presbyterianism, while others held that " new presbyter was but old priest writ large," and so pressed on to Independency. It was early in Elizabeth's reign that the zeal of these extreme brethren, inflamed by persecution, gave rise to the sect of Separatists, who flatly denied the royal supremacy over ecclesiastical affairs, and asserted the right to set up churches of their own, with pastors and elders and rules of discipline, independent of queen or bishop.

In 1567 the first congregation of this sort, consisting of about a hundred persons assembled in a hall in Anchor Lane in London, was forcibly broken up and thirty-one of the number were sent to jail and kept there for nearly a year. By 1576 the Separatists had come to be recognized as a sect, under the lead of Robert Brown, a man of high social position, related to the great Lord Burleigh. Brown fled to Holland, where he preached to a congregation of English exiles, and wrote books which were smuggled into England and privately circulated there, much to the disgust, not only of the queen, but of all parties, Puritans as well as High Churchmen. The great majority of Puritans, whose aim was not to leave the church, but to stay in it and control it, looked with dread and disapproval upon these extremists who seemed likely to endanger their success by forcing them into deadly opposition to the crown. Just as in the years which ushered in our

Robert Brown and the Separatists.

late Civil War, the opponents of the Republicans sought to throw discredit upon them by confusing them with the little sect of Abolitionists; and just as the Republicans, in resenting the imputation, went so far as to frown upon the Abolitionists, so that in December, 1860, men who had just voted for Mr. Lincoln were ready to join in breaking up "John Brown meetings" in Boston; so it was with religious parties in the reign of Elizabeth. The opponents of the Puritans pointed to the Separatists, and cried, "See whither your anarchical doctrines are leading!" and in their eagerness to clear themselves of this insinuation, the leading Puritans were as severe upon the Separatists as anybody. It is worthy of note that in both instances the imputation, so warmly resented, was true. Under the pressure of actual hostilities the Republicans did become Abolitionists, and in like manner, when in England it came to downright warfare the Puritans became Separatists. But meanwhile it fared ill with the little sect which everybody hated and despised. Their meetings were broken up by mobs. In an old pamphlet describing a "tumult in Fleet Street, raised by the disorderly preachment, pratings, and prattlings of a swarm of Separatists," one reads such sentences as the following: "At length they catcht one of them alone, but they kickt him so vehemently as if they meant to beat him into a jelly. It is ambiguous whether they have kil'd him or no, but for a certainty they did knock him about as if they meant to pull him to pieces. I confesse it had been no matter if they had beaten the whole tribe in the like manner." For their leaders the penalty was more serious. The denial of the queen's ecclesiastical supremacy could be treated as high treason, and two of Brown's friends, convicted of circulating his books, were sent to the gallows. In spite of these dangers Brown returned to England in 1585. William the Silent had lately been murdered, and heresy in Holland was not yet safe from the long arm of the Spaniard. Brown trusted in Lord Burleigh's ability to protect him, but in 1588, finding himself in imminent danger, he suddenly recanted and accepted a comfortable living under the bishops who had just condemned him. His followers were already known as Brownists; henceforth their enemies took pains to call them so and twit them with holding doctrines too weak for making martyrs.

The flimsiness of Brown's moral texture prevented him from becoming the leader in the Puritan exodus to New England. That honour was reserved for William Brewster, son of a country gentleman who had for many years been postmaster at Scrooby. The office was then one of high responsibility and influence. After taking his degree at Cambridge, Brewster became private secretary to Sir William Davison, whom he accompanied on his mission to the Netherlands. When Davison's public career came to an end in 1587, Brewster returned to Scrooby, and soon afterward succeeded his father as postmaster, in which position he remained until 1607. During the interval Elizabeth died, and James Stuart came from Scotland to take her place on the throne.

William Brewster.

The feelings with which the late queen had regarded Puritanism were mild compared with the sentiments entertained by her successor. For some years he had been getting worsted in his struggle with the Presbyterians of the northern kingdom. His vindictive memory treasured up the day when a mighty Puritan preacher had in public twitched him by the sleeve and called him "God's silly vassal." "I tell you, sir," said Andrew Melville on that occasion, "there are two kings and two kingdoms in Scotland. There is Christ Jesus the King, and his kingdom the Kirk, whose subject James VI. is, and of whose kingdom not a king, nor a lord, nor a head, but a member. And they whom Christ hath called to watch over his kirk and govern his spiritual kingdom have sufficient power and authority so to do both together and severally." In this bold and masterful speech we have the whole political philosophy of Puritanism, as in a nutshell. Under the guise of theocratic fanaticism, and in words as arrogant as ever fell from priestly lips, there was couched the assertion of the popular will against despotic privilege. Melville could say such things to the king's face and walk away unharmed, because there stood behind him a people fully aroused to the conviction that there is an eternal law of God, which kings no less than scullions must obey.[1] Melville knew this full well, and so did James know it in the bitterness of his heart. He would have no such mischievous work in England. He despised Elizabeth's grand national policy which

James Stuart and Andrew Melville.

---

[1] Green, *History of the English People*, iii. 47.

his narrow intellect could not comprehend. He could see that in fighting Spain and aiding Dutchmen and Huguenots she was strengthening the very spirit that sought to pull monarchy down. In spite of her faults, which were neither few nor small, the patriotism of that fearless woman was superior to any personal ambition. It was quite otherwise with James. He was by no means fearless, and he cared more for James Stuart than for either England or Scotland. He had an overweening opinion of his skill in kingcraft. In coming to Westminster it was his policy to use his newly acquired power to break down the Puritan party in both kingdoms and to fasten episcopacy upon Scotland. In pursuing this policy he took no heed of English national sentiment, but was quite ready to defy and insult it, even to the point of making — before children who remembered the Armada had yet reached middle age — an alliance with the hated Spaniard. In such wise James succeeded in arraying against the monarchical principle the strongest forces of English life, — the sentiment of nationality, the sentiment of personal freedom, and the uncompromising religious fervour of Calvinism; and out of this invincible combination of forces has been wrought the nobler and happier state of society in which we live to-day.

Scarcely ten months had James been king of England when he invited the leading Puritan clergymen to meet himself and the bishops in a conference at Hampton Court, as he wished to learn what changes they would like to make in the government and ritual of the church. In the course of the discussion he lost his temper and stormed, as was his wont. The mention of the word "presbytery" lashed him into fury. "A Scottish presbytery," he cried, "agreeth as well with a monarchy as God and the Devil. Then Jack and Tom and Will and Dick shall meet, and at their pleasures censure me and my council, and all our proceedings. . . . Stay, I pray you, for one seven years, before you demand that from me, and if then you find me pursy and fat, and my windpipes stuffed, I will perhaps hearken to you. . . . Until you find that I grow lazy, let that alone." One of the bishops declared that in this significant tirade his Majesty spoke by special inspiration from Heaven! The Puritans saw that their only hope lay in resistance. If any doubt remained, it was dispelled by the vicious threat with which the king broke up the conference. "I will *make* them conform," said he, "or I will harry them out of the land."

King James's view of the political situation.

These words made a profound sensation in England, as well they might, for they heralded the struggle which within half a century was to deliver up James's son to the executioner. The Parliament of 1604 met in angrier mood than any Parliament which had assembled at Westminster since the dethronement of Richard II. Among the churches non-conformity began more decidedly to assume the form of secession. The key-note of the conflict was struck at Scrooby. Staunch Puritan as he was, Brewster had not hitherto favoured the extreme measures of the Separatists. Now he withdrew from the church, and gathered together a company of men and women who met on Sundays for divine service in his own drawing-room at Scrooby Manor. In organizing this independent Congregationalist society, Brewster was powerfully aided by John Robinson, a native of Lincolnshire. Robinson was then thirty years of age, and had taken his master's degree at Cambridge in 1600. He was a man of great learning and rare sweetness of temper, and was moreover distinguished for a broad and tolerant habit of mind too seldom found among the Puritans of that day. Friendly and unfriendly writers alike bear witness to his spirit of Christian charity and the comparatively slight value which he attached to orthodoxy in points of doctrine; and we can hardly be wrong in supposing that the comparatively tolerant behaviour of the Plymouth colonists, whereby they were contrasted with the settlers of Massachusetts, was in some measure due to the abiding influence of the teachings of this admirable man. Another important member of the Scrooby congregation was William Bradford, of the neighbouring village of Austerfield, then a lad of seventeen years, but already remarkable for maturity of intelligence and weight of character. Afterward governor of Plymouth for nearly thirty years, he became the historian of his colony; and to his picturesque chronicle, written in pure and vigorous English, we are indebted for most that we know of the migration that started from Scrooby and ended in Plymouth.

<small>The congregation of Separatists at Scrooby.</small>

It was in 1606 — two years after King James's

truculent threat — that this independent church of Scrooby was organized. Another year had not elapsed before its members had suffered so much at the hands of officers of the law, that they began to think of following the example of former heretics and escaping to Holland. After an unsuccessful attempt in the autumn of 1607, they at length succeeded a few months later in accomplishing their flight to Amsterdam, where they hoped to find a home. But here they found the English exiles who had preceded them so fiercely involved in doctrinal controversies, that they decided to go further in search of peace and quiet. This decision, which we may ascribe to Robinson's wise counsels, served to keep the society of Pilgrims from getting divided and scattered. They reached Leyden in 1609, just as the Spanish government had sullenly abandoned the hopeless task of conquer- *The flight to Holland.* ing the Dutch, and had granted to Holland the Twelve Years Truce. During eleven of these twelve years the Pilgrims remained in Leyden, supporting themselves by various occupations, while their numbers increased from 300 to more than 1000. Brewster opened a publishing house, devoted mainly to the issue of theological books. Robinson accepted a professorship in the university, and engaged in the defence of Calvinism against the attacks of Episcopius, the successor of Arminius. The youthful Bradford devoted himself to the study of languages, — Dutch, French, Latin, Greek, and finally Hebrew; wishing, as he said, to " see with his own eyes the ancient oracles of God in all their native beauty." During their sojourn in Leyden, the Pilgrims were introduced to a strange and novel spectacle, — the systematic legal toleration of all persons, whether Catholic or Protestant, who called themselves followers of Christ. Not that there was not plenty of intolerance in spirit, but the policy inaugurated by the idolized William the Silent held it in check by law. All persons who came to Holland, and led decorous lives there, were protected in their opinions and customs. By contemporary writers in other countries this eccentric behaviour of the Dutch government was treated with unspeakable scorn. "All strange religions flock thither," says one; it is "a common harbour of all heresies," a "cage of unclean birds," says another; "the great mingle mangle of religion," says a third.[1] In spite of the relief from persecution, however, the Pilgrims were not fully satisfied with their new home. The expiration of the truce with Spain might prove that this relief was only temporary; and at any rate, complete toleration did not fill the measure of their wants. Had they come to Holland as scattered bands of refugees, they might have been absorbed into the Dutch population, as Huguenot refugees have been absorbed in Germany, England, and America. But they had come as an organized community, and absorption into a foreign nation was something to be dreaded. They wished to preserve their English speech and English traditions, keep up their organization, and find some favoured spot where they might lay the corner-stone of a great Christian state. The spirit of nationality was

Why the Pilgrims did not stay there.

---

[1] Steele's *Life of Brewster*, p. 161.

strong in them; the spirit of self-government was strong in them; and the only thing which could satisfy these feelings was such a migration as had not been seen since ancient times, a migration like that of Phokaians to Massilia or Tyrians to Carthage.

It was too late in the world's history to carry out such a scheme upon European soil. Every acre of territory there was appropriated. The only favourable outlook was upon the Atlantic coast of America, where English cruisers had now successfully disputed the pretensions of Spain, and where after forty years of disappointment and disaster a flourishing colony had at length been founded in Virginia. The colonization of the North American coast had now become part of the avowed policy of the British government. In 1606 a great joint-stock company was formed for the establishment of two colonies in America. The branch which was to take charge of the proposed southern colony had its headquarters in London; the management of the northern branch was at Plymouth in Devonshire. Hence the two branches are commonly spoken of as the London and Plymouth companies. The former was also called the Virginia Company, and the latter the North Virginia Company, as the name of Virginia was then loosely applied to the entire Atlantic coast north of Florida. The London Company had jurisdiction from 34° to 38° north latitude; the Plymouth Company had jurisdiction from 45° down to 41°; the intervening territory, between 38° and 41° was to go to whichever company should first plant a self-supporting colony. The local The London and Plymouth companies.

government of each colony was to be entrusted to a council resident in America and nominated by the king; while general supervision over both colonies was to be exercised by a council resident in England.

In pursuance of this general plan, though with some variations in detail, the settlement of Jamestown had been begun in 1607, and its success was now beginning to seem assured. On the other hand all the attempts which had been made to the north of the fortieth parallel had failed miserably. As early as 1602 Bartholomew Gosnold, with 32 men, had landed on the headland which they named Cape Cod from the fish found thereabouts in great numbers. This was the first English name given to any spot in that part of America, and so far as known these were the first Englishmen that ever set foot there. They went on and gave names to Martha's Vineyard and the Elizabeth Islands in Buzzard's Bay; and on Cuttyhunk they built some huts with the intention of remaining, but after a month's experience they changed their mind and went back to England. Gosnold's story interested other captains, and on Easter Sunday, 1605, George Weymouth set sail for North Virginia, as it was called. He found Cape Cod and coasted northward as far as the Kennebec river, up which he sailed for many miles. Weymouth kidnapped five Indians and carried them to England, that they might learn the language and acquire a wholesome respect for the arts of civilization and the resistless power of white men. His glowing accounts of the spacious har-

First exploration of the New England coast.

bours, the abundance of fish and game, the noble trees, the luxuriant herbage, and the balmy climate, aroused general interest in England, and doubtless had some influence upon the formation, in the following year, of the great joint-stock company just described. The leading spirit of the Plymouth Company was Sir John Popham, chief-justice of England, and he was not disposed to let his friends of the southern branch excel him in promptness. Within three months after the founding of Jamestown, a party of 120 colonists, led by the judge's kinsman George Popham, landed at the mouth of the Kennebec, and proceeded to build a rude village of some fifty cabins, with storehouse, chapel, and block-house. When they landed in August they doubtless shared Weymouth's opinion of the climate. These Englishmen had heard of warm countries like Italy and cold countries like Russia; harsh experience soon taught them that there are climates in which the summer of Naples may alternate with the winter of Moscow. The president and many others fell sick and died. News came of the death of Sir John Popham in England, and presently the weary and disappointed settlers abandoned their enterprise and returned to their old homes. Their failure spread abroad in England the opinion that North Virginia was uninhabitable by reason of the cold, and no further attempts were made upon that coast until in 1614 it was visited by Captain John Smith.

The romantic career of this gallant and garrulous hero did not end with his departure from the infant colony at Jamestown. By a curious destiny his fame is associated with the beginnings of both the southern and the northern portions of the United States. To Virginia Smith may be said to have given its very existence as a commonwealth; to New England he gave its name. In 1614 he came over with two ships to North Virginia, explored its coast minutely from the Penobscot river to Cape Cod, and thinking it a country of such extent and importance as to deserve a name of its own, rechristened it New England. On returning home he made a very good map of the coast and dotted it with English names suggested by Prince Charles. Of these names Cape Elizabeth, Cape Ann, Charles River, and Plymouth still remain where Smith placed them. In 1615 Smith again set sail for the New World, this time with a view to planting a colony under the auspices of the Plymouth Company, but his talent for strange adventures had not deserted him. He was taken prisoner by a French fleet, carried hither and thither on a long cruise, and finally set ashore at Rochelle, whence, without a penny in his pocket, he contrived to make his way back to England. Perhaps Smith's life of hardship may have made him prematurely old. After all his wild and varied experience he was now only in his thirty-seventh year, but he does not seem to have gone on any more voyages. The remaining sixteen years of his life were spent quietly in England in writing books, publishing maps, and otherwise stimulating the public interest in the colonization of the New World. But as for the rocky coast of New England, which he had explored and named, he declared that he was

John Smith.

not so simple as to suppose that any other motive than riches would "ever erect there a commonwealth or draw company from their ease and humours at home, to stay in New England."

In this opinion, however, the bold explorer was mistaken. Of all migrations of peoples the settlement of New England is preëminently the one in which the almighty dollar played the smallest part, however important it may since have become as a motive power. It was left for religious enthusiasm to achieve what commercial enterprise had failed to accomplish. By the summer of 1617 the Pilgrim society at Leyden had decided to send a detachment of its most vigorous members to lay the foundations of a Puritan state in America. There had been much discussion as to the fittest site for such a colony. Many were in favour of Guiana, which Sir Walter Raleigh had described in such glowing colours; but it was thought that the tropical climate would be ill-suited to northern men of industrious and thrifty habit, and the situation, moreover, was dangerously exposed to the Spaniards. Half a century had scarcely elapsed since the wholesale massacre of Huguenots in Florida. Virginia was then talked of, but Episcopal ideas had already taken root there. New England, on the other hand, was considered too cold. Popham's experience was not encouraging. But the country about the Delaware river afforded an opportunity for erecting an independent colony under the jurisdiction of the London Company, and this seemed the best course to pursue. Sir Edwin Sandys, the leading spirit in the

The Pilgrims at Leyden decide to make a settlement near the Delaware river.

London Company, was favourably inclined toward Puritans, and through him negotiations were begun. Capital to the amount of £7000 was furnished by seventy merchant adventurers in England, and the earnings of the settlers were to be thrown into a common stock until these subscribers should have been remunerated. A grant of land was obtained from the London Company, and the king was asked to protect the emigrants by a charter, but this was refused. James, however, made no objections to their going, herein showing himself less of a bigot than Louis XIV. in later days, who would not suffer a Huguenot to set foot in Canada, though France was teeming with Huguenots who would have been glad enough to go. When James inquired how the colonists expected to support themselves, some one answered, most likely by fishing. "Very good," quoth the king, " it was the Apostles' own calling." He declared that no one should molest them so long as they behaved themselves properly. From this unwonted urbanity it would appear that James anticipated no trouble from the new colony. A few Puritans in America could not do much to annoy him, and there was of course a fair chance of their perishing, as so many other colonizers had perished.

The congregation at Leyden did not think it wise to cut loose from Holland until they should have secured a foothold in America. It was but an advance guard that started out from Delft haven late in July, 1620, in the rickety ship Speedwell, with Brewster and Bradford, and sturdy Miles Standish, a trained soldier whose aid was welcome, though he does not seem to have belonged to the congregation. Robinson remained at Leyden, and never came to America. After a brief stop at Southampton, where they met the Mayflower with friends from London, the Pilgrims again set sail in the two ships. The Speedwell sprang a leak, and they stopped at Dartmouth for repairs. Again they started, and had put three hundred miles of salt water between themselves and Land's End, when the Speedwell leaked so badly that they were forced to return. When they dropped anchor at Plymouth in Devonshire, about twenty were left on shore, and the remainder, exactly one hundred in number, crowded into the Mayflower and on the 6th of September started once more to cross the Atlantic. The capacity of the little ship was 180 tons, and her strength was but slight. In a fierce storm in mid-ocean a mainbeam amidships was wrenched and cracked, and but for a huge iron screw which one of the passengers had brought from Delft, they might have gone to the bottom. The foul weather prevented any accurate calculation of latitude and longitude, and they were so far out in their reckoning that when they caught sight of land on the 9th of November, it was to Cape Cod that they had come. Their patent gave them no authority to settle here, as it was beyond the jurisdiction of the London Company. They turned their prow southward, but encountering perilous shoals and a stiff headwind they desisted and sought shelter in Cape Cod bay. On the 11th they decided to find some place of abode in this neighbourhood, anticipating no difficulty in getting

Voyage of the Mayflower.

a patent from the Plymouth Company, which was anxious to obtain settlers. For five weeks they stayed in the ship while little parties were exploring the coast and deciding upon the best site for a town. It was purely a coincidence that the spot which they chose had already received from John Smith the name of Plymouth, the beautiful port in Devonshire from which the Mayflower had sailed.

<small>Founding of Plymouth.</small>

There was not much to remind them of home in the snow-covered coast on which they landed. They had hoped to get their rude houses built before the winter should set in, but the many delays and mishaps had served to bring them ashore in the coldest season. When the long winter came to an end, fifty-one of the hundred Pilgrims had died, — a mortality even greater than that before which the Popham colony had succumbed. But Brewster spoke truth when he said, "It is not with us as with men whom small things can discourage or small discontentments cause to wish themselves at home again." At one time the living were scarcely able to bury the dead; only Brewster, Standish, and five other hardy ones were well enough to get about. At first they were crowded under a single roof, and as glimpses were caught of dusky savages skulking among the trees, a platform was built on the nearest hill and a few cannon were placed there in such wise as to command the neighbouring valleys and plains. By the end of the first summer the platform had grown to a fortress, down from which to the harbour led a village street with seven houses finished and others going up. Twenty-six acres had been cleared, and a plentiful harvest gathered in; venison, wild fowl, and fish were easy to obtain. When provisions and fuel had been laid in for the ensuing winter, Governor Bradford appointed a day of Thanksgiving. Town-meetings had already been held, and a few laws passed. The history of New England had begun.

This had evidently been a busy summer for the forty-nine survivors. On the 9th of November, the anniversary of the day on which they had sighted land, a ship was descried in the offing. She was the Fortune, bringing some fifty more of the Leyden company. It was a welcome reinforcement, but it diminished the rations of food that could be served during the winter, for the Fortune was not well supplied. When she set sail for England, she carried a little cargo of beaver-skins and choice wood for wainscoting to the value of £500 sterling, as a first instalment of the sum due to the merchant adventurers. But this cargo never reached England, for the Fortune was overhauled by a French cruiser and robbed of everything worth carrying away.

For two years more it was an anxious and difficult time for the new colony. By 1624 its success may be said to have become assured. That the Indians in the neighbourhood had not taken advantage of the distress of the settlers in that first winter, and massacred every one of them, was due to a remarkable circumstance. Early in 1617 a frightful pestilence had swept over New England and slain, it is thought, more than half the Indian population between the Penobscot river and Narragansett bay. Many of the Indians were inclined to attribute this calamity to the murder of two or three white fishermen the year before. They had not got over the superstitious dread with which the first sight of white men had inspired them, and now they believed that the strangers held the demon of the plague at their disposal and had let him loose upon the red men in revenge for the murders they had committed. This wholesome delusion kept their tomahawks quiet for a while. When they saw the Englishmen establishing themselves at Plymouth, they at first held a powwow in the forest, at which the new-comers were cursed with all the elaborate ingenuity that the sorcery of the medicine-men could summon for so momentous an occasion; but it was deemed best to refrain from merely human methods of attack. It was not until the end of the first winter that any of them mustered courage to visit the palefaces. Then an Indian named Samoset, who had learned a little English from fishermen and for his own part was inclined to be friendly, came one day into the village with words of welcome. He was so kindly treated that presently Massasoit, principal sachem of the Wampanoags, who dwelt between Narragansett and Cape Cod bays, came with a score of painted and feathered warriors and squatting on a green rug and cushions in the governor's log-house smoked the pipe of peace, while Standish with half-a-dozen musketeers stood quietly by. An offensive and defensive alliance was then and there made between King

Why the colony was not attacked by the Indians.

Massasoit and King James, and the treaty was faithfully kept for half a century. Some time afterward, when Massasoit had fallen sick and lay at death's door, his life was saved by Edward Winslow, who came to his wigwam and skilfully nursed him. Henceforth the Wampanoag thought well of the Pilgrim. The powerful Narragansetts, who dwelt on the farther side of the bay, felt differently, and thought it worth while to try the effect of a threat. A little while after the Fortune had brought its reinforcement, the Narragansett sachem Canonicus sent a messenger to Plymouth with a bundle of newly-made arrows wrapped in a snake-skin. The messenger threw it in at the governor's door and made off with unseemly haste. Bradford understood this as a challenge, and in this he was confirmed by a friendly Wampanoag. The Narragansetts could muster 2000 warriors, for whom forty or fifty Englishmen, even with fire-arms, were hardly a fair match; but it would not do to show fear. Bradford stuffed the snake-skin with powder and bullets, and sent it back to Canonicus, telling him that if he wanted war he might come whenever he liked and get his fill of it. When the sachem saw what the skin contained, he was afraid to touch it or have it about, and medicine-men, handling it no doubt gingerly enough, carried it out of his territory.

It was a fortunate miscalculation that brought the Pilgrims to New England. Had they ventured upon the lands between the Hudson and the Delaware, they would probably have fared worse. They would soon have come into collision with the

Dutch, and not far from that neighbourhood dwelt the Susquehannocks, at that time one of the most powerful and ferocious tribes on the continent. For the present the new-comers were less likely to be molested in the Wampanoag country than anywhere else. In the course of the year 1621 they obtained their grant from the Plymouth Company. This grant was not made to them directly but to the joint-stock company of merchant adventurers with whom they were associated. But the alliance between the Pilgrims and these London merchants was not altogether comfortable; there was too much divergence between their aims. In 1627 the settlers, wishing to be entirely independent, bought up all the stock and paid for it by instalments from the fruits of their labour. By 1633 they had paid every penny, and become the undisputed owners of the country they had occupied.

Such was the humble beginning of that great Puritan exodus from England to America which had so much to do with founding and peopling the United States. These Pilgrims of the Mayflower were but the pioneers of a mighty host. Historically their enterprise is interesting not so much for what it achieved as for what it suggested. Of itself the Plymouth colony could hardly have become a wealthy and powerful state. Its growth was extremely slow. After ten years its numbers were but three hundred. In 1643, when the exodus had come to an end, and the New England Confederacy was formed, the population of Plymouth was but three thousand. In an established community, indeed, such a rate of increase would be rapid, but it was not sufficient to raise in New England a power which could overcome Indians and Dutchmen and Frenchmen, and assert its will in opposition to the crown. It is when we view the founding of Plymouth in relation to what came afterward, that it assumes the importance which belongs to the beginning of a new era.

We have thus seen how it was that the political aspirations of James I. toward absolute sovereignty resulted in the beginnings of the Puritan exodus to America. In the next chapter we shall see how the still more arbitrary policy of his ill-fated son all at once gave new dimensions to that exodus and resulted in the speedy planting of a high-spirited and powerful New England.

CHAPTER III.

THE PLANTING OF NEW ENGLAND.

WHEN Captain George Weymouth in the summer of 1605 sailed into the harbour of Plymouth in Devonshire, with his five kidnapped savages and his glowing accounts of the country since known as New England, the garrison of that fortified seaport was commanded by Sir Ferdinando Gorges. The Christian name of this person now strikes us as rather odd, but in those days it was not so uncommon in England, and it does not necessarily indicate a Spanish or Italian ancestry for its bearer. Gorges was a man of considerable ability, but not of high character. On the downfall of his old patron the Earl of Essex he had contrived to save his own fortunes by a course of treachery and ingratitude. He had served in the Dutch war against Spain, and since 1596 had been military governor of Plymouth. The sight of Weymouth's Indians and the recital of his explorations awakened the interest of Gorges in the colonization of North America. He became one of the most active members of the Plymouth, or North Virginia, Company established in the following year. It was he who took the leading part in fitting out the two ships with which John Smith started on his unsuccessful expedition in 1615. In the following years he continued to send out voyages of exploration, became largely interested in the fisheries, and at length in 1620 succeeded in obtaining a new patent for the Plymouth Company, by which it was made independent of the London Company, its old yoke-fellow and rival. This new document created a corporation of forty patentees who, sitting in council as directors of their enterprise, were known as the Council for New England. Sir Ferdinando Gorges, and the Council for New England. The president of this council was King James's unpopular favourite the Duke of Buckingham, and its most prominent members were the earls of Pembroke and Lenox, Sir Ferdinando Gorges, and Shakespeare's friend the Earl of Southampton. This council was empowered to legislate for its American territory, to exercise martial law there and expel all intruders, and to exercise a monopoly of trade within the limits of the patent. Such extensive powers, entrusted to a company of which Buckingham was the head, excited popular indignation, and in the great struggle against monopolies which was then going on, the Plymouth Company did not fail to serve as a target for attacks. It started, however, with too little capital to enter upon schemes involving immediate outlay, and began almost from the first to seek to increase its income by letting or selling portions of its territory, which extended from the latitude of Philadelphia to that of Quebec, thus encroaching upon regions where Holland and France were already gaining a foothold. It was from this company that the merchant adventurers associated with the Mayflower Pilgrims obtained their new patent in the summer of 1621, and for the next fifteen years all settlers in New England based their claims to the soil upon territorial rights conveyed to them by the Plymouth Company. The grants, however, were often ignorantly and sometimes unscrupulously made, and their limits were so ill-defined that much quarrelling ensued.

During the years immediately following the voyage of the Mayflower, several attempts at settlement were made about the shores of Massachusetts bay. One of the merchant adventurers, Thomas Weston, took it into his head in 1622 to separate from his partners and send out a colony of seventy men on his own account. These men made a settlement at Wessagusset, some twenty-five miles north of Plymouth. They were a disorderly, thriftless rabble, picked up from the London streets, and soon got into trouble with the Indians; after a year they were glad to get back to England as best they could, and in this the Plymouth settlers willingly aided them. In June of that same year 1622 there arrived on the scene a picturesque but ill understood personage, Thomas Morton, " of Clifford's Inn, Gent.," as he tells on the title-page of his quaint and delightful book, the " New English Canaan." Bradford disparagingly says that he " had been a kind of petie-fogger of Furnifell's Inn "; but the churchman Samuel Maverick declares that he was a " gentleman of good qualitie." He was an agent of Sir Ferdinando Gorges, and came with some thirty followers to make the beginnings of a royalist and Episcopal settlement in the Massachu-

Wessagusset and Merrymount.

setts bay. He was naturally regarded with ill favour by the Pilgrims as well as by the later Puritan settlers, and their accounts of him will probably bear taking with a grain or two of salt.

In 1625 there came one Captain Wollaston, with a gang of indented white servants, and established himself on the site of the present town of Quincy. Finding this system of industry ill suited to northern agriculture, he carried most of his men off to Virginia, where he sold them. Morton took possession of the site of the settlement, which he called Merrymount. There, according to Bradford, he set up a " schoole of athisme," and his men did quaff strong waters and comport themselves " as if they had anew revived and celebrated the feasts of ye Roman Goddes Flora, or the beastly practices of ye madd Bachanalians." Charges of atheism have been freely hurled about in all ages. In Morton's case the accusation seems to have been based upon the fact that he used the Book of Common Prayer. His men so far maintained the ancient customs of merry England as to plant a Maypole eighty feet high, about which they frolicked with the redskins, while furthermore they taught them the use of firearms and sold them muskets and rum. This was positively dangerous, and in the summer of 1628 the settlers at Merrymount were dispersed by Miles Standish. Morton was sent to England, but returned the next year, and presently again repaired to Merrymount.

By this time other settlements were dotted about the coast. There were a few scattered cottages or cabins at Nantasket and at the mouth of the Piscataqua, while Samuel Maverick had fortified himself on Noddle's Island, and William Blackstone already lived upon the Shawmut peninsula, since called Boston. These two gentlemen were no friends to the Puritans; they were churchmen and representatives of Sir Ferdinando Gorges.

The case was very different with another of these earliest settlements, which deserves especial mention as coming directly in the line of causation which led to the founding of Massachusetts by Puritans. For some years past the Dorchester adventurers — a small company of merchants in the shire town of Dorset — had been sending vessels to catch fish off the New England coast. In 1623 these men conceived the idea of planting a small village as a fishing station, and setting up a church and preacher therein, for the spiritual solace of the fishermen and sailors. In pursuance of this scheme a small party occupied Cape Ann, where after two years they got into trouble with the men of Plymouth. Several grants and assignments had made it doubtful where the ownership lay, and although this place was not near their own town, the men of Plymouth claimed it. The dispute was amicably arranged by Roger Conant, an independent settler who had withdrawn from Plymouth because he did not fully sympathize with the Separatist views of the people there. The next step was for the Dorchester adventurers to appoint Conant as their manager, and the next was for them to abandon their enterprise, dissolve their partnership, and leave the remnant of the little colony to shift for

The Dorchester adventurers.

itself. The settlers retained their tools and cattle, and Conant found for them a new and safer situation at Naumkeag, on the site of the present Salem. So far little seemed to have been accomplished; one more seemed added to the list of failures.

But the excellent John White, the Puritan rector of Trinity Church in Dorchester, had meditated carefully about these things. He saw that many attempts at colonization had failed because they made use of unfit instruments, "a multitude of rude ungovernable persons, the very scum of the land." So Virginia had failed in its first years, and only succeeded when settled by worthy and industrious people under a strong government. The example of Plymouth, as contrasted with Wessagusset, taught a similar lesson. We desire, said White, "to raise a bulwark against the kingdom of Antichrist." Learn wisdom, my countrymen, from the ruin which has befallen the Protestants at Rochelle and in the Palatinate; learn "to avoid the plague while it is foreseen, and not to tarry as they did till it overtook them." The Puritan party in England *John White and his noble scheme.* was numerous and powerful, but the day of strife was not far off and none might foretell its issue. Clearly it was well to establish a strong and secure retreat in the New World, in case of disaster in the Old. What had been done at Plymouth by a few men of humble means might be done on a much greater scale by an association of leading Puritans, including men of wealth and wide social influence. Such arguments were urged in timely pamphlets, of one of which White is supposed to have been the author. The matter was discussed in London, and inquiry was made whether fit men could be found "to engage their persons in the voyage." "It fell out that among others they lighted at last on Master Endicott, a man well known to divers persons of good note, who manifested much willingness to accept of the offer as soon as it was tendered." All were thereby much encouraged, the schemes of White took definite shape, and on the 19th of March, 1628, a tract of land was obtained from the Council for New England, consisting of all the territory included between three miles north of the Merrimack and three miles south of the Charles in one direction, and the Atlantic and Pacific Oceans in the other.

This liberal grant was made at a time when people still supposed the Pacific coast to be not far west of Henry Hudson's river. The territory was granted to an association of six gentlemen, only one of whom — John Endicott — figures conspicuously in the history of New England. The grant was <small>Conflicting grants sow seeds of trouble.</small> made in the usual reckless style, and conflicted with various patents which had been issued before. In 1622 Gorges and John Mason had obtained a grant of all the land between the rivers Kennebec and Merrimack, and the new grant encroached somewhat upon this. The difficulty seems to have been temporarily adjusted by some sort of compromise which restricted the new grant to the Merrimack, for in 1629 we find Mason's title confirmed to the region between that river and the Piscataqua, while later on Gorges appears as proprietor of the territory between the Piscataqua and the Kennebec. A more serious difficulty was the claim of Robert Gorges, son of Sir Ferdinando. That young man had in 1623 obtained a grant of some 300 square miles in Massachusetts, and had gone to look after it, but had soon returned discouraged to England and shortly afterward died. But his claim devolved upon his surviving brother, John Gorges, and Sir Ferdinando, in consenting to the grant to Endicott and his friends, expressly reserved the rights of his sons. No such reservation, however, was mentioned in the Massachusetts charter, and the colonists never paid the slightest heed to it. In these conflicting claims were sown seeds of trouble which bore fruit for more than half a century.

In such cases actual possession is apt to make nine points in the law, and accordingly Endicott was sent over, as soon as possible, with sixty persons, to reinforce the party at Naumkeag and supersede Conant as its leader. On Endicott's arrival in September, 1628, the settlers were at first inclined to dispute his authority, but they were soon conciliated, and in token of this amicable adjustment the place was called by the Hebrew name of Salem, or "peace." *John Endicott and the founding of Salem.*

Meanwhile Mr. White and the partners in England were pushing things vigorously. Their scheme took a wider scope. They were determined to establish something more than a trading company. From Charles I. it was sometimes easy to get promises because he felt himself under no obligation to keep them. In March, 1629, a royal charter was granted, creating a corporation, under the legal style of the Governor and Company of Massachusetts Bay in New England. The affairs of this corporate body were to be managed by a governor, deputy-governor, and a council of eighteen assistants, to be elected annually by the company. They were empowered to make such laws as they liked for their settlers, provided they did not contravene the laws of England, — a proviso susceptible of much latitude of interpretation. The place where the company was to hold its meetings was not mentioned in the charter. The law-officers of the crown at first tried to insert a condition that the government must reside in England, but the grantees with skilful argument succeeded in preventing this. Nothing was said in the charter about religious liberty, for a twofold reason : the crown would not have granted it, and it was not what the grantees wanted ; such a provision would have been liable to hamper them seriously in carrying out their scheme. They preferred to keep in their own hands the question as to how much or how little religious liberty they should claim or allow. Six small ships were presently fitted out, and upon them were embarked 300 men, 80 women, and 26 children, with 140 head of cattle, 40 goats, and abundance of arms, ammunition, and tools. The principal leader of this company was Francis Higginson, of St. John's College, Cambridge, rector of a church in Leicestershire, who had been deprived of his living for non-conformity. With him were associated two other ministers, also graduates of Cambridge. All three were members of the council. By the arrival of this company at

The Company of Massachusetts Bay.

Salem, Endicott now became governor of a colony larger than any yet started in New England, — larger than Plymouth after its growth of nearly nine years.

The time was at length ripe for that great Puritan exodus of which the voyage of the Mayflower had been the premonitory symptom. The grand crisis for the Puritans had come, the moment when decisive action could no longer be deferred. It was not by accident that the rapid development of John White's enterprise into the Company of Massachusetts Bay coincided exactly with the first four years of the reign of Charles I. They were years well fitted to bring such a scheme to quick maturity. The character of Charles was such as to exacerbate the evils of his father's reign. James could leave some things alone in the comfortable hope that all would by and by come out right, but Charles was not satisfied without meddling everywhere. Both father and son cherished some good intentions; both were sincere believers in their narrow theory of kingcraft. For wrongheaded obstinacy, utter want of tact, and bottomless perfidy, there was little to choose between them. The humorous epitaph of the grandson " whose word no man relies on " might have served for them all. But of this unhappy family Charles I. was eminently the dreamer. He lived in a world of his own, and was slow in rendering thought into action; and this made him rely upon the quick-witted but unwise and unscrupulous Buckingham,[1] who was silly enough to make feeble

Charles I.

[1] Gardiner, *Puritan Revolution*, p. 50.

attempts at unpopular warfare without consulting Parliament. During each of Charles's first four years there was an angry session of Parliament, in which, through the unwillingness of the popular leaders to resort to violence, the king's policy seemed able to hold its ground. Despite all protest the king persisted in levying strange taxes and was to some extent able to collect them. Men who refused to pay enforced loans were thrown into jail and the writ of *habeas corpus* was denied them. Meanwhile the treatment of Puritans became more and more vexatious. It was clear enough that Charles meant to become an absolute monarch, like Louis XIII., but Parliament began by throwing all the blame upon the unpopular minister and seeking to impeach him.

On the 5th of June, 1628, the House of Commons presented the most extraordinary spectacle, perhaps in all its history. The famous Petition of Right had been passed by both Houses, and the royal answer had just been received. Its tone was that of gracious assent, but it omitted the necessary legal formalities, and the Commons well knew what this meant. They were to be tricked with sweet words, and the petition was not to acquire the force of a statute. How was it possible to deal with such a slippery creature? There was but one way of saving the dignity of the throne without sacrificing the liberty of the people, and that was to hold the king's ministers responsible to Parliament, in anticipation of modern methods. It was accordingly proposed to impeach the Duke of Buckingham

<small>Remarkable scene in the House of Commons.</small>

before the House of Lords. The Speaker now "brought an imperious message from the king, ... warning them ... that he would not tolerate any aspersion upon his ministers." Nothing daunted by this, Sir John Eliot arose to lead the debate, when the Speaker called him to order in view of the king's message. "Amid a deadly stillness" Eliot sat down and burst into tears. For a moment the House was overcome with despair. Deprived of all constitutional methods of redress, they suddenly saw yawning before them the direful alternative — slavery or civil war. Since the day of Bosworth a hundred and fifty years had passed without fighting worthy of mention on English soil, such an era of peace as had hardly ever before been seen on the earth; now half the nation was to be pitted against the other half, families were to be divided against themselves, as in the dreadful days of the Roses, and with what consequences no one could foresee. "Let us sit in silence," quoth Sir Dudley Digges, "we are miserable, we know not what to do!" Nay, cried Sir Nathaniel Rich, "we *must* now speak, or forever hold our peace." Then did grim Mr. Prynne and Sir Edward Coke mingle their words with sobs, while there were few dry eyes in the House. Presently they found their voices, and used them in a way that wrung from the startled king his formal assent to the Petition of Right.

There is something strangely pathetic and historically significant [1] in the emotion of these stern,

---

[1] It is now 204 years since a battle has been fought in England. The last was Sedgmoor in 1685. For four centuries, since Bosworth, in 1485, the English people have lived in peace in their

fearless men. The scene was no less striking on the 2d of the following March, when, "amid the cries and entreaties of the Speaker held down in his chair by force," while the Usher of the Black Rod was knocking loudly at the bolted door, and the tramp of the king's soldiers was heard in the courtyard, Eliot's clear voice rang out the defiance that whoever advised the levy of tonnage and poundage without a grant from Parliament, or whoever voluntarily paid those duties, was to be counted an enemy to the kingdom and a betrayer of its liberties. As shouts of "Aye, aye," resounded on every side, " the doors were flung open, and the members poured forth in a throng." The noble Eliot went to end his days in the Tower, and for eleven years no Parliament sat again in England.[1]

It was in one and the same week that Charles I. thus began his experiment of governing without a Parliament, and that he granted a charter to the Company of Massachusetts Bay. He was very far, as we shall see, from realizing the import of what he was doing. To the Puritan leaders it was evident that a great struggle was at hand. Affairs at home might well seem des-

Desperate nature of the crisis.

own homes, except for the brief episode of the Great Rebellion, and Monmouth's slight affair. This long peace, unparalleled in history, has powerfully influenced the English and American character for good. Since the Middle Ages most English warfare has been warfare at a distance, and that does not nourish the brutal passions in the way that warfare at home does. An instructive result is to be seen in the mildness of temper which characterized the conduct of our stupendous Civil War. Nothing like it was ever seen before.

[1] Picton's *Cromwell*, pp. 61, 67; Gardiner, *Puritan Revolution*, p. 72.

perate, and the news from abroad was not encouraging. It was only four months since the surrender of Rochelle had ended the existence of the Huguenots as an armed political party. They had now sunk into the melancholy condition of a tolerated sect which may at any moment cease to be tolerated. In Germany the terrible Thirty Years War had just reached the darkest moment for the Protestants. Fifteen months were yet to pass before the immortal Gustavus was to cross the Baltic and give to the sorely harassed cause of liberty a fresh lease of life. The news of the cruel Edict of Restitution in this same fateful month of March, 1629, could not but give the English Puritans great concern. Everywhere in Europe the champions of human freedom seemed worsted. They might well think that never had the prospect looked so dismal; and never before, as never since, did the venture of a wholesale migration to the New World so strongly recommend itself as the only feasible escape from a situation that was fast becoming intolerable. Such were the anxious thoughts of the leading Puritans in the spring of 1629, and in face of so grave a problem different minds came naturally to different conclusions. Some were for staying in England to fight it out to the bitter end; some were for crossing the ocean to create a new England in the wilderness. Either task was arduous enough, and not to be achieved without steadfast and sober heroism.

On the 26th of August twelve gentlemen, among the most eminent in the Puritan party, held a meeting at Cambridge, and resolved to lead a migration to New England, provided the charter of the Massachusetts Bay Company and the government established under it could be transferred to that country. On examination it appeared that no legal obstacle stood in the way. Accordingly such of the old officers as did not wish to take part in the emigration resigned their places, which were forthwith filled by these new leaders. For governor the choice fell upon John Winthrop, a wealthy gentleman from Groton in Suffolk, who was henceforth to occupy the foremost place among the founders of New England. Winthrop was at this time forty-one years of age, having been born in the memorable year of the Armada. He was a man of remarkable strength and beauty of character, grave and modest, intelligent and scholarlike, intensely religious and endowed with a moral sensitiveness that was almost morbid, yet liberal withal in his opinions and charitable in disposition. When his life shall have been adequately written, as it never has been, he will be recognized as one of the very noblest figures in American history. From early youth he had that same power of winning confidence and commanding respect for which Washington was so remarkable; and when he was selected as the Moses of the great Puritan exodus, there was a wide-spread feeling that extraordinary results were likely to come of such an enterprise.

Transfer of the charter; John Winthrop and Thomas Dudley.

In marked contrast to Winthrop stands the figure of the man associated with him as deputy-governor. Thomas Dudley came of an ancient family, the history of which, alike in the old and in the new England, has not been altogether creditable. He represented the elder branch of that Norman family, to the younger branch of which belonged the unfortunate husband of Lady Jane Grey and the unscrupulous husband of Amy Robsart. There was, however, very little likeness to Elizabeth's gay lover in grim Thomas Dudley. His Puritanism was bleak and stern, and for Christian charity he was not eminent. He had a foible for making verses, and at his death there was found in his pocket a poem of his, containing a quatrain wherein the intolerance of that age is neatly summed up : —

> "Let men of God in courts and churches watch
> O'er such as do a Toleration hatch,
> Lest that ill egg bring forth a cockatrice
> To poison all with heresy and vice."

Such was the spirit of most of the Puritans of that day, but in the manifestation of it there were great differences, and here was the strong contrast between Dudley and Winthrop. In the former we have the typical narrow-minded, strait-laced Calvinist for whom it is so much easier to entertain respect than affection. But Winthrop's character, as we look at the well-known portrait ascribed to Van Dyck, is revealed in a face expressive of what was finest in the age of Elizabeth, the face of a spiritual brother of Raleigh and Sidney.

The accession of two men so important as Winthrop and Dudley served to bring matters speedily to a crisis. Their embarkation in April, 1630, was the signal for a general movement on the part of the English Puritans. Before Christmas of that year seventeen ships had come to New England, bringing more than 1000 passengers. This huge wave of immigration quite overwhelmed and bore away the few links of possession by which Gorges had thus far kept his hold upon the country. In January, 1629, John Gorges had tried to assert the validity of his late brother's claim by executing conveyances covering portions of it. One of these was to John Oldham, a man who had been harshly treated at Plymouth, and might be supposed very ready to defend his rights against settlers of the Puritan company. Gorges further maintained that he retained possession of the country through the presence of his brother's tenants, Blackstone, Maverick, Walford, and others on the shores of the bay. In June, 1629, Endicott had responded by sending forward some fifty persons from Salem to begin the settlement of Charlestown. Shortly before Winthrop's departure from England, Gorges had sent that singular personage Sir Christopher Gardiner to look after his interests in the New World, and there he was presently found established near the mouth of the Neponset river, in company with "a comly yonge woman whom he caled his cousin." But these few claimants were now at once lost in the human tide which poured over Charlestown, Boston, Newtown, Watertown, Roxbury, and Dorchester. The settlement at Merrymount was again dispersed, and Morton sent back to London; Gardiner fled to the coast of Maine and thence sailed for England in 1632. The Puritans had indeed occupied the country in force.

Founding of Massachusetts.

Here on the very threshold we are confronted by facts which show that not a mere colonial plantation, but a definite and organized state was in process of formation. The emigration was not like that of Jamestown or of Plymouth. It sufficed at once to make the beginnings of half a dozen towns, and the question as to self-government immediately sprang up. Early in 1631 a tax of £60 was assessed upon the settlements, in order to pay for building frontier fortifications at Newtown. This incident was in itself of small dimensions, as incidents in newly founded states are apt to be. But in its historic import it may serve to connect the England of John Hampden with the New England of Samuel Adams. The inhabitants of Watertown at first declined to pay this tax, which was assessed by the Board of Assistants, on the ground that English freemen cannot rightfully be taxed save by their own consent. This protest led to a change in the constitution of the infant colony, and here, at once, we are introduced to the beginnings of American constitutional history. At first it was thought that public business could be transacted by a primary assembly of all the freemen in the colony meeting four times in the year; but the number of freemen increased so fast that this was almost at once (in October, 1630) found to be impracticable. The right of choosing the governor and making the laws was then left to the Board of Assistants; and in May, 1631, it was further decided that the assistants need not be chosen afresh every year, but might keep their seats during good behaviour or

The question as to self-government raised at Watertown.

until ousted by special vote of the freemen. If the settlers of Massachusetts had been ancient Greeks or Romans, this would have been about as far as they could go in the matter; the choice would have been between a primary assembly and an assembly of notables. It is curious to see Englishmen passing from one of these alternatives to the other. But it was only for a moment. The protest of the Watertown men came in time to check these proceedings, which began to have a decidedly oligarchical look. To settle the immediate question of the tax, two deputies were sent from each settlement to advise with the Board of Assistants; while the power of choosing each year the governor and assistants was resumed by the freemen. Two years later, in order to reserve to the freemen the power of making laws without interfering too much with the ordinary business of life, the colonists fell back upon the old English rural plan of electing deputies or representatives to a general court.

At first the deputies sat in the same chamber with the assistants, but at length in 1644 they were formed into a second chamber with increased powers, and the way in which this important constitutional change came about is worth remembering, as an illustration of the smallness of the state which so soon was to play a great part in history. As Winthrop puts it, "there fell out a great business upon a very small occasion." To a certain Captain Keayne, of Boston, a rich man deemed to be hard and overbearing toward the poor, there was brought a stray pig, whereof he gave due public notice through the town

<small>Story of the stray pig.</small>

crier, yet none came to claim it till after he had killed a pig of his own which he kept in the same stye with the stray. A year having passed by, a poor woman named Sherman came to see the stray and to decide if it were one that she had lost. Not recognizing it as hers, she forthwith laid claim to the slaughtered pig. The case was brought before the elders of the church of Boston, who decided that the woman was mistaken. Mrs. Sherman then accused the captain of theft, and brought the case before a jury, which exonerated the defendant with £3 costs. The captain then sued Mrs. Sherman for defamation of character and got a verdict for £40 damages, a round sum indeed to assess upon the poor woman. But long before this it had appeared that she had many partisans and supporters; it had become a political question, in which the popular protest against aristocracy was implicated. Not yet browbeaten, the warlike Mrs. Sherman appealed to the General Court. The length of the hearing shows the importance which was attached to the case. After seven days of discussion the vote was taken. Seven assistants and eight deputies approved the former decisions, two assistants and fifteen deputies condemned them, while seven deputies refrained from voting. In other words, Captain Keayne had a decided majority among the more aristocratic assistants, while Mrs. Sherman seemed to prevail with the more democratic deputies. Regarding the result as the vote of a single body, the woman had a plurality of two; regarding it as the vote of a double body, her cause had prevailed in the lower house, but was lost by the veto of the upper. No decision was reached at the time, but after a year of discussion the legislature was permanently separated into two houses, each with a veto power upon the other; and this was felt to be a victory for the assistants.

As for the ecclesiastical polity of the new colony, it had begun to take shape immediately upon the arrival of Endicott's party at Salem. The clergymen, Samuel Skelton and Francis Higginson, consecrated each other, and a church covenant and confession of faith were drawn up by Higginson. Thirty persons joining in this covenant constituted the first church in the colony; and several brethren appointed by this church proceeded formally to ordain the two ministers by the laying on of hands. In such simple wise was the first Congregational church in Massachusetts founded. The simple fact of removal from England converted all the Puritan emigrants into Separatists, as Robinson had already predicted. Some, however, were not yet quite prepared for so radical a measure. These proceedings gave umbrage to two of the Salem party, who attempted forthwith to set up a separate church in conformity with episcopal models. A very important question was thus raised at once, but it was not allowed to disturb the peace of the colony. Endicott was a man of summary methods. He immediately sent the two malcontents back to England; and thus the colonial church not only seceded from the national establishment, but the principle was virtually laid down that the Episcopal form of worship would not be tolerated in the colony. For the present

<small>The triumph of Separatism.</small>

such a step was to be regarded as a measure of self-defence on the part of the colonists. Episcopacy to them meant actual and practical tyranny — the very thing they had crossed the ocean expressly to get away from — and it was hardly to be supposed that they would encourage the growth of it in their new home. One or two surpliced priests, conducting worship in accordance with the Book of Common Prayer, might in themselves be excellent members of society; but behind the surpliced priest the colonist saw the intolerance of Laud and the despotism of the Court of High Commission. In 1631 a still more searching measure of self-protection was adopted. It was decided that "no man shall be admitted to the freedom of this body politic, but such as are members of some of the churches within the limits of the same." Into the merits of this measure as illustrating the theocratic ideal of society which the Puritans sought to realize in New England, we shall inquire hereafter. At present we must note that, as a measure of self-protection, this decree was intended to keep out of the new community all emissaries of Strafford and Laud, as well as such persons as Morton and Gardiner and other agents of Sir Ferdinando Gorges.

By the year 1634 the scheme of the Massachusetts Company had so far prospered that nearly 4000 Englishmen had come over, and some twenty villages on or near the shores of the bay had been founded. The building of permanent houses, roads, fences, and bridges had begun to go on quite briskly; farms were beginning to yield a return for the labour of the husbandman; lumber, furs, and salted fish were beginning to be sent to England in exchange for manufactured articles; 4000 goats and 1500 head of cattle grazed in the pastures, and swine innumerable rooted in the clearings and helped to make ready the land for the ploughman. Political meetings were held, justice was administered by magistrates after old English precedents, and church services were performed by a score of clergymen, nearly all graduates of Cambridge, though one or two had their degrees from Oxford, and nearly all of whom had held livings in the Church of England. The most distinguished of these clergymen, John Cotton, in his younger days a Fellow and Tutor of Emmanuel College, had for more than twenty years been rector of St. Botolph's, when he left the most magnificent parish church in England to hold service in the first rude meeting-house of the new Boston. From Emmanuel College came also Thomas Hooker and John Harvard. Besides these clergymen, so many of the leading persons concerned in the emigration were university men that it was not long before a university began to seem indispensable to the colony. In 1636 the General Court appropriated £400 toward the establishment of a college at Newtown.

Founding of Harvard College. In 1638 John Harvard, dying childless, bequeathed his library and the half of his estate to the new college, which the Court forthwith ordered to be called by his name; while in honour of the mother university the name of the town was changed to Cambridge.

It has been said that the assembly which decreed the establishment of Harvard College was "the first body in which the people, by their representatives, ever gave their own money to found a place of education."[1] The act was a memorable one if we have regard to all the circumstances of the year in which it was done. On every side danger was in the air. Threatened at once with an Indian war, with the enmity of the home government, and with grave dissensions among themselves, the year 1636 was a trying one indeed for the little community of Puritans, and their founding a college by public taxation just at this time is a striking illustration of their unalterable purpose to realize, in this new home, their ideal of an educated Christian society.

<small>Threefold danger in the year 1636.</small>

That the government of Charles I. should view with a hostile eye the growth of a Puritan state in New England is not at all surprising. The only fit ground for wonder would seem to be that Charles should have been willing at the outset to grant a charter to the able and influential Puritans who organized the Company of Massachusetts Bay. Probably, however, the king thought at first that it would relieve him at home if a few dozen of the Puritan leaders could be allowed to concentrate their minds upon a project of colonization in America. It might divert attention for a moment from his own despotic schemes. Very likely the scheme would prove a failure and the Massachusetts colony incur a fate like that of Roanoke Island; and at all events the wealth of the Puritans might better be sunk in a remote and perilous enterprise than

<small>1. From the king, who prepares to attack the infant colony but is foiled by dissensions at home.</small>

[1] Quincy, *History of Harvard University*, ii. 654.

employed at home in organizing resistance to the crown. Such, very likely, may have been the king's motive in granting the Massachusetts charter two days after turning his Parliament out of doors. But the events of the last half-dozen years had come to present the case in a new light. The young colony was not languishing. It was full of sturdy life; it had wrought mischief to the schemes of Gorges; and what was more, it had begun to take unheard-of liberties with things ecclesiastical and political. Its example was getting to be a dangerous one. It was evidently worth while to put a strong curb upon Massachusetts. Any promise made to his subjects Charles regarded as a promise made under duress which he was quite justified in breaking whenever it suited his purpose to do so. Enemies of Massachusetts were busy in England. Schismatics from Salem and revellers from Merrymount were ready with their tales of woe, and now Gorges and Mason were vigorously pressing their territorial claims. They bargained with the king. In February, 1635, the moribund Council for New England surrendered its charter and all its corporate rights in America, on condition that the king should disregard all the various grants by which these rights had from time to time been alienated, and should divide up the territory of New England in severalty among the members of the Council. In pursuance of this scheme Gorges and Mason, together with half a dozen noblemen, were allowed to parcel out New England among themselves as they should see fit. In this way the influence of the Marquis of Hamilton, with the Earls of Arundel, Surrey, Carlisle, and Stirling, might be actively enlisted against the Massachusetts Company. A writ of *quo warranto* was brought against it; and it was proposed to send Sir Ferdinando to govern New England with viceregal powers like those afterward exercised by Andros.

For a moment the danger seemed alarming; but, as Winthrop says, " the Lord frustrated their design." It was noted as a special providence that the ship in which Gorges was to sail was hardly off the stocks when it fell to pieces. Then the most indefatigable enemy of the colony, John Mason, suddenly died. The king issued his famous writ of ship-money and set all England by the ears; and, to crown all, the attempt to read the Episcopal liturgy at St. Giles's church in Edinburgh led straight to the Solemn League and Covenant. Amid the first mutterings of the Great Rebellion the proceedings against Massachusetts were dropped, and the unheeded colony went on thriving in its independent course. Possibly too some locks at Whitehall may have been turned with golden keys,[1] for the company was rich, and the king was ever open to such arguments. But when the news of his evil designs had first reached Boston the people of the infant colony showed no readiness to yield to intimidation. In their measures there was a decided smack of what was to be realized a hundred and forty years later. Orders were immediately issued for fortifying Castle Island in the harbour and the heights at Charlestown and Dorchester. Militia companies were put in training,

[1] C. F. Adams, *Sir Christopher Gardiner, Knight*, p. 31.

and a beacon was set up on the highest hill in Boston, to give prompt notice to all the surrounding country of any approaching enemy.

While the ill will of the home government thus kept the colonists in a state of alarm, there were causes of strife at work at their very doors, of which they were fain to rid themselves as soon as possible. Among all the Puritans who came to New England there is no more interesting figure than the learned, quick-witted pugnacious Welshman, Roger Williams. He was over-fond of logical subtleties and delighted in controversy. There was scarcely any subject about which he did not wrangle, from the sinfulness of persecution to the propriety of women wearing veils in church. Yet, with all this love of controversy, there has perhaps never lived a more gentle and kindly soul. Within five years from the settlement of Massachusetts this young preacher had announced the true principles of religious liberty with a clearness of insight quite remarkable in that age. Roger Williams had been aided in securing an education by the great lawyer Sir Edward Coke, and had lately taken his degree at Pembroke College, Cambridge; but the boldness with which he declared his opinions had aroused the hostility of Laud, and in 1631 he had come over to Plymouth, whence he removed two years later to Salem, and became pastor of the church there. The views of Williams, if logically carried out, involved the entire separation of church from state, the equal protection of all forms of religious faith, the repeal of all laws compelling attendance

2. From religious dissensions; Roger Williams.

on public worship, the abolition of tithes and of all forced contributions to the support of religion. Such views are to-day quite generally adopted by the more civilized portions of the Protestant world; but it is needless to say that they were not the views of the seventeenth century, in Massachusetts or elsewhere. For declaring such opinions as these on the continent of Europe, anywhere except in Holland, a man like Williams would in that age have run great risk of being burned at the stake. In England, under the energetic misgovernment of Laud, he would very likely have had to stand in the pillory with his ears cropped, or perhaps, like Bunyan and Baxter, would have been sent to jail. In Massachusetts such views were naturally enough regarded as anarchical, but in Williams's case they were further complicated by grave political imprudence. He wrote a pamphlet in which he denied the right of the colonists to the lands which they held in New England under the king's grant. He held that the soil belonged to the Indians, that the settlers could only obtain a valid title to it by purchase from them, and that the acceptance of a patent from a mere intruder, like the king, was a sin requiring public repentance. This doctrine was sure to be regarded in England as an attack upon the king's supremacy over Massachusetts, and at the same time an incident occurred in Salem which made it all the more unfortunate. The royal colours under which the little companies of militia marched were emblazoned with the red cross of St. George. The uncompromising Endicott loathed this emblem as tainted with Popery, and one day he publicly defaced the flag of the Salem company by cutting out the cross. The enemies of Massachusetts misinterpreted this act as a defiance aimed at the royal authority, and they attributed it to the teachings of Williams. In view of the king's unfriendliness these were dangerous proceedings. Endicott was summoned before the General Court at Boston, where he was publicly reprimanded and declared incapable of holding office for a year. A few months afterward, in January, 1636, Williams was ordered by the General Court to come to Boston and embark in a ship that was about to set sail for England. But he escaped into the forest, and made his way through the snow to the wigwam of Massasoit. He was a rare linguist, and had learned to talk fluently in the language of the Indians, and now he passed the winter in trying to instill into their ferocious hearts something of the gentleness of Christianity. In the spring he was privately notified by Winthrop that if he were to steer his course to Narragansett bay he would be secure from molestation; and such was the beginning of the settlement of Providence.

Shortly before the departure of Williams, there came to Boston one of the greatest Puritan statesmen of that heroic age, the younger Henry Vane.

Henry Vane and Anne Hutchinson.

It is pleasant to remember that the man who did so much to overthrow the tyranny of Strafford, who brought the military strength of Scotland to the aid of the hard-pressed Parliament, who administered the navy with which Blake won his astonishing victories, who dared even withstand Cromwell at the height of his power when his measures became too violent, — it is pleasant to remember that this admirable man was once the chief magistrate of an American commonwealth. It is pleasant for a Harvard man to remember that as such he presided over the assembly that founded our first university. Thorough republican and enthusiastic lover of liberty, he was spiritually akin to Jefferson and to Samuel Adams. Like Williams he was a friend to toleration, and like Williams he found Massachusetts an uncomfortable home. In 1636 he was only twenty-four years of age, "young in years," and perhaps not yet "in sage counsel old." He was chosen governor for that year, and his administration was stormy. Among those persons who had followed Mr. Cotton from Lincolnshire was Mrs. Anne Hutchinson, a very bright and capable lady, if perhaps somewhat impulsive and indiscreet. She had brought over with her, says Winthrop, "two dangerous errors: first, that the person of the Holy Ghost dwells in a justified person; second, that no sanctification can help to evidence to us our justification." Into the merits of such abstruse doctrines it is not necessary for the historian to enter. One can hardly repress a smile as one reflects how early in the history of Boston some of its characteristic social features were developed. It is curious to read of lectures there in 1636, lectures by a lady, and transcendentalist lectures withal! Never did lectures in Boston arouse greater excitement than Mrs. Hutchinson's. Many of her hearers forsook the teachings of the regular ministers, to follow her

She was very effectively supported by her brother-in-law, Mr. Wheelwright, an eloquent preacher, and for a while she seemed to be carrying everything before her. She won her old minister Mr. Cotton, she won the stout soldier Captain Underhill, she won Governor Vane himself; while she incurred the deadly hatred of such men as Dudley and Cotton's associate John Wilson. The church at Boston was divided into two hostile camps. The sensible Winthrop marvelled at hearing men distinguished " by being under a covenant of grace or a covenant of works, as in other countries between Protestants and Papists," and he ventured to doubt whether any man could really tell what the difference was. The theological strife went on until it threatened to breed civil disaffection among the followers of Mrs. Hutchinson. A peculiar bitterness was given to the affair, from the fact that she professed to be endowed with the spirit of prophecy and taught her partisans that it was their duty to follow the biddings of a supernatural light; and there was nothing which the orthodox Puritan so steadfastly abhorred as the anarchical pretence of living by the aid of a supernatural light. In a strong and complex society the teachings of Mrs. Hutchinson would have awakened but a languid speculative interest, or perhaps would have passed by unheeded. In the simple society of Massachusetts in 1636, physically weak and as yet struggling for very existence, the practical effect of such teachings may well have been deemed politically dangerous. When things came to such a pass that the forces of the colony were mustered for an Indian campaign and the men of Boston were ready to shirk the service because they suspected their chaplain to be "under a covenant of works," it was naturally thought to be high time to put Mrs. Hutchinson down. In the spring of 1637 Winthrop was elected governor, and in August Vane returned to England. His father had at that moment more influence with the king than any other person except Strafford, and the young man had indiscreetly hinted at an appeal to the home government for the protection of the Antinomians, as Mrs. Hutchinson's followers were called. But an appeal from America to England was something which Massachusetts would no more tolerate in the days of Winthrop than in the days of Hancock and Adams. Soon after Vane's departure, Mrs. Hutchinson and her friends were ordered to leave the colony. It was doubtless an odious act of persecution, yet of all such acts which stain the history of Massachusetts in the seventeenth century, it is just the one for which the plea of political necessity may really be to some extent accepted.

We now begin to see how the spreading of the New England colonization, and the founding of distinct communities, was hastened by these differences of opinion on theological questions or on questions concerning the relations between church and state. Of Mrs. Hutchinson's friends and adherents, some went northward, and founded the towns of Exeter and Hampton. Some time before Portsmouth and Dover had been settled by followers of Mason and Gorges. In 1641 these towns were added to the domain of Massachusetts, and so the matter stood until 1679, when we shall see Charles II. marking them off as a separate province, under a royal government. Such were the beginnings of New Hampshire. Mrs. Hutchinson herself, however, with the rest of her adherents, bought the island of Aquedneck from the Indians, and settlements were made at Portsmouth and Newport. After a quarter of a century of turbulence, these settlements coalesced with Williams's colony at Providence, and thus was formed the state of Rhode Island. After her husband's death in 1642, Mrs. Hutchinson left Aquedneck and settled upon some land to the west of Stamford and supposed to be within the territory of the New Netherlands. There in the following year she was cruelly murdered by Indians, together with nearly all her children and servants, sixteen victims in all. One of her descendants was the illustrious Thomas Hutchinson, the first great American historian, and last royal governor of Massachusetts.

To the dangers arising from the ill-will of the crown, and from these theological quarrels, there was added the danger of a general attack by the savages. Down to this time, since the landing of the Pilgrims at Plymouth, the settlers of New England had been in no way molested by the natives. Massasoit's treaty with the Pilgrims was scrupulously observed on both sides, and kept the Wampanoags quiet for fifty-four years. The somewhat smaller tribe which took its name from the *Massawachusett*, or Great Hill, of Milton, kept on friendly terms with the settlers about Boston, because these red men coveted the powerful aid of the white strangers in case of war with their hereditary foes the Tarratines, who dwelt in the Piscataqua country. It was only when the English began to leave these coast regions and press into the interior that trouble arose. The western shores of Narragansett bay were possessed by the numerous and warlike tribe of that name, which held in partial subjection the Nyantics near Point Judith. To the west of these, and about the Thames river, dwelt the still more formidable Pequots, a tribe which for bravery and ferocity asserted a preëminence in New England not unlike that which the Iroquois league of the Mohawk valley was fast winning over all North America east of the Mississippi. North of the Pequots, the squalid villages of the Nipmucks were scattered over the beautiful highlands that stretch in long ridges from Quinsigamond to Nichewaug, and beyond toward blue Monadnock. Westward, in the lower Connecticut valley, lived the Mohegans, a small but valiant tribe, now for some time held tributary to their Pequot cousins, and very restive under the yoke. The thickly wooded mountain ranges between the Connecticut and the Hudson had few human inhabitants. These hundred miles of crag and forest were a bulwark none too wide or strong against the incursions of the terrible Mohawks, whose name sent a shiver of fear throughout savage New England, and whose forbearance the Nipmucks and Mohegans were fain to ensure by a yearly payment of blackmail. Each summer there came two Mohawk elders, secure in the dread that Iroquois prowess had everywhere inspired; and up

3. From the Indians: the Pequot supremacy.

and down the Connecticut valley they seized the tribute of weapons and wampum, and proclaimed the last harsh edict issued from the savage council at Onondaga. The scowls that greeted their unwelcome visits were doubtless nowhere fiercer than among the Mohegans, thus ground down between Mohawk and Pequot as between the upper and the nether millstone.

Among the various points in which civilized man surpasses the savage none is more conspicuous than the military brute force which in the highest civilization is always latent though comparatively seldom exerted. The sudden intrusion of English warfare into the Indian world of the seventeenth century may well have seemed to the red men a supernatural visitation, like the hurricane or the earthquake. The uncompromising vigour with which the founders of Massachusetts carried on their work was viewed in some quarters with a dissatisfaction which soon thrust the English migration into the very heart of the Indian country.

The first movement, however, was directed against the encroachments of the New Netherlands. In October, 1634, some men of Plymouth, led by William Holmes, sailed up the Connecticut river, and, after bandying threats with a party of Dutch who had built a rude fort on the site of Hartford, passed on and fortified themselves on the site of Windsor. Next year Governor Van Twiller sent a company of seventy men to drive away these intruders, but after reconnoitring the situation the Dutchmen thought it best not to make an attack. Their little strong-

First movements into Connecticut.

hold at Hartford remained unmolested by the English, and, in order to secure the communication between this advanced outpost and New Amsterdam, Van Twiller decided to build another fort at the mouth of the river, but this time the English were beforehand. Rumours of Dutch designs may have reached the ears of Lord Say and Sele and Lord Brooke — "fanatic Brooke," as Scott calls him in "Marmion" — who had obtained from the Council for New England a grant of territory on the shores of the Sound. These noblemen chose as their agent the younger John Winthrop, son of the Massachusetts governor, and this new-comer arrived upon the scene just in time to drive away Van Twiller's vessel and build an English fort which in honour of his two patrons he called "Say-Brooke."

Had it not been for seeds of discontent already sown in Massachusetts, the English hold upon the Connecticut valley might perhaps have been for a few years confined to these two military outposts at Windsor and Saybrook. But there were people in Massachusetts who did not look with favour upon the aristocratic and theocratic features in its polity. The provision that none but church-members should vote or hold office was by no means unanimously approved. We see it in the course of another generation putting altogether too much temporal power into the hands of the clergy, and we can trace the growth of the opposition to it until in the reign of Charles II. it becomes a dangerous source of weakness to Massachusetts. At the outset the opposition seems to

Disaffection in Massachusetts.

have been strongest in Dorchester, Newtown, and Watertown. When the Board of Assistants undertook to secure for themselves permanency of tenure, together with the power of choosing the governor and making the laws, these three towns sent deputies to Boston to inspect the charter and see if it authorized any such stretch of power. They were foremost in insisting that representatives chosen by the towns must have a share in the general government. Men who held such opinions were naturally unwilling to increase the political weight of the clergy, who, during these early disputes and indeed until the downfall of the charter, were inclined to take aristocratic views and to sympathize with the Board of Assistants. Cotton declared that democracy was no fit government either for church or for commonwealth, and the majority of the ministers agreed with him. Chief among those who did not was the learned and eloquent Thomas Hooker, pastor of the church at Newtown. When Winthrop, in a letter to Hooker, defended the restriction of the suffrage on the ground that " the best part is always the least, and of that best part the wiser part is always the lesser ; " Hooker replied that " in matters which concern the common good, a general council, chosen by all, to transact businesses which concern all, I conceive most suitable to rule and most safe for relief of the whole." It is interesting to meet, on the very threshold of American history, with such a lucid statement of the strongly contrasted views which a hundred and fifty years later were to be represented on a national scale by Hamilton and Jefferson. There were many in Newtown who took Hooker's view of the matter; and there, as also in Watertown and Dorchester, which in 1633 took the initiative in framing town governments with selectmen, a strong disposition was shown to evade the restrictions upon the suffrage.

While such things were talked about in the summer of 1633 the adventurous John Oldham was making his way through the forest and over the mountains into the Connecticut valley, and when he returned to the coast his glowing accounts set some people to thinking. Two years afterward a few pioneers from Dorchester pushed through the wilderness as far as the Plymouth men's fort at Windsor, while a party from Watertown went farther and came to a halt upon the site of Wethersfield. A larger party, bringing cattle and such goods as they could carry, set out in the autumn and succeeded in reaching Windsor. Their winter supplies were sent around by water to meet them, but early in November the ships had barely passed the Saybrook fort when they found the river blocked with ice and were obliged to return to Boston. The sufferings of the pioneers, thus cut off from the world, were dreadful. Their cattle perished, and they were reduced to a diet of acorns and ground-nuts. Some seventy of them, walking on the frozen river to Saybrook, were so fortunate as to find a crazy little sloop jammed in the ice. They succeeded in cutting her adrift, and steered themselves back to Boston. Others surmounted greater obstacles in struggling back through the snow over the region which the Pull-

<small>Connecticut pioneers.</small>

man car now traverses, regardless of seasons, in three hours. A few grim heroes, the nameless founders of a noble commonwealth, stayed on the spot and defied starvation. In the next June, 1636, the Newtown congregation, a hundred or more in number, led by their sturdy pastor, and bringing with them 160 head of cattle, made the pilgrimage to the Connecticut valley. Women and children took part in this pleasant summer journey; Mrs. Hooker, the pastor's wife, being too ill to walk, was carried on a litter. Thus, in the memorable year in which our great university was born, did Cambridge become, in the true Greek sense of a much-abused word, the *metropolis* or " mother town " of Hartford. The migration at once became strong in numbers. During the past twelvemonth a score of ships had brought from England to Massachusetts more than 3000 souls, and so great an accession made further movement easy. Hooker's pilgrims were soon followed by the Dorchester and Watertown congregations, and by the next May 800 people were living in Windsor, Hartford, and Wethersfield. As we read of these movements, not of individuals, but of organic communities, united in allegiance to a church and its pastor, and fervid with the instinct of self-government, we seem to see Greek history renewed, but with centuries of added political training. For one year a board of commissioners from Massachusetts governed the new towns, but at the end of that time the towns chose representatives and held a General Court at Hartford, and thus the separate existence of Connecticut was begun. As for Springfield, which was settled about the same time by a party from Roxbury, it remained for some years doubtful to which state it belonged. At the opening session of the General Court, May 31, 1638, Mr. Hooker preached a sermon of wonderful power, in which he maintained that "the foundation of authority is laid in the free consent of the people," "that the choice of public magistrates belongs unto the people by God's own allowance," and that "they who have power to appoint officers and magistrates have the right also to set the bounds and limitations of the power and place unto which they call them." On the 14th of January, 1639, all the freemen of the three towns assembled at Hartford and adopted a written constitution in which the hand of the great preacher is clearly discernible. It is worthy of note that this document contains none of the conventional references to a "dread sovereign" or a "gracious king," nor the slightest allusion to the British or any other government outside of Connecticut itself, nor does it prescribe any condition of church-membership for the right of suffrage. It was the first written constitution known to history, that created a government,[1] and it marked the beginnings of American democracy, of which Thomas Hooker deserves more than any other man to be called the father. The government of the United States today is in lineal descent more nearly related to that

The first written constitution.

---

[1] The compact drawn up in the Mayflower's cabin was not, in the strict sense a constitution, which is a document defining and limiting the functions of government. Magna Charta partook of the nature of a written constitution, as far as it went, but it did not create a government.

of Connecticut than to that of any of the other thirteen colonies. The most noteworthy feature of the Connecticut republic was that it was a federation of independent towns, and that all attributes of sovereignty not expressly granted to the General Court remained, as of original right, in the towns. Moreover, while the governor and council were chosen by a majority vote of the whole people, and by a suffrage that was almost universal, there was for each township an equality of representation in the assembly.[1] This little federal republic was allowed to develop peacefully and normally; its constitution was not violently wrenched out of shape like that of Massachusetts at the end of the seventeenth century. It silently grew till it became the strongest political structure on the continent, as was illustrated in the remarkable military energy and the unshaken financial credit of Connecticut during the Revolutionary War; and in the chief crisis of the Federal Convention of 1787 Connecticut, with her compromise which secured equal state representation in one branch of the national government and popular representation in the other, played the controlling part.

Before the little federation of towns had framed its government, it had its Indian question to dispose of. Three years before the migration led by Hooker, a crew of eight traders, while making their way up the river to the Dutch station on the site of Hartford, had been murdered by a party of Indians subject to Sassacus, chief sachem of the Pequots. Negotiations concerning this outrage had gone on

[1] See Johnston's *Connecticut*, p. 321, a very brilliant book.

between Sassacus and the government at Boston, and the Pequots had promised to deliver up the murderers, but had neglected to do so. In the summer of 1636 some Indians on Block Island subject to the Narragansetts murdered the pioneer John Oldham, who was sailing on the Sound, and captured his little vessel. At this, says Underhill, "God stirred up the hearts" of Governor Vane and the rest of the magistrates. They were determined to make an end of the Indian question and show the savages that such things would not be endured. First an embassy was sent to Canonicus and his nephew Miantonomo, chief sachems of the Narragansetts, who hastened to disclaim all responsibility for the murder, and to throw the blame entirely upon the Indians of the island. Vane then sent out three vessels under command of Endicott, who ravaged Block Island, burning wigwams, sinking canoes, and slaying dogs, for the men had taken to the woods. Endicott then crossed to the mainland to reckon with the Pequots. He demanded the surrender of the murderers, with a thousand fathoms of wampum for damages; and not getting a satisfactory answer, he attacked the Indians, killed a score of them, seized their ripe corn, and burned and spoiled what he could. But such reprisals served only to enrage the red men. Lyon Gardiner, commander of the Saybrook fort, complained to Endicott: "You come hither to raise these wasps about my ears; then you will take wing and flee away." The immediate effect was to incite Sassacus to do his utmost to compass the ruin of the English. The superstitious awe

Origin of the Pequot War.

with which the white men were at first regarded
had been somewhat lessened by familiar contact
with them, as in Æsop's fable of the fox and the
lion. The resources of Indian diplomacy were exhausted in the attempt to unite the Narragansett
warriors with the Pequots in a grand crusade
against the white men. Such a combination could
hardly have been as formidable as that which was
effected forty years afterward in King Philip's
war; for the savages had not as yet become accustomed to fire-arms, and the English settlements did
not present so many points exposed to attack; but
there is no doubt that it might have wrought fearful havoc. We can, at any rate, find no difficulty
in comprehending the manifold perplexity of the
Massachusetts men at this time, threatened as they
were at once by an Indian crusade, by the machinations of a faithless king, and by a bitter theological quarrel at home, in this eventful year when
they laid aside part of their incomes to establish
Harvard College.

The schemes of Sassacus were unsuccessful.
The hereditary enmity of the Narragansetts toward their Pequot rivals was too strong to be
lightly overcome. Roger Williams, taking advantage of this feeling, so worked upon
the minds of the Narragansett chiefs
that in the autumn of 1636 they sent
an embassy to Boston and made a treaty of alliance with the English. The Pequots were thus
left to fight out their own quarrel; and had they
still been separated from the English by the distance between Boston and the Thames river, the

Sassacus is foiled by Roger Williams.

feud might very likely have smouldered until the drift of events had given a different shape to it. But as the English had in this very year thrown out their advanced posts into the lower Connecticut valley, there was clearly no issue from the situation save in deadly war. All through the winter of 1636-37 the Connecticut towns were kept in a state of alarm by the savages. Men going to their work were killed and horribly mangled. A Wethersfield man was kidnapped and roasted alive. Emboldened by the success of this feat, the Pequots attacked Wethersfield, massacred ten people, and carried away two girls. Wrought up to desperation by these atrocities, the Connecticut men appealed to Massachusetts and Plymouth for aid, and put into service ninety of their own number, under command of John Mason, an excellent and sturdy officer who had won golden opinions from Sir Thomas Fairfax, under whom he had served in the Netherlands. It took time to get men from Boston, and all that Massachusetts contributed to the enterprise at its beginning was that eccentric daredevil John Underhill, with a force of twenty men. Seventy friendly Mohegans, under their chief Uncas, eager to see vengeance wrought upon their Pequot oppressors, accompanied the expedition. From the fort at Saybrook this little company set sail on the twentieth of May, 1637, and landed in brilliant moonlight near Point Judith, where they were reinforced by four hundred Narragansetts and Nyantics. From this point they turned westward toward the stronghold of the

The Pequots take the war-path alone;

Pequots, near the place where the town of Stonington now stands. As they approached the dreaded spot the courage of the Indian allies gave out, and they slunk behind, declaring that Sassacus was a god whom it was useless to think of attacking. The force with which Mason and Underhill advanced to the fray consisted of just seventy-seven Englishmen. Their task was to assault and carry an entrenched fort or walled village containing seven hundred Pequots. The fort was a circle of two or three acres in area, girdled by a palisade of sturdy sapling-trunks, set firm and deep into the ground, the narrow interstices between them serving as loopholes wherefrom to reconnoitre any one passing by and to shoot at assailants. At opposite sides of this stronghold were two openings barely large enough to let any one go through. Within this enclosure were the crowded wigwams. The attack was skilfully managed, and was a complete surprise. A little before daybreak Mason, with sixteen men, occupied one of the doors, while Underhill made sure of the other. The Indians in panic sought first one outlet and then the other, and were ruthlessly shot down, whichever way they turned. A few succeeded in breaking loose, but these were caught and tomahawked by the Indian allies, who, though afraid to take the risks of the fight, were ready enough to help slay the fugitives. The English threw firebrands among the wigwams, and soon the whole village was in a light blaze, and most of the savages suffered the horrible death which they were so fond of inflict-

And are exterminated.

ing upon their captives. Of the seven hundred Pequots in the stronghold, but five got away with their lives. All this bloody work had been done in less than an hour, and of the English there had been two killed and sixteen wounded. It was the end of the Pequot nation. Of the remnant which had not been included in this wholesale slaughter, most were soon afterwards destroyed piecemeal in a running fight which extended as far westward as the site of Fairfield. Sassacus fled across the Hudson river to the Mohawks, who slew him and sent his scalp to Boston, as a peace-offering to the English. The few survivors were divided between the Mohegans and Narragansetts and adopted into those tribes. Truly the work was done with Cromwellian thoroughness. The tribe which had lorded it so fiercely over the New England forests was all at once wiped out of existence. So terrible a vengeance the Indians had never heard of. If the name of Pequot had hitherto been a name of terror, so now did the Englishmen win the inheritance of that deadly prestige. Not for eight-and-thirty years after the destruction of the Pequots, not until a generation of red men had grown up that knew not Underhill and Mason, did the Indian of New England dare again to lift his hand against the white man.

Such scenes of wholesale slaughter are not pleasant reading in this milder age. But our forefathers felt that the wars of Canaan afforded a sound precedent for such cases; and, indeed, if we remember what the soldiers of Tilly and Wallenstein were doing at this very time in Germany, we shall realize that the work of Mason and Underhill would not have been felt by any one in that age to merit censure or stand in need of excuses. As a matter of practical policy the annihilation of the Pequots can be condemned only by those who read history so incorrectly as to suppose that savages, whose business is to torture and slay, can always be dealt with according to the methods in use between civilized peoples. A mighty nation, like the United States, is in honour bound to treat the red man with scrupulous justice and refrain from cruelty in punishing his delinquencies. But if the founders of Connecticut, in confronting a danger which threatened their very existence, struck with savage fierceness, we cannot blame them. The world is so made that it is only in that way that the higher races have been able to preserve themselves and carry on their progressive work.

The overthrow of the Pequots was a cardinal event in the planting of New England. It removed the chief obstacle to the colonization of the Connecticut coast, and brought the inland settlements into such unimpeded communication with those on tide-water as to prepare the way for the formation of the New England confederacy. Its first fruits were seen in the direction taken by the next wave of migration, which ended the Puritan exodus from England to America. About a month after the storming of the palisaded village there arrived in Boston a company of wealthy London merchants, with their families. The most prominent among them, Theophilus Eaton, was a member of the Company of Mas-

The colony of New Haven.

sachusetts Bay. Their pastor, John Davenport, was an eloquent preacher and a man of power. He was a graduate of Oxford, and in 1624 had been chosen vicar of St. Stephen's parish, in Coleman street, London. When he heard that Cotton and Hooker were about to sail for America, he sought earnestly to turn them from what he deemed the error of their ways, but instead he became converted himself and soon incurred the especial enmity of Laud, so that it became necessary for him to flee to Amsterdam. In 1636 he returned to England, and in concert with Eaton organized a scheme of emigration that included men from Yorkshire, Hertfordshire, and Kent. The leaders arrived in Boston in the midst of the Antinomian disputes, and although Davenport won admiration for his skill in battling with heresy, he may perhaps have deemed it preferable to lead his flock to some new spot in the wilderness where such warfare might not be required. The merchants desired a fine harbour and good commercial situation, and the reports of the men who returned from hunting the Pequots told them of just such a spot at Quinnipiack on Long Island Sound. Here they could carry out their plan of putting into practice a theocratic ideal even more rigid than that which obtained in Massachusetts, and arrange their civil as well as ecclesiastical affairs in accordance with rules to be obtained from a minute study of the Scriptures.

In the spring of 1638 the town of New Haven was accordingly founded. The next year a swarm from this new town settled Milford, while another party, freshly arrived from England, made the beginnings of Guilford. In 1640 Stamford was added to the group, and in 1643 the four towns were united into the republic of New Haven, to which Southold, on Long Island, and Branford were afterwards added. As being a confederation of independent towns, New Haven resembled Connecticut. In other respects the differences between the two reflected the differences between Davenport and Hooker; the latter was what would now be called more radical than Winthrop or Cotton, the former was more conservative. In the New Haven colony none but church-members could vote, and this measure at the outset disfranchised more than half the settlers in New Haven town, nearly half in Guilford, and less than one fifth in Milford. This result was practically less democratic than in Massachusetts where it was some time before the disfranchisement attained such dimensions. The power of the clergy reached its extreme point in New Haven, where each of the towns was governed by seven ecclesiastical officers known as "pillars of the church." These magistrates served as judges, and trial by jury was dispensed with, because no authority could be found for it in the laws of Moses. The legislation was quaint enough, though the famous "Blue Laws"

Legend of the "Blue Laws." of New Haven, which have been made the theme of so many jests at the expense of our forefathers, never really existed. The story of the Blue Laws was first published in 1781 by the Rev. Samuel Peters, a Tory refugee in London, who took delight in horrifying our British cousins with tales of wholesale tarring and feathering done by the patriots of the Revolution. In point of strict veracity Dr. Peters reminds one of Baron Munchausen; he declares that the river at Bellows Falls flows so fast as to float iron crowbars, and he gravely describes sundry animals who were evidently cousins to the Jabberwok. The most famous passage of his pretended code is that which enacts that " no woman shall kiss her child on the Sabbath," and that " no one shall play on any instrument of music except the drum, trumpet, or jewsharp."

When the Long Parliament met in 1640, the Puritan exodus to New England came to an end. During the twenty years which had elapsed since the voyage of the Mayflower, the population had grown to 26,000 souls. Of this number scarcely 500 had arrived before 1629. It is a striking fact, since it expresses a causal relation and not a mere coincidence, that the eleven years, 1629–1640, during which Charles I. governed England without a parliament, were the same eleven years that witnessed the planting of New England. For more than a century after this there was no considerable migration to this part of North America. Puritan England now found employment for all its energies and all its enthusiasm at home. The struggle with the king and the efforts toward reorganization under Cromwell were to occupy it for another score of years, and then, by the time of the Restoration the youthful creative energy of Puritanism had spent itself. The influence of this great movement

End of the Puritan exodus.

was indeed destined to grow wider and deeper with the progress of civilization, but after 1660 its creative work began to run in new channels and assume different forms.

It is curious to reflect what might have been the result, to America and to the world, had things in England gone differently between 1620 and 1660. Had the policy of James and Charles been less formidable, the Puritan exodus might never have occurred, and the Virginian type of society, varied perhaps by a strong Dutch infusion, might have become supreme in America. The western continent would have lost in richness and variety of life, and it is not likely that Europe would have made a corresponding gain, for the moral effect of the challenge, the struggle, and the overthrow of monarchy in England was a stimulus sorely needed by neighbouring peoples. It is not always by avoiding the evil, it is rather by grappling with it and conquering it that character is strengthened and life enriched, and there is no better example of this than the history of England in the seventeenth century.

What might have been.

On the other hand, if the Stuart despotism had triumphed in England, the Puritan exodus would doubtless have been swelled to huge dimensions. New England would have gained strength so quickly that much less irritation than she actually suffered between 1664 and 1689 would probably have goaded her into rebellion. The war of independence might have been waged a century sooner than it was. It is not easy to point to any especial advantage that could have come to America from this; one is rather inclined to think of the peculiarly valuable political training of the eighteenth century that would have been lost. Such surmises are for the most part idle. But as concerns Europe, it is plain to be seen, for reasons stated in my first chapter, that the decisive victory of Charles I. would have been a calamity of the first magnitude. It would have been like the Greeks losing Marathon or the Saracens winning Tours, supposing the worst consequences ever imagined in those hypothetical cases to have been realized. Or taking a more contracted view, we can see how England, robbed of her Puritan element, might still have waxed in strength, as France has done in spite of losing the Huguenots; but she could not have taken the proud position that she has come to occupy as mother of nations. Her preëminence since Cromwell's time has been chiefly due to her unrivalled power of planting self-supporting colonies, and that power has had its roots in English self-government. It is the vitality of the English Idea that is making the language of Cromwell and Washington dominant in the world.

CHAPTER IV.

THE NEW ENGLAND CONFEDERACY.

THE Puritan exodus to New England, which came to an end about 1640, was purely and exclusively English. There was nothing in it that came from the continent of Europe, nothing that was either Irish or Scotch, very little that was Welsh. As Palfrey says, the population of 26,000 that had been planted in New England by 1640 "thenceforward continued to multiply on its own soil for a century and a half, in remarkable seclusion from other communities." During the whole of this period New England received but few immigrants; and it was not until after the Revolutionary War that its people had fairly started on their westward march into the state of New York and beyond, until now, after yet another century, we find some of their descendants dwelling in a homelike Salem and a Portland of charming beauty on the Pacific coast. Three times between the meeting of the Long Parliament and the meeting of the Continental Congress did the New England colonies receive a slight infusion of non-English blood. In 1652, after his victories at Dunbar and Worcester, Cromwell sent 270 of his Scottish prisoners to Boston, where the descendants of some of them

The exodus was purely English.

still dwell. After the revocation of the Edict of Nantes in 1685, 150 families of Huguenots came to Massachusetts. And finally in 1719, 120 Presbyterian families came over from the north of Ireland, and settled at Londonderry in New Hampshire, and elsewhere. In view of these facts it may be said that there is not a county in England of which the population is more purely English than the population of New England at the end of the eighteenth century. From long and careful research, Mr. Savage, the highest authority on this subject, concludes that more than 98 in 100 of the New England people at that time could trace their origin to England in the narrowest sense, excluding even Wales. As already observed, every English shire contributed something to the emigration, but there was a marked preponderance of people from the East Anglian counties.

The population of New England was nearly as homogeneous in social condition as it was in blood. The emigration was preëminent for its respectability. Like the best part of the emigration to Virginia, it consisted largely of country squires and yeomen. The men who followed Winthrop were thrifty and prosperous in their old homes from which their devotion to an idea made them voluntary exiles. They attached so much importance to regular industry and decorous behaviour that for a long time the needy and shiftless people who usually make trouble in new colonies were not tolerated among them. Hence the early history of New England is remarkably free from those scenes of violence

Respectable character of the emigration.

and disorder which have so often made hideous the first years of new communities. Of negro slaves there were very few, and these were employed wholly in domestic service; there were not enough of them to affect the industrial life of New England or to be worth mentioning as a class. Neither were there many of the wretched people, kidnapped from the jails and slums of English sea-ports, such as in those early days when negro labour was scarce, were sent by ship-loads to Virginia, to become the progenitors of the "white trash." There were a few indented white servants, usually of the class known as "redemptioners," or immigrants who voluntarily bound themselves to service for a stated time in order to defray the cost of their voyage from Europe. At a later time there were many of these "redemptioners" in the middle colonies, but in New England they were very few; and as no stigma of servitude was attached to manual labour, they were apt at the end of their terms of service to become independent farmers; thus they ceased to be recognizable as a distinct class of society. Nevertheless the common statement that no traces of the "mean white" are to be found in New England is perhaps somewhat too sweeping. Interspersed among those respectable and tidy mountain villages, once full of such vigorous life, one sometimes comes upon little isolated groups of wretched hovels whose local reputation is sufficiently indicated by such terse epithets as "Hardscrabble" or "Hellhuddle." Their denizens may in many instances be the degenerate offspring of a sound New England stock, but they sometimes show strong points of resemblance to that "white trash" which has come to be a recognizable strain of the English race; and one cannot help suspecting that while the New England colonies made every effort to keep out such riff raff, it may nevertheless have now and then crept in. However this may be, it cannot be said that this element ever formed a noticeable feature in the life of colonial New England. As regards their social derivation, the settlers of New England were homogeneous in character to a remarkable degree, and they were drawn from the sturdiest part of the English stock. In all history there has been no other instance of colonization so exclusively effected by picked and chosen men. The colonists knew this, and were proud of it, as well they might be. It was the simple truth that was spoken by William Stoughton when he said, in his election sermon of 1688: "God sifted a whole nation, that He might send choice grain into the wilderness."

This matter comes to have more than a local interest, when we reflect that the 26,000 New Englanders of 1640 have in two hundred and fifty years increased to something like 15,000,000. From these men have come at least one-fourth of the present population of the United States. Striking as this fact may seem, it is perhaps less striking than the fact of the original migration when duly considered. In these times, when great steamers sail every day from European ports, bringing immigrants to a country not less advanced in material civilization than the country which they leave, the daily arrival of a thousand new citizens has come to be a commonplace event. But in the seventeenth century the transfer of more than twenty thousand well-to-do people within twenty years from their comfortable homes in England to the American wilderness was by no means a commonplace event. It reminds one of the migrations of ancient peoples, and in the quaint thought of our forefathers it was aptly likened to the exodus of Israel from the Egyptian house of bondage.

In this migration a principle of selection was at work which insured an extraordinary uniformity of character and of purpose among the settlers. To this uniformity of purpose, combined with complete homogeneity of race, is due the preponderance early acquired by New England in the history of the American people. In view of this, it is worth while to inquire what were the real aims of the settlers of New England. What was the common purpose which brought these men together in their resolve to create for themselves new homes in the wilderness?

This is a point concerning which there has been a great deal of popular misapprehension, and there has been no end of nonsense talked about it. It has been customary first to assume that the Puritan migration was undertaken in the interests of religious liberty, and then to upbraid the Puritans for forgetting all about religious liberty as soon as people came among them who disagreed with their opinions. But this view of the case is not sup-

<small>The migration was not intended to promote what we call religious liberty.</small>

ported by history. It is quite true that the Puritans were chargeable with gross intolerance; but it is not true that in this they were guilty of inconsistency. The notion that they came to New England for the purpose of establishing religious liberty, in any sense in which we should understand such a phrase, is entirely incorrect. It is neither more nor less than a bit of popular legend. If we mean by the phrase "religious liberty" a state of things in which opposite or contradictory opinions on questions of religion shall exist side by side in the same community, and in which everybody shall decide for himself how far he will conform to the customary religious observances, nothing could have been further from their thoughts. There is nothing they would have regarded with more genuine abhorrence. If they could have been forewarned by a prophetic voice of the general freedom — or, as they would have termed it, license — of thought and behaviour which prevails in this country to-day, they would very likely have abandoned their enterprise in despair.[1] The philosophic student of history often has occasion to see how God is wiser than man. In other words, he is often brought to realize how fortunate it is that the leaders in great historic events cannot foresee the remote results of the labours to which they have zealously consecrated their lives. It is part of the irony of human destiny that the end we really accomplish by striving with might and main is apt to be something quite different from the end we dreamed of

[1] See the passionate exclamation of Endicott, below, p. 190.

as we started on our arduous labour. So it was with the Puritan settlers of New England. The religious liberty that we enjoy to-day is largely the consequence of their work; but it is a consequence that was unforeseen, while the direct and conscious aim of their labours was something that has never been realized, and probably never will be.

The aim of Winthrop and his friends in coming to Massachusetts was the construction of a theocratic state which should be to Christians, under the New Testament dispensation, all that the theocracy of Moses and Joshua and Samuel had been to the Jews in Old Testament days. They should be to all intents and purposes freed from the jurisdiction of the Stuart king, and so far as possible the text of the Holy Scriptures should be their guide both in weighty matters of general legislation and in the shaping of the smallest details of daily life. In such a scheme there was no room for religious liberty as we understand it. No doubt the text of the Scriptures may be interpreted in many ways, but among these men there was a substantial agreement as to the important points, and nothing could have been further from their thoughts than to found a colony which should afford a field for new experiments in the art of right living. The state they were to found was to consist of a united body of believers; citizenship itself was to be co-extensive with church-membership; and in such a state there was apparently no more room for heretics than there was in Rome or Madrid. This was the idea which drew Winthrop and his followers

Theocratic ideal of the Puritans.

from England at a time when — as events were soon to show — they might have stayed there and defied persecution with less trouble than it cost them to cross the ocean and found a new state.

Such an ideal as this, considered by itself and apart from the concrete acts in which it was historically manifested, may seem like the merest fanaticism. But we cannot dismiss in this summary way a movement which has been at the source of so much that is great in American history: mere fanaticism has never produced such substantial results. Mere fanaticism is sure to aim at changing the constitution of human society in some essential point, to undo the work of evolution, and offer in some indistinctly apprehended fashion to remodel human life. But in these respects the Puritans were intensely conservative. The impulse by which they were animated was a profoundly ethical impulse — the desire to lead godly lives, and to drive out sin from the community — the same ethical impulse which animates the glowing pages of Hebrew poets and prophets, and which has given to the history and literature of Israel their commanding influence in the world. The Greek, says Matthew Arnold, held that the perfection of happiness was to have one's thoughts hit the mark; but the Hebrew held that it was to serve the Lord day and night. It was a touch of this inspiration that the Puritan caught from his earnest and reverent study of the sacred text, and that served to justify and intensify his yearning for a better life, and to give it the character of a

The impulse which sought to realize itself in the Puritan ideal was an ethical impulse.

grand and holy ideal. Yet with all this religious enthusiasm, the Puritan was in every fibre a practical Englishman with his full share of plain common-sense. He avoided the error of mediæval anchorites and mystics in setting an exaggerated value upon otherworldliness. In his desire to win a crown of glory hereafter he did not forget that the present life has its simple duties, in the exact performance of which the welfare of society mainly consists. He likewise avoided the error of modern radicals who would remodel the fundamental institutions of property and of the family, and thus disturb the very groundwork of our ethical ideals. The Puritan's ethical conception of society was simply that which has grown up in the natural course of historical evolution, and which in its essential points is therefore intelligible to all men, and approved by the common-sense of men, however various may be the terminology — whether theological or scientific — in which it is expounded. For these reasons there was nothing essentially fanatical or impracticable in the Puritan scheme: in substance it was something that great bodies of men could at once put into practice, while its quaint and peculiar form was something that could be easily and naturally outgrown and set aside.

Yet another point in which the Puritan scheme of a theocratic society was rational and not fanatical was its method of interpreting the Scriptures. That method was essentially rationalistic in two ways. First, the Puritan laid no claim to the possession of any peculiar inspiration or divine light whereby he

In interpreting Scripture, the Puritan appealed to his reason.

might be aided in ascertaining the meaning of the sacred text; but he used his reason just as he would in any matter of business, and he sought to convince, and expected to be convinced, by rational argument, and by nothing else. Secondly, it followed from this denial of any peculiar inspiration that there was no room in the Puritan commonwealth for anything like a priestly class, and that every individual must hold his own opinions at his own personal risk. The consequences of this rationalistic spirit have been very far-reaching. In the conviction that religious opinion must be consonant with reason, and that religious truth must be brought home to each individual by rational argument, we may find one of the chief causes of that peculiarly conservative yet flexible intelligence which has enabled the Puritan countries to take the lead in the civilized world of to-day. Free discussion of theological questions, when conducted with earnestness and reverence, and within certain generally acknowledged limits, was never discountenanced in New England. On the contrary, there has never been a society in the world in which theological problems have been so seriously and persistently discussed as in New England in the colonial period. The long sermons of the clergymen were usually learned and elaborate arguments of doctrinal points, bristling with quotations from the Bible, or from famous books of controversial divinity, and in the long winter evenings the questions thus raised afforded the occasion for lively debate in every household. The clergy were, as a rule, men of learning, able to read both Old and New Testaments in the original languages, and familiar with the best that had been talked and written, among Protestants at least, on theological subjects. They were also, for the most part, men of lofty character, and they were held in high social esteem on account of their character and scholarship, as well as on account of their clerical position. But in spite of the reverence in which they were commonly held, it would have been a thing quite unheard of for one of these pastors to urge an opinion from the pulpit on the sole ground of his personal authority or his superior knowledge of Scriptural exegesis. The hearers, too, were quick to detect novelties or variations in doctrine; and while there was perhaps no more than the ordinary human unwillingness to listen to a new thought merely because of its newness, it was above all things needful that the orthodox soundness of every new suggestion should be thoroughly and severely tested. This intense interest in doctrinal theology was part and parcel of the whole theory of New England life; because, as I have said, it was taken for granted that each individual must hold his own opinions at his own personal risk in the world to come.

Value of theological discussion. Such perpetual discussion, conducted under such a stimulus, afforded in itself no mean school of intellectual training. Viewed in relation to the subsequent mental activity of New England, it may be said to have occupied a position somewhat similar to that which the polemics of the mediæval schoolmen occupied in relation to the European thought of the Renaissance, and of the age of Hobbes and Descartes. At the same time the Puritan theory of life lay at the bottom of the whole system of popular education in New England. According to that theory, it was absolutely essential that every one should be taught from early childhood how to read and understand the Bible. So much instruction as this was assumed to be a sacred duty which the community owed to every child born within its jurisdiction. In ignorance, the Puritans maintained, lay the principal strength of popery in religion as well as of despotism in politics; and so, to the best of their lights, they cultivated knowledge with might and main. But in this energetic diffusion of knowledge they were unwittingly preparing the complete and irreparable destruction of the theocratic ideal of society which they had sought to realize by crossing the ocean and settling in New England. This universal education, and this perpetual discussion of theological questions, were no more compatible with rigid adherence to the Calvinistic system than with submission to the absolute rule of Rome. The inevitable result was the liberal and enlightened Protestantism which is characteristic of the best American society at the present day, and which is continually growing more liberal as it grows more enlightened — a Protestantism which, in the natural course of development, is coming to realize the noble ideal of Roger Williams, but from the very thought of which such men as Winthrop and Cotton and Endicott would have shrunk with dismay.

In this connection it is interesting to note the

similarity between the experience of the Puritans in New England and in Scotland with respect to the influence of their religious theory of life upon general education. Nowhere has Puritanism, with its keen intelligence and its iron tenacity of purpose, played a greater part than it has played in the history of Scotland. And one need not fear contradiction in saying that no other people in modern times, in proportion to their numbers, have achieved so much in all departments of human activity as the people of Scotland have achieved. It would be superfluous to mention the preëminence of Scotland in the industrial arts since the days of James Watt, or to recount the glorious names in philosophy, in history, in poetry and romance, and in every department of science, which since the middle of the eighteenth century have made the country of Burns and Scott, of Hume and Adam Smith, of Black and Hunter and Hutton and Lyell, illustrious for all future time. Now this period of magnificent intellectual fruition in Scotland was preceded by a period of Calvinistic orthodoxy quite as rigorous as that of New England. The ministers of the Scotch Kirk in the seventeenth century cherished a theocratic ideal of society not unlike that which the colonists of New England aimed at realizing. There was the same austerity, the same intolerance, the same narrowness of interests, in Scotland that there was in New England. Mr. Buckle, in the book which thirty years ago seemed so great and stimulating, gave us a graphic picture of this state of society,

Comparison with the case of Scotland.

and the only thing which he could find to say about it, as the result of his elaborate survey, was that the spirit of the Scotch Kirk was as thoroughly hostile to human progress as the spirit of the Spanish Inquisition! If this were really so, it would be difficult indeed to account for the period of brilliant mental activity which immediately followed. But in reality the Puritan theory of life led to general education in Scotland as it did in New England, and for precisely the same reasons, while the effects of theological discussion in breaking down the old Calvinistic exclusiveness have been illustrated in the history of Edinburgh as well as in the history of Boston.

It is well for us to bear in mind the foregoing considerations as we deal with the history of the short-lived New England Confederacy. The story is full of instances of an intolerant and domineering spirit, especially on the part of Massachusetts, and now and then this spirit breaks forth in ugly acts of persecution. In considering these facts, it is well to remember that we are observing the workings of a system which contained within itself a curative principle; and it is further interesting to observe how political circumstances contributed to modify the Puritan ideal, gradually breaking down the old theocratic exclusiveness and strengthening the spirit of religious liberty.

Scarcely had the first New England colonies been established when it was found desirable to unite them into some kind of a confederation. It is worthy of note that the separate existence of so many colonies was at the outset largely the result of religious differences. The uniformity of purpose, great as it was, fell far short of completeness. Could all have agreed, or had there been religious toleration in the modern sense, there was still room enough for all in Massachusetts; and a compact settlement would have been in much less danger from the Indians. But in the founding of Connecticut the theocratic idea had less weight, and in the founding of New Haven it had more weight, than in Massachusetts. The existence of Rhode Island was based upon that principle of full toleration which the three colonies just mentioned alike abhorred, and its first settlers were people banished from Massachusetts. With regard to toleration Plymouth occupied a middle ground; without admitting the principles of Williams, the people of that colony were still fairly tolerant in practice. Of the four towns of New Hampshire, two had been founded by Antinomians driven from Boston, and two by Episcopal friends of Mason and Gorges. It was impossible that neighbouring communities, characterized by such differences of opinion, but otherwise homogeneous in race and in social condition, should fail to react upon one another and to liberalize one another. Still more was this true when they attempted to enter into a political union. When, for example, Massachusetts in 1641–43 annexed the New Hampshire townships, she was of necessity obliged to relax in their case her policy of insisting upon religious conformity as a test of citizenship. So in forming the New England Confederacy, there were some mat-

Existence of so many colonies due to slight religious differences.

THE NEW ENGLAND CONFEDERACY. 155

ters of dispute that had to be passed over by mutual consent or connivance.

The same causes which had spread the English settlements over so wide a territory now led, as an indirect result, to their partial union into a confederacy. The immediate consequence of the westward movement had been an Indian war. Several savage tribes were now interspersed between the settlements, so that it became desirable that the military force should be brought, as far as possible, under one management. The colony of New Netherlands, moreover, had begun to assume importance, and the settlements west of the Connecticut river had already occasioned hard words between Dutch and English, which might at any moment be followed by blows. In the French colonies at the north, with their extensive Indian alliances under Jesuit guidance, the Puritans saw a rival power which was likely in course of time to prove troublesome. With a view to more efficient self-defence, therefore, in 1643 the four colonies of Massachusetts, Plymouth, Connecticut, and New Haven formed themselves into a league, under the style of "The United Colonies of New England." These four little states now contained thirty-nine towns, with an aggregate population of 24,000. To the northeast of Massachusetts, which now extended to the Piscataqua, a small colony had at length been constituted under a proprietary charter somewhat similar to that held by the Calverts in Maryland. Of this new province or palatinate of Maine the aged Sir Ferdinando Gorges was Lord Proprie-

It led to a notable attempt at federation.

tary, and he had undertaken not only to establish the Church of England there, but also to introduce usages of feudal jurisdiction like those remaining in the old country. Such a community was not likely to join the Confederacy; apart from other reasons, its proprietary constitution and the feud between the Puritans and Gorges would have been sufficient obstacles.

As for Rhode Island, on the other hand, it was regarded with strong dislike by the other colonies. It was a curious and noteworthy consequence of the circumstances under which this little state was founded that for a long time it became the refuge of all the fanatical and turbulent people who could not submit to the strict and orderly governments of Connecticut or Massachusetts. All extremes met on Narragansett bay. There were not only sensible advocates of religious liberty, but theocrats as well who saw flaws in the theocracy of other Puritans. The English world was then in a state of theological fermentation. People who fancied themselves favoured with direct revelations from Heaven; people who thought it right to keep the seventh day of the week as a Sabbath instead of the first day; people who cherished a special predilection for the Apocalypse and the Book of Daniel; people with queer views about property and government; people who advocated either too little marriage or too much marriage; all such eccentric characters as are apt to come to the surface in periods of religious excitement found in Rhode Island a favoured spot where they could prophesy without let or

Turbulence of dissent in Rhode Island.

hindrance. But the immediate practical result of so much discordance in opinion was the impossibility of founding a strong and well-ordered government. The early history of Rhode Island was marked by enough of turbulence to suggest the question whether, after all, at the bottom of the Puritan's refusal to recognize the doctrine of private inspiration, or to tolerate indiscriminately all sorts of opinions, there may not have been a grain of shrewd political sense not ill adapted to the social condition of the seventeenth century. In 1644 and again in 1648 the Narragansett settlers asked leave to join the Confederacy; but the request was refused on the ground that they had no stable government of their own. They were offered the alternative of voluntary annexation either to Massachusetts or to Plymouth, or of staying out in the cold; and they chose the latter course. Early in 1643 they had sent Roger Williams over to England to obtain a charter for Rhode Island. In that year Parliament created a Board of Commissioners, with the Earl of Warwick at its head, for the superintendence of colonial affairs; and noth- *The Earl of Warwick and his Board of Commissioners.* ing could better illustrate the loose and reckless manner in which American questions were treated in England than the first proceedings of this board. It gave an early instance of British carelessness in matters of American geography. In December, 1643, it granted to Massachusetts all the territory on the mainland of Narragansett bay; and in the following March it incorporated the townships of Newport and Portsmouth, which stood on the island, together with Providence, which stood on the mainland, into an independent colony empowered to frame a government and make laws for itself. With this second document Williams returned to Providence in the autumn of 1644. Just how far it was intended to cancel the first one, nobody could tell, but it plainly afforded an occasion for a conflict of claims.

The league of the four colonies is interesting as the first American experiment in federation. By the articles it was agreed that each colony should retain full independence so far as concerned the management of its internal affairs, but that the confederate government should have entire control over all dealings with the Indians or with foreign powers. The administration of the league was put into the hands of a board of eight Federal Commissioners, two from each colony. Constitution of the Confederacy. The commissioners were required to be church-members in good standing. They could choose for themselves a president or chairman out of their own number, but such a president was to have no more power than the other members of the Board. If any measure were to come up concerning which the commissioners could not agree, it was to be referred for consideration to the legislatures or general courts of the four colonies. Expenses for war were to be charged to each colony in proportion to the number of males in each between sixteen years of age and sixty. A meeting of the Board might be summoned by any two magistrates whenever the public safety might seem to require it; but a regular meeting was to be held once every year.

In this scheme of confederacy all power of taxation was expressly left to the several colonies. The scheme provided for a mere league, not for a federal union. The government of the Commissioners acted only upon the local governments, not upon individuals. The Board had thus but little executive power, and was hardly more than a consulting body. Another source of weakness in the confederacy was the overwhelming preponderance of Massachusetts. Of the 24,000 people in the confederation, 15,000 belonged to Massachusetts, while the other three colonies had only about 3,000 each. Massachusetts accordingly had to carry the heaviest burden, both in the furnishing of soldiers and in the payment of war expenses, while in the direction of affairs she had no more authority than one of the small colonies. As a natural consequence, Massachusetts tried to exert more authority than she was entitled to by the articles of confederation; and such conduct was not unnaturally resented by the small colonies, as betokening an unfair and domineering spirit. In spite of these drawbacks, however, the league was of great value to New England. On many occasions it worked well as a high court of jurisdiction, and it made the military strength of the colonies more available than it would otherwise have been. But for the interference of the British government, which brought it to an untimely end, the Confederacy might have been gradually amended so as to become enduring. After its downfall it was pleasantly remembered by the people of New England;

It was only a league, not a federal union.

in times of trouble their thoughts reverted to it; and the historian must in fairness assign it some share in preparing men's minds for the greater work of federation which was achieved before the end of the following century.

Its formation involved a tacit assumption of sovereignty. The formation of such a confederacy certainly involved something very like a tacit assumption of sovereignty on the part of the four colonies. It is worthy of note that they did not take the trouble to ask the permission of the home government in advance. They did as they pleased, and then defended their action afterward. In England the act of confederation was regarded with jealousy and distrust. But Edward Winslow, who was sent over to London to defend the colonies, pithily said: "If we in America should forbear to unite for offence and defence against a common enemy till we have leave from England, our throats might be all cut before the messenger would be half seas through." Whether such considerations would have had weight with Charles I. or not was now of little consequence. His power of making mischief soon came to an end, and from the liberal and sagacious policy of Cromwell the Confederacy had not much to fear. Nevertheless the fall of Charles I. brought up for the first time that question which a century later was to acquire surpassing interest, — the question as to the supremacy of Parliament over the colonies.

Down to this time the supreme control over colonial affairs had been in the hands of the king and his privy council, and the Parliament had not disputed it. In 1624 they had grumbled at James I.'s high-handed suppression of the Virginia Company, but they had not gone so far as to call in question the king's supreme authority over the colonies. In 1628, in a petition to Charles I. relating to the Bermudas, they had fully admitted this royal authority. But the fall of Charles I. for the moment changed all this. Among the royal powers devolved upon Parliament was the prerogative of superintending the affairs of the colonies. Such, at least, was the theory held in England, and it is not easy to see how any other theory could logically have been held; but the Americans never formally admitted it, and in practice they continued to behave toward Parliament very much as they had behaved toward the crown, yielding just as little obedience as possible. When the Earl of Warwick's commissioners in 1644 seized upon a royalist vessel in Boston harbour, the legislature of Massachusetts debated the question whether it was compatible with the dignity of the colony to permit such an act of sovereignty on the part of Parliament. It was decided to wink at the proceeding, on account of the strong sympathy between Massachusetts and the Parliament which was overthrowing the king. At the same time the legislature sent over to London a skilfully worded protest against any like exercise of power in future. In 1651 Parliament ordered Massachusetts to surrender the charter obtained from Charles I. and take out a new one from Parliament, in which the relations of the colony to the

Fall of Charles I. brings up the question as to supremacy of Parliament over the colonies.

home government should be made the subject of fresh and more precise definition. To this request the colony for more than a year vouchsafed no answer; and finally, when it became necessary to do something, instead of sending back the charter, the legislature sent back a memorial, setting forth that the people of Massachusetts were quite contented with their form of government, and hoped that no change would be made in it. War between England and Holland, and the difficult political problems which beset the brief rule of Cromwell, prevented the question from coming to an issue, and Massachusetts was enabled to preserve her independent and somewhat haughty attitude.

During the whole period of the Confederacy, however, disputes kept coming up which through endless crooked ramifications were apt to end in an appeal to the home government, and thus raise again and again the question as to the extent of its imperial supremacy. For our present purpose, it is enough to mention three of these cases: 1, the adventures of Samuel Gorton; 2, the Presbyterian cabal; 3, the persecution of the Quakers. Other cases in point are those of John Clarke and the Baptists, and the relations of Massachusetts to the northeastern settlements; but as it is not my purpose here to make a complete outline of New England history, the three cases enumerated will suffice.

The first case shows, in a curious and instructive way, how religious dissensions were apt to be complicated with threats of an Indian war on the one hand and peril from Great Britain on the other; and as we come to realize the triple danger, we can perhaps make some allowances for the high-handed measures with which the Puritan governments sometimes sought to avert it. As I have elsewhere tried to show, the genesis of the persecuting spirit is to be found in the conditions of primitive society, where "above all things the prime social and political necessity is social cohesion within the tribal limits, for unless such social cohesion be maintained, the very existence of the tribe is likely to be extinguished in bloodshed." The persecuting spirit "began to pass away after men had become organized into great nations, covering a vast extent of territory, and secured by their concentrated military strength against the gravest dangers of barbaric attack."[1] Now as regards these considerations, the Puritan communities in the New England wilderness were to some slight extent influenced by such conditions as used to prevail in primitive society; and this will help us to understand the treatment of the Antinomians and such cases as that with which we have now to deal.

Genesis of the persecuting spirit.

Among the supporters of Mrs. Hutchinson, after her arrival at Aquedneck, was a sincere and courageous, but incoherent and crotchetty man named Samuel Gorton. In the denunciatory language of that day he was called a "proud and pestilent seducer," or, as the modern newspaper would say, a "crank." It is well to make due allowances for the prejudice so con-

Samuel Gorton.

[1] *Excursions of an Evolutionist*, pp. 250, 255.

spicuous in the accounts given by his enemies, who felt obliged to justify their harsh treatment of him. But we have also his own writings from which to form an opinion as to his character and views. Lucidity, indeed, was not one of his strong points as a writer, and the drift of his argument is not always easy to decipher; but he seems to have had some points of contact with the Familists, a sect established in the sixteenth century in Holland. The Familists held that the essence of religion consists not in adherence to any particular creed or ritual, but in cherishing the spirit of divine love. The general adoption of this point of view was to inaugurate a third dispensation, superior to those of Moses and Christ, the dispensation of the Holy Ghost. The value of the Bible lay not so much in the literal truth of its texts as in their spiritual import; and by the union of believers with Christ they came to share in the ineffable perfection of the Godhead. There is much that is modern and enlightened in such views, which Gorton seems to some extent to have shared. He certainly set little store by ritual observances and maintained the equal right of laymen with clergymen to preach the gospel. Himself a London clothier, and thanking God that he had not been brought up in "the schools of human learning," he set up as a preacher without ordination, and styled himself "professor of the mysteries of Christ." He seems to have cherished that doctrine of private inspiration which the Puritans especially abhorred. It is not likely that he had any distinct comprehension of his own views, for distinctness was just what they lacked.[1] But they were such as in the seventeenth century could not fail to arouse fierce antagonism, and if it was true that wherever there was a government Gorton was against it, perhaps that only shows that wherever

[1] A glimmer of light upon Gorton may be got from reading the title-page of one of his books: "AN INCORRUPTIBLE KEY, composed of the CX PSALME, wherewith you may open the Rest of the Holy Scriptures; Turning itself only according to the Composure and Art of that Lock, of the Closure and Secresie of that great Mystery of God manifest in the Flesh, but justified only by the Spirit, which it evidently openeth and revealeth, out of Fall and Resurrection, Sin and Righteousness, Ascension and Descension, Height and Depth, First and Last, Beginning and Ending, Flesh and Spirit, Wisdome and Foolishnesse, Strength and Weakness, Mortality and Immortality, Jew and Gentile, Light and Darknesse, Unity and Multiplication, Fruitfulness and Barrenness, Curse and Blessing, Man and Woman, Kingdom and Priesthood, Heaven and Earth, Allsufficiency and Deficiency, God and Man. And out of every Unity made up of twaine, it openeth that great two-leafed Gate, which is the sole Entrie into the City of God, of New Jerusalem, *into which none but the King of glory can enter;* and as that Porter openeth the Doore of the Sheepfold, *by which whosoever entreth is the Shepheard of the Sheep;* See Isa. 45. 1. Psal. 24. 7, 8, 9, 10. John 10. 1, 2, 3; Or, (according to the Signification of the Word translated *Psalme,*) it is a Pruning-Knife, to lop off from the Church of Christ all superfluous Twigs *of earthly and carnal Commandments*, Leviticall Services or Ministery, and fading and vanishing Priests, or Ministers, who are taken away and cease, and are not established and confirmed by Death, as holding no Correspondency with the princely Dignity, Office, and Ministry of our *Melchisedek*, who is the only Minister and Ministry of the Sanctuary, and of that true Tabernacle which the Lord pitcht, and not Man. For it supplants the Old Man, and implants the New; abrogates the Old Testament or Covenant, and confirms the New, unto a thousand Generations, or in Generations forever. By Samuel Gorton, *Gent.*, and at the time of penning hereof, in the Place of Judicature (upon Aquethneck, alias Road Island) of Providence Plantations in the Nanhyganset Bay, New England. Printed in the Yeere 1647."

there was a government it was sure to be against him.

In the case of such men as Gorton, however, — and the type is by no means an uncommon one, — their temperament usually has much more to do with getting them into trouble than their opinions. Gorton's temperament was such as to keep him always in an atmosphere of strife. Other heresiarchs suffered persecution in Massachusetts, but Gorton was in hot water everywhere. His arrival in any community was the signal for an immediate disturbance of the peace. His troubles began in Plymouth, where the wife of the pastor preferred his teachings to those of her husband. In 1638 he fled to Aquedneck, where his first achievement was a schism among Mrs. Hutchinson's followers, which ended in some staying to found the town of Portsmouth while others went away to found Newport. Presently Portsmouth found him intolerable, flogged and banished him, and after his departure was able to make up its quarrel with Newport. He next made his way with a few followers to Pawtuxet, within the jurisdiction of Providence, and now it is the broad-minded and gentle Roger Williams who complains of his "bewitching and madding poor Providence." The question is here suggested what could it have been in Gorton's teaching that enabled him thus to "bewitch" these little communities? We may be sure that it could not have been the element of modern liberalism suggested in the Familistic doctrines above cited. That was the feature then least likely to appeal to the minds of common people, and most likely to appeal to Williams. More probably such success as Gorton had in winning followers was due to some of the mystical rubbish which abounds in his pages and finds in a modern mind no doorway through which to enter.

Williams disapproved of Gorton, but was true to his principles of toleration and would not take part in any attempt to silence him. But in 1641 we find thirteen leading citizens of Providence, headed by William Arnold,[1] sending a memorial to Boston, asking for assistance and counsel in regard to this disturber of the peace. How was Massachusetts to treat such an appeal? She could not presume to meddle with the affair unless she could have permanent jurisdiction over Pawtuxet; otherwise she was a mere intruder. *Providence protests against him.* How strong a side-light does this little incident throw upon the history of the Roman republic, and of all relatively strong communities when confronted with the problem of preserving order in neighbouring states that are too weak to preserve it for themselves! Arnold's argument, in his appeal to Massachusetts, was precisely the same as that by which the latter colony excused herself for banishing the Antinomians. He simply says that Gorton and his company "are not fit persons to be received, and made members of a body in so weak a state as our town is in at

[1] Father of Benedict Arnold, afterward governor of Rhode Island, and owner of the stone windmill (apparently copied from one in Chesterton, Warwickshire) which was formerly supposed by some antiquarians to be a vestige of the Northmen. Governor Benedict Arnold was great-grandfather of the traitor.

present;" and he adds, "There is no state but in the first place will seek to preserve its own safety and peace." Whatever might be the abstract merits of Gorton's opinions, his conduct was politically dangerous; and accordingly the jurisdiction over Pawtuxet was formally conceded to Massachusetts. Thereupon that colony, assuming jurisdiction, summoned Gorton and his men to Boston, to prove their title to the lands they occupied. They of course regarded the summons as a flagrant usurpation of authority, and instead of obeying it they withdrew to Shawomet, on the western shore of Narragansett bay, where they bought a tract of land from the principal sachem of the Narragansetts, Miantonomo. The immediate rule over this land belonged to two inferior chiefs, who ratified the sale at the time, but six months afterward disavowed the ratification, on the ground that it had been given under duress from their overlord Miantonomo. Here was a state of things which might easily bring on an Indian war. The two chiefs appealed to Massachusetts for protection, and were accordingly summoned, along with Miantonomo, to a hearing at Boston. Here we see how a kind of English protectorate over the native tribes had begun to grow up so soon after the destruction of the Pequots. Such a result was inevitable. After hearing the arguments, the legislature decided to defend the two chiefs, provided they would put themselves under the jurisdiction of Massachusetts. This was done, while further complaints against Gorton came from the citizens

He flees to Shawomet, where he buys land of the Indians.

of Providence. Gorton and his men were now peremptorily summoned to Boston to show cause why they should not surrender their land at Shawomet and to answer the charges against them. On receiving from Gorton a defiant reply, couched in terms which some thought blasphemous, the government of Massachusetts prepared to use force.

Meanwhile the unfortunate Miantonomo had rushed upon his doom. The annihilation of the Pequots had left the Mohegans and Narragansetts contending for the foremost place among the native tribes. Between the rival sachems, Uncas and Miantonomo, the hatred was deep and deadly. As soon as the Mohegan perceived that trouble was brewing between Miantonomo and the government at Boston, he improved the occasion by gathering a few Narragansett scalps. Miantonomo now took the war-path and was totally defeated by Uncas in a battle on the Great Plain in the present township of Norwich. Encumbered with a coat of mail which his friend Gorton had given him, Miantonomo was overtaken and captured. By ordinary Indian usage he Miantonomo and Uncas. would have been put to death with fiendish torments, as soon as due preparations could be made and a fit company assembled to gloat over his agony; but Gorton sent a messenger to Uncas, threatening dire vengeance if harm were done to his ally. This message puzzled the Mohegan chief. The appearance of a schism in the English counsels was more than he could quite fathom. When the affair had somewhat more fully developed itself, some of the Indians spoke of the white men as divided into two rival tribes, the Gortonoges and Wattaconoges.[1] Roger Williams tells us that the latter term, applied to the men of Boston, meant coat-wearers. Whether it is to be inferred that the Gortonoges went about in what in modern parlance would be called their "shirt-sleeves," the reader must decide.

In his perplexity Uncas took his prisoner to Hartford, and afterward, upon the advice of the governor and council, sent him to Boston, that his fate might be determined by the Federal Commissioners who were there holding their first regular meeting. It was now the turn of the commissioners to be perplexed. According to English law there was no good reason for putting Miantonomo to death. The question was whether they should interfere with the Indian custom by which his life was already forfeit to his captor. The magistrates already suspected the Narragansetts of cherishing hostile designs. To set their sachem at liberty, especially while the Gorton affair remained unsettled, might be dangerous; and it would be likely to alienate Uncas from the English. In their embarrassment the commissioners sought spiritual guidance. A synod of forty or fifty clergymen, from all parts of New England, was in session at Boston, and the question was referred to a committee of five of their number. The decision was prompt that Miantonomo must die. He was sent back to Hartford to be slain by Uncas, but two messengers accompanied him, to see that no

[1] Gorton, *Simplicitie's Defence against Seven-headed Policy*, p. 88.

tortures were inflicted. A select band of Mohegan warriors journeyed through the forest with the prisoner and the two Englishmen, until they came to the plain where the battle had been fought. Then at a signal from Uncas, the war- <small>Death of Miantonomo.</small> rior walking behind Miantonomo silently lifted his tomahawk and sank it into the brain of the victim who fell dead without a groan. Uncas cut a warm slice from the shoulder and greedily devoured it, declaring that the flesh of his enemy was the sweetest of meat and gave strength to his heart. Miantonomo was buried there on the scene of his defeat, which has ever since been known as the Sachem's Plain. This was in September, 1643, and for years afterward, in that month, parties of Narragansetts used to visit the spot and with frantic gestures and hideous yells lament their fallen leader. A heap of stones was raised over the grave, and no Narragansett came near it without adding to the pile. After many a summer had passed and the red men had disappeared from the land, a Yankee farmer, with whom thrift prevailed over sentiment, cleared away the mound and used the stones for the foundation of his new barn.[1]

One cannot regard this affair as altogether creditable to the Federal Commissioners and their clerical advisers. One of the clearest-headed and most impartial students of our history observes that " if the English were to meddle in the matter at all, it was their clear duty to enforce as far as

---

[1] De Forest, *History of the Indians of Connecticut*, Hartford, 1850, p. 198.

might be the principles recognized by civilized men. When they accepted the appeal made by Uncas they shifted the responsibility from the Mohegan chief to themselves."[1] The decision was doubtless based purely upon grounds of policy. Miantonomo was put out of the way because he was believed to be dangerous. In the thirst for revenge that was aroused among the Narragansetts there was an alternative source of danger, to which I shall hereafter refer.[2] It is difficult now to decide, as a mere question of safe policy, what the English ought to have done. The chance of being dragged into an Indian war, through the feud between Narragansetts and Mohegans, was always imminent. The policy which condemned Miantonomo was one of timidity, and fear is merciless.

The Federal Commissioners heartily approved the conduct of Massachusetts toward Gorton, and adopted it in the name of the United Colonies. After a formal warning, which passed unheeded, a company of forty men, under Edward Johnson of Woburn and two other officers, was sent to Shawomet. Some worthy citizens of Providence essayed to play the part of mediators, and after some parley the Gortonites offered to submit to arbitration. The proposal was conveyed to Boston, and the clergy were again consulted. They declared it beneath the dignity of Massachusetts to negotiate "with a few fugitives living without law or government," and they would no more compound with Gorton's "blas-

Expedition against Shawomet.

---

[1] Doyle, *Puritan Colonies*, i. 324.
[2] See below, p. 222, note.

phemous revilings" than they would bargain with the Evil One. The community must be "purged" of such wickedness, either by repentance or by punishment. The ministers felt that God would hold the community responsible for Gorton and visit calamities upon them unless he were silenced.[1] The arbitration was refused, Gorton's blockhouse was besieged and captured, and the agitator was carried with nine of his followers to Boston, where they were speedily convicted of heresy and sedition. Before passing judgment the General Court as usual consulted with the clergy who recommended a sentence of death. *Trial and sentence of the heretics.* Their advice was adopted by the assistants, but the deputies were more merciful, and the heretics were sentenced to imprisonment at the pleasure of the court. In this difference between the assistants and the deputies, we observe an early symptom of that popular revolt against the ascendancy of the clergy which was by and by to become so much more conspicuous and effective in the affair of the Quakers. Another symptom might be seen in the circumstance that so much sympathy was expressed for the Gortonites, especially by women, that after some months of imprisonment and abuse the heretics were banished under penalty of death.

Gorton now went to England and laid his tale of woe before the parliamentary Board of Commissioners. The Earl of War- *Gorton appeals to Parliament.* wick behaved with moderation. He declined to commit himself to an opinion as to the

---

[1] See my *Excursions of an Evolutionist*, pp. 239–242, 250–255, 286–289.

merits of the quarrel, but Gorton's title to Shawomet was confirmed. He returned to Boston with an order to the government to allow him to pass unmolested through Massachusetts, and hereafter to protect him in the possession of Shawomet. If this little commonwealth of 15,000 inhabitants had been a nation as powerful as France, she could not have treated the message more haughtily. By a majority of one vote it was decided not to refuse so trifling a favour as a passage through the country for just this once; but as for protecting the new town of Warwick which the Gortonites proceeded to found at Shawomet, although it was several times threatened by the Indians, and the settlers appealed to the parliamentary order, that order Massachusetts flatly and doggedly refused to obey.[1]

In the discussions of which these years were so full, "King Winthrop," as his enemy Morton called him, used some very significant language. By a curious legal fiction of the Massachusetts charter the colonists were supposed to hold their land as in the manor of East Greenwich near London, and it was argued that they were represented in Parliament by the members of the county or borough which contained that manor, and were accordingly subject to the jurisdiction of Parliament. It was further argued that since the king had no absolute sovereignty in-

Winthrop's prophetic opinion.

---

[1] Gorton's life at Warwick, after all these troubles, seems to have been quiet and happy. He died in 1677 at a great age. In 1771 Dr. Ezra Stiles visited, in Providence, his last surviving disciple, born in 1691. This old man said that Gorton wrote in heaven, and none can understand his books except those who live in heaven while on earth.

THE NEW ENGLAND CONFEDERACY. 175

dependent of Parliament he could not by charter impart any such independent sovereignty to others. Winthrop did not dispute these points, but observed that the safety of the commonwealth was the supreme law, and if in the interests of that safety it should be found necessary to renounce the authority of Parliament, the colonists would be justified in doing so.[1] This was essentially the same doctrine as was set forth ninety-nine years later by young Samuel Adams in his Commencement Oration at Harvard.

The case of the Presbyterian cabal admits of briefer treatment than that of Gorton. There had now come to be many persons in Massachusetts who disapproved of the provision which restricted the suffrage to members of the Independent or Congregational churches of New England, and in 1646 the views of these people were presented in a petition to the General Court. The petitioners asked "that their civil disabilities might be removed, and that all members of the churches of England and Scotland might be admitted to communion with the New England churches. If this could not be granted they prayed to be released from all civil burdens. Should the court refuse to entertain their complaint, they would be obliged to bring their case before Parliament."[2] The leading signers of this menacing petition were William Vassall, Samuel Maverick, and Dr. Robert Child. Maverick we have already met. From the day when the ships of the

The Presbyterian cabal.

---

[1] Doyle, *Puritan Colonies*, i. 369.
[2] Doyle, i. 372.

first Puritan settlers had sailed past his log fortress on Noddle's Island, he had been their enemy; "a man of loving and curteous behaviour," says Johnson, "very ready to entertaine strangers, yet an enemy to the reformation in hand, being strong for the lordly prelatical power." Vassall was not a denizen of Massachusetts, but lived in Scituate, in the colony of Plymouth, where there were no such restrictions upon the suffrage. Child was a learned physician who after a good deal of roaming about the world had lately taken it into his head to come and see what sort of a place Massachusetts was. Although these names were therefore not such as to lend weight to such a petition, their request would seem at first sight reasonable enough. At a superficial glance it seems conceived in a modern spirit of liberalism. In reality it was nothing of the sort. In England it was just the critical moment of the struggle between Presbyterians and Independents which had come in to complicate the issues of the great civil war. Vassall, Child, and Maverick seem to have been the leading spirits in a cabal for the establishment of Presbyterianism in New England, and in their petition they simply took advantage of the discontent of the disfranchised citizens in Massachusetts in order to put in an entering wedge. This was thoroughly understood by the legislature of Massachusetts, and accordingly the petition was dismissed and the petitioners were roundly fined. Just as Child was about to start for England with his grievances, the magistrates overhauled his papers and discovered a petition to the parliamentary Board of Commissioners, suggesting that Presbyterianism should be established in New England, and that a viceroy or governor-general should be appointed to rule there. To the men of Massachusetts this last suggestion was a crowning horror. It seemed scarcely less than treason. The signers of this petition were the same who had signed the petition to the General Court. They were now fined still more heavily and imprisoned for six months. By and by they found their way, one after another, to London, while the colonists sent Edward Winslow, of Plymouth, as an advocate to thwart their schemes. Winslow was assailed by Child's brother in a spicy pamphlet entitled "New England's Jonas cast up at London," and replied after the same sort, entitling his pamphlet "New England's Salamander discovered." The cabal accomplished nothing because of the decisive defeat of Presbyterianism in England. "Pride's Purge" settled all that.

The petition of Vassall and his friends was the occasion for the meeting of a synod of churches at Cambridge, in order to complete the organization of Congregationalism. In 1648 the work of the synod was embodied in the famous Cambridge Platform, which adopted the Westminster Confession as its creed, carefully defined the powers of the clergy, and declared it to be the duty of magistrates to suppress heresy. In 1649 the General Court laid this platform before the congregations; in 1651 it was adopted; and this event may be regarded as completing the theocratic organization of the Puritan commonwealth in Massachusetts. *The Cambridge Platform; deaths of Winthrop and Cotton.*

It was immediately preceded and followed by the deaths of the two foremost men in that commonwealth. John Winthrop died in 1649 and John Cotton in 1652. Both were men of extraordinary power. Of Winthrop it is enough to say that under his skilful guidance Massachusetts had been able to pursue the daring policy which had characterized the first twenty years of her history, and which in weaker hands would almost surely have ended in disaster. Of Cotton it may be said that he was the most eminent among a group of clergymen who for learning and dialectical skill have seldom been surpassed. Neither Winthrop nor Cotton approved of toleration upon principle. Cotton, in his elaborate controversy with Roger Williams, frankly asserted that persecution is not wrong in itself; it is wicked for falsehood to persecute truth, but it is the sacred duty of truth to persecute falsehood. This was the theologian's view. Winthrop's was that of a man of affairs. They had come to New England, he said, in order to make a society after their own model; all who agreed with them might come and join that society; those who disagreed with them might go elsewhere; there was room enough on the American continent. But while neither Winthrop nor Cotton understood the principle of religious liberty, at the same time neither of them had the temperament which persecutes. Both were men of genial disposition, sound common-sense, and exquisite tact. Under their guidance no such tragedy would have been possible as that which was about to leave its ineffaceable stain upon the annals of Massachusetts.

It was most unfortunate that at this moment the places of these two men should have been taken by two as arrant fanatics as ever drew breath. For thirteen out of the fifteen years following Winthrop's death, the governor of Massachusetts was John Endicott, a sturdy pioneer, whose services to the colony had been great. He was honest and conscientious, but passionate, domineering, and very deficient in tact. At the same time Cotton's successor in position and influence was John Norton, a man of pungent wit, unyielding temper, and melancholy mood. He was possessed by a morbid fear of Satan, whose hirelings he thought were walking up and down over the earth in the visible semblance of heretics and schismatics. Under such leaders the bigotry latent in the Puritan commonwealth might easily break out in acts of deadly persecution.

Endicott and Norton take the lead.

The occasion was not long in coming. Already the preaching of George Fox had borne fruit, and the noble sect of Quakers was an object of scorn and loathing to all such as had not gone so far as they toward learning the true lesson of Protestantism. Of all Protestant sects the Quakers went furthest in stripping off from Christianity its non-essential features of doctrine and ceremonial. Their ideal was not a theocracy but a separation between church and state. They would abolish all distinction between clergy and laity, and could not be coaxed or bullied into paying tithes. They also refused to render military service, or to take the oath of allegiance. In these ways they came at once into

The Quakers, and their views.

antagonism both with church and with state. In doctrine their chief peculiarity was the assertion of an "Inward Light" by which every individual is to be guided in his conduct of life. They did not believe that men ceased to be divinely inspired when the apostolic ages came to an end, but held that at all times and places the human soul may be enlightened by direct communion with its Heavenly Father. Such views involved the most absolute assertion of the right of private judgment; and when it is added that in the exercise of this right many Quakers were found to reject the dogmas of original sin and the resurrection of the body, to doubt the efficacy of baptism, and to call in question the propriety of Christians turning the Lord's Day into a Jewish Sabbath, we see that they had in some respects gone far on the road toward modern rationalism. It was not to be expected that such opinions should be treated by the Puritans in any other spirit than one of extreme abhorrence and dread. The doctrine of the "Inward Light," or of private inspiration, was something especially hateful to the Puritan. To the modern rationalist, looking at things in the dry light of history, it may seem that this doctrine was only the Puritan's own appeal to individual judgment, stated in different form; but the Puritan could not so regard it. To such a fanatic as Norton this inward light was but a reflection from the glare of the bottomless pit, this private inspiration was the beguiling voice of the Devil. As it led the Quakers to strange and novel conclusions, this inward light seemed to array itself in hostility to that final court of appeal for all good Protestants, the sacred text of the Bible. The Quakers were accordingly regarded as infidels who sought to deprive Protestantism of its only firm support. They were wrongly accused of blasphemy in their treatment of the Scriptures. Cotton Mather says that the Quakers were in the habit of alluding to the Bible as the Word of the Devil. Such charges, from passionate and uncritical enemies, are worthless except as they serve to explain the bitter prejudice with which the Quakers were regarded. They remind one of the silly accusation brought against Wyclif two centuries earlier, that he taught his disciples that God ought to obey the Devil;[1] and they are not altogether unlike the assumptions of some modern theologians who take it for granted that any writer who accepts the Darwinian theory must be a materialist.

But worthless as Mather's statements are, in describing the views of the Quakers, they are valuable as indicating the temper in which these disturbers of the Puritan theocracy were regarded. In accusing them of rejecting the Bible and making a law unto themselves, Mather simply put on record a general belief which he shared. Nor can it be doubted that the demeanour of the Quaker enthusiasts was sometimes such as to seem to warrant the belief that their anarchical doctrines entailed, as a natural consequence, disorderly and disreputable conduct. In those days all manifestations of dissent were apt to be violent, and the persecution which they

Violent manifestations of dissent.

[1] Milman, *Latin Christianity*, vii. 390.

encountered was likely to call forth strange and unseemly vagaries. When we remember how the Quakers, in their scorn of earthly magistrates and princes, would hoot at the governor as he walked up the street; how they used to rush into church on Sundays and interrupt the sermon with untimely remarks; how Thomas Newhouse once came into the Old South Meeting-House with a glass bottle in each hand, and, holding them up before the astonished congregation, knocked them together and smashed them, with the remark, "Thus will the Lord break you all in pieces"; how Lydia Wardwell and Deborah Wilson ran about the streets in the primitive costume of Eve before the fall, and called their conduct "testifying before the Lord"; we can hardly wonder that people should have been reminded of the wretched scenes enacted at Münster by the Anabaptists of the preceding century.

Such incidents, however, do not afford the slightest excuse for the cruel treatment which the Quakers received in Boston, nor do they go far toward explaining it. Persecution began immediately, before the new-comers had a chance to behave themselves well or ill. Their mere coming to Boston was taken as an act of invasion. It was indeed an attack upon the Puritan theocratic idea. Of all the sectaries of that age of sects, the Quakers were the most aggressive. There were at one time more than four thousand of them in English jails; yet when any of them left England, it was less to escape persecution than to preach their doctrines far and wide over the earth. Their missionaries found their way to Paris, to Vienna; even to Rome, where they testified under the very roof of the Vatican. In this dauntless spirit they came to New England to convert its inhabitants, or at any rate to establish the principle that in whatever community it might please them to stay, there they would stay in spite of judge or hangman. At first they came to Barbadoes, whence two of their number, Anne Austin and Mary Fisher, sailed for Boston. When they landed, on a May morning in 1656, Endicott happened to be away from Boston, but the deputy-governor, Richard Bellingham, was equal to the occasion. He arrested the two women and locked them up in jail, where, for fear they might proclaim their heresies to the crowd gathered outside, the windows were boarded up. There was no law as yet enacted against Quakers, but a council summoned for the occasion pronounced their doctrines blasphemous and devilish. The books which the poor women had with them were seized and publicly burned, and the women themselves were kept in prison half-starved for five weeks until the ship they had come in was ready to return to Barbadoes. Soon after their departure Endicott came home. He found fault with Bellingham's conduct as too gentle; if he had been there he would have had the hussies flogged.

Anne Austin and Mary Fisher.

Five years afterward Mary Fisher went to Adrianople and tried to convert the Grand Turk, who treated her with grave courtesy and allowed her to prophesy unmolested. This is one of the numerous incidents that, on a superficial view of history, might be cited in support of the opinion that there has been on the whole more tolerance in the Mussulman than in the Christian world. Rightly interpreted, however, the fact has no such implication. In Massachusetts the preaching of Quaker doctrines might (and did) lead to a revolution; in Turkey it was as harmless as the barking of dogs. Governor Endicott was afraid of Mary Fisher; Mahomet III. was not.

No sooner had the two women been shipped from Boston than eight other Quakers arrived from London. They were at once arrested. While they were lying in jail the Federal Commissioners, then in session at Plymouth, recommended that laws be forthwith enacted to keep these dreaded heretics out of the land. Next year they stooped so far as to seek the aid of Rhode Island, the colony which they had refused to admit into their confederacy. "They sent a letter to the authorities of that colony, signing themselves their loving friends and neighbours, and beseeching them to preserve the whole body of colonies against 'such a pest' by banishing and excluding all Quakers, a measure to which 'the rule of charity did oblige them.'" Roger Williams was then president of Rhode Island, and in full accord with his noble spirit was the reply of the assembly. "We have no law amongst us whereby to punish any for only declaring by words their minds and understandings concerning the things and ways of God as to salvation and our eternal condition." As for these Quakers we find that where they are "most of all suffered to declare

Noble conduct of Rhode Island.

themselves freely and only opposed by arguments in discourse, there they least of all desire to come." Any breach of the civil law shall be punished, but the "freedom of different consciences shall be respected." This reply enraged the confederated colonies, and Massachusetts, as the strongest and most overbearing, threatened to cut off the trade of Rhode Island, which forthwith appealed to Cromwell for protection. The language of the appeal is as touching as its broad Christian spirit is grand. It recognizes that by stopping trade the men of Massachusetts will injure themselves, yet, it goes on to say, "for the safeguard of their religion they may seem to neglect themselves in that respect; for what will not men do for their God?" But whatever fortune may befall, "let us not be compelled to exercise any civil power over men's consciences."[1]

Roger Williams appeals to Cromwell.

There could never, of course, be a doubt as to who drew up this state paper. During his last visit to England, three years before, Roger Williams had spent several weeks at Sir Harry Vane's country house in Lincolnshire, and he had also been intimately associated with Cromwell and Milton. The views of these great men were the most advanced of that age. They were coming to understand the true principle upon which toleration should be based.[2] Vane had said in Parliament, "Why should the labours of any be suppressed, if sober, though never so different? We now profess to seek God, we desire to see light!"

---

[1] Doyle, ii. 133, 134; *Rhode Island Records*, i. 377, 378.

[2] See my *Excursions of an Evolutionist*, pp. 247, 289–293.

This Williams called a "heavenly speech." The sentiment it expressed was in accordance with the practical policy of Cromwell, and in the appeal of the president of Rhode Island to the Lord Protector one hears the tone with which friend speaks to friend.

In thus protecting the Quakers, Williams never for a moment concealed his antipathy to their doctrines. The author of "George Fox digged out of his Burrowes," the sturdy controversialist who in his seventy-third year rowed himself in a boat the whole length of Narragansett bay to engage in a theological tournament against three Quaker champions, was animated by nothing less than the broadest liberalism in his bold reply to the Federal Commissioners in 1657. The event showed that under his guidance the policy of Rhode Island was not only honourable but wise.

Laws passed against the Quakers. The four confederated colonies all proceeded to pass laws banishing Quakers and making it a penal offence for shipmasters to bring them to New England. These laws differed in severity. Those of Connecticut, in which we may trace the influence of the younger John Winthrop, were the mildest; those of Massachusetts were the most severe, and as Quakers kept coming all the more in spite of them, they grew harsher and harsher. At first the Quaker who persisted in returning was to be flogged and imprisoned at hard labour, next his ears were to be cut off, and for a third offence his tongue was to be bored with a hot iron. At length in 1658, the Federal Commissioners, sitting at Boston with

Endicott as chairman, recommended capital punishment. It must be borne in mind that the general reluctance toward prescribing or inflicting the death penalty was much weaker then than now. On the statute-books there *The death penalty.* were not less than fifteen capital crimes, including such offences as idolatry, witchcraft, blasphemy, marriage within the Levitical degrees, "presumptuous sabbath-breaking," and cursing or smiting one's parents.[1] The infliction of the penalty, however, lay practically very much within the discretion of the court, and was generally avoided except in cases of murder or other heinous felony. In some of these ecclesiastical offences the statute seems to have served the purpose of a threat, and was therefore perhaps the more easily enacted. Yet none of the colonies except Massachusetts now adopted the suggestion of the Federal Commissioners and threatened the Quakers with death.

In Massachusetts the opposition was very strong indeed, and its character shows how wide the divergence in sentiment had already become between the upper stratum of society and the people in general. This divergence was one result of the excessive weight given to the clergy by the restriction of the suffrage to church members. One might almost say that it was not the people of Massachusetts, after all, that shed the blood of the Quakers; it was Endicott and the clergy. The bill establishing death as the penalty for returning after banishment was passed in the upper house

---

[1] *Colonial Laws of Massachusetts*, pp. 14–16; Levermore's *Republic of New Haven*, p. 153.

without serious difficulty; but in the lower house it was at first defeated. Of the twenty-six deputies fifteen were opposed to it, but one of these fell sick and two were intimidated, so that finally the infamous measure was passed by a vote of thirteen against twelve. Probably it would not have passed but for a hopeful feeling that an occasion for putting it into execution would not be likely to arise. It was hoped that the mere threat would prove effective. Endicott begged the Quakers to keep away, saying earnestly that he did not desire their death; but the more resolute spirits were not deterred by fear of the gallows. In September, 1659, William Robinson, Marmaduke Stevenson, and Mary Dyer, who had come to Boston expressly to defy the cruel law, were banished. Mrs. Dyer was a lady of good family, wife of the secretary of Rhode Island. She had been an intimate friend of Mrs. Hutchinson. While she went home to her husband, Stevenson and Robinson went only to Salem and then faced about and came back to Boston. Mrs. Dyer also returned. All three felt themselves under divine command to resist and defy the persecutors. On the 27th of October they were led to the gallows on Boston Common, under escort of a hundred soldiers. Many people had begun to cry shame on such proceedings, and it was thought necessary to take precautions against a tumult. The victims tried to address the crowd, but their voices were drowned by the beating of drums. While the Rev. John Wilson railed and scoffed at them from the foot of the gallows the two brave men were hanged. The halter had been placed upon Mrs. Dyer when her son, who had come in all haste from Rhode Island, obtained her reprieve on his promise to take her away. The bodies of the two men were denied Christian burial and thrown uncovered into a pit. All the efforts of husband and son were unable to keep Mrs. Dyer at home. In the following spring she returned to Boston and on the first day of June was again taken to the gallows. At the last moment she was offered freedom if she would only promise to go away and stay, but she refused. "In obedience to the will of the Lord I came," said she, "and in his will I abide faithful unto death." And so she died.

Public sentiment in Boston was now turning so strongly against the magistrates that they began to weaken in their purpose. But there was one more victim. In November, 1660, William Leddra returned from banishment. The case was clear enough, but he was kept in prison four months and every effort was made to induce him to promise to leave the colony, but in vain. In the following March he too was put to death. A few days before the execution, as Leddra was being questioned in court, a memorable scene occurred. Wenlock Christison was one of those who had been banished under penalty of death. On his return he made straight for the town-house, strode into the court-room, and with uplifted finger addressed the judges in words of authority. "I am come here to warn you," said he, "that ye shed no more innocent blood." He

Wenlock Christison's defiance, and victory.

was instantly seized and dragged off to jail. After three months he was brought to trial before the Court of Assistants. The magistrates debated for more than a fortnight as to what should be done. The air was thick with mutterings of insurrection, and they had lost all heart for their dreadful work. Not so the savage old man who presided, frowning gloomily under his black skull cap. Losing his patience at last, Endicott smote the table with fury, upbraided the judges for their weakness, and declared himself so disgusted that he was ready to go back to England.[1] "You that will not consent, record it," he shouted, as the question was again put to vote, "I thank God I am not afraid to give judgment." Christison was condemned to death, but the sentence was never executed. In the interval the legislature assembled, and the law was modified. The martyrs had not died in vain. Their cause was victorious. A revolution had been effected. The Puritan ideal of a commonwealth composed of a united body of believers was broken down, never again to be restored. The principle had been admitted that the heretic might come to Massachusetts and stay there.

It was not in a moment, however, that these results were fully realized. For some years longer Quakers were fined, imprisoned, and now and then tied to the cart's tail and whipped from one town to another. But these acts of persecution came to be more and more discountenanced by public opinion until at length they ceased.

[1] See my remarks above, p. 145.

It was on the 25th of May, 1660, just one week before the martyrdom of Mary Dyer, that Charles II. returned to England to occupy his father's throne. One of the first papers laid before him was a memorial in behalf of the oppressed Quakers in New England. In the course of the following year he sent a letter to Endicott and the other New England governors, ordering them to suspend proceedings against the Quakers, and if any were then in prison, to send them to England for trial. Christison's victory had already been won, but the "King's Missive" was now partially obeyed by the release of all prisoners. As for sending anybody to England for trial, that was something that no New England government could ever be made to allow. *The "King's Missive."*

Charles's defence of the Quakers was due, neither to liberality of disposition nor to any sympathy with them, but rather to his inclinations toward Romanism. Unlike in other respects, Quakers and Catholics were alike in this, that they were the only sects which the Protestant world in general agreed in excluding from toleration. Charles wished to secure toleration for Catholics, and he could not prudently take steps toward this end without pursuing a policy broad enough to diminish persecution in other directions, and from these circumstances the Quakers profited. At times there was something almost like a political alliance between Quaker and Catholic, as instanced in the relations between William Penn and Charles's brother, the Duke of York. *Why Charles II. interfered to protect the Quakers.*

Besides all this, Charles had good reason to feel that the governments of New England were assuming too many airs of sovereignty. There were plenty of people at hand to work upon his mind. The friends of Gorton and Child and Vassall were loud with their complaints. Samuel Maverick swore that the people of New England were all rebels, and he could prove it. The king was assured that the Confederacy was "a war combination, made by the four colonies when they had a design to throw off their dependence on England, and for that purpose." The enemies of the New England people, while dilating upon the rebellious disposition of Massachusetts, could also remind the king that for several years that colony had been coining and circulating shillings and sixpences with the name "Massachusetts" and a tree on one side, and the name "New England" with the date on the other. There was no recognition of England upon this coinage, which was begun in 1652 and kept up for more than thirty years. Such pieces of money used to be called "pine-tree shillings"; but, so far as looks go, the tree might be anything, and an adroit friend of New England once gravely assured the king that it was meant for the royal oak in which his majesty hid himself after the battle of Worcester!

Against the colony of New Haven the king had a special grudge. Two of the regicide judges, who had sat in the tribunal which condemned his father, escaped to New England in 1660 and were well received there. They were gentlemen of high position. Edward Whalley was a cousin of Cromwell and Hampden. He had distinguished himself at Naseby and Dunbar, and had risen to the rank of lieutenant-general. He had commanded at the capture of Worcester, where it is interesting to observe that the royalist commander who surrendered to him was Sir Henry Washington, own cousin to the grandfather of George Washington. The other regicide, William Goffe, as a major-general in Cromwell's army, had won such distinction that there were some who pointed to him as the proper person to succeed the Lord Protector on the death of the latter. He had married Whalley's daughter. Soon after the arrival of these gentlemen, a royal order for their arrest was sent to Boston. If they had been arrested and sent back to England, their severed heads would soon have been placed over Temple Bar. The king's detectives hotly pursued them through the woodland paths of New England, and they would soon have been taken but for the aid they got from the people. Many are the stories of their hairbreadth escapes. Sometimes they took refuge in a cave on a mountain near New Haven, sometimes they hid in friendly cellars; and once, being hard put to it, they skulked under a wooden bridge, while their pursuers on horseback galloped by overhead. After lurking about New Haven and Milford for two or three years, on hearing of the expected arrival of Colonel Nichols and his commission, they sought a more secluded hiding-place near Hadley, a village lately settled far up the Connecticut river, within the jurisdiction of Massachusetts. Here the avengers lost the trail,

The regicide judges.

the pursuit was abandoned, and the weary regicides were presently forgotten. The people of New Haven had been especially zealous in shielding the fugitives. Mr. Davenport had not only harboured them in his own house, but on the Sabbath before their expected arrival he had preached a very bold sermon, openly advising his people to aid and comfort them as far as possible.[1] The colony, moreover, did not officially recognize the restoration of Charles II. to the throne until that event had been commonly known in New England for more than a year. For these reasons the wrath of the king was specially roused against New Haven, when circumstances combined to enable him at once to punish this disloyal colony and deal a blow at the Confederacy.

We have seen that in restricting the suffrage to church members New Haven had followed the example of Massachusetts, but Connecticut had

---

[1] The daring passage in the sermon is thus given in Bacon's *Historical Discourses*, New Haven, 1838: "Withhold not countenance, entertainment, and protection from the people of God — whom men may call fools and fanatics — if any such come to you from other countries, as from France or England, or any other place. Be not forgetful to entertain strangers. Remember those that are in bonds, as bound with them. The Lord required this of Moab, saying, 'Make thy shadow as the night in the midst of the noonday; hide the outcasts; bewray not him that wandereth. Let mine outcasts dwell with thee, Moab; be thou a covert to them from the face of the spoiler.' Is it objected — 'But so I may expose myself to be spoiled or troubled'? He, therefore, to remove this objection, addeth, 'For the extortioner is at an end, the spoiler ceaseth, the oppressors are consumed out of the land.' While we are attending to our duty in owning and harbouring Christ's witnesses, God will be providing for their and our safety, by destroying those that would destroy his people."

not; and at this time there was warm controversy between the two younger colonies as to the wisdom of such a policy. As yet none of the colonies save Massachusetts had obtained a charter, and Connecticut was naturally anxious to obtain one. Whether through a complaisant spirit connected with this desire, or through mere accident, Connecticut had been prompt in acknowledging the restoration of Charles II.; and in August, 1661, she dispatched the younger Winthrop to England to apply for a charter. Winthrop was a man of winning address and of wide culture. His scientific tastes were a passport to the favour of the king at a time when the Royal Society was being founded, of which Winthrop himself was soon chosen a fellow. In every way the occasion was an auspicious one. The king looked upon the rise of the New England Confederacy with unfriendly eyes. Massachusetts was as yet the only member of the league that was really troublesome; and there seemed to be no easier way to weaken her than to raise up a rival power by her side, and extend to it such privileges as might awaken her jealousy. All the more would such a policy be likely to succeed if accompanied by measures of which Massachusetts must necessarily disapprove, and the suppression of New Haven would be such a measure.

New Haven annexed to Connecticut.

In accordance with these views, a charter of great liberality was at once granted to Connecticut, and by the same instrument the colony of New Haven was deprived of its separate existence and annexed to its stronger neighbour. As if to emphasize the motives which had led to this display of royal favour toward Connecticut, an equally liberal charter was granted to Rhode Island. In the summer of 1664 Charles II. sent a couple of ships-of-war to Boston harbour, with 400 troops under command of Colonel Richard Nichols, who had been appointed, along with Samuel Maverick and two others as royal commissioners, to look after the affairs of the New World. Colonel Nichols took his ships to New Amsterdam, and captured that important town. After his return the commissioners held meetings at Boston, and for a time the Massachusetts charter seemed in danger. But the Puritan magistrates were shrewd, and months were frittered away to no purpose. Presently the Dutch made war upon England, and the king felt it to be unwise to irritate the people of Massachusetts beyond endurance. The turbulent state of English politics which followed still further absorbed his attention, and New England had another respite of several years.

In New Haven a party had grown up which was dissatisfied with its extreme theocratic policy and approved of the union with Connecticut. Davenport and his followers, the founders of the colony, were beyond measure disgusted. They spurned "the Christless rule" of the sister colony. Many of them took advantage of the recent conquest of New Netherland, and a strong party, led by the Rev. Abraham Pierson, of Branford, migrated to the banks of the Passaic in June, 1667, and laid the foundations of Newark. For some years to come the theocratic idea that

Founding of Newark.

had given birth to New Haven continued to live on in New Jersey. As for Mr. Davenport, he went to Boston and ended his days there. Cotton Mather, writing at a later date, when the theocratic scheme of the early settlers had been manifestly outgrown and superseded, says of Davenport: "Yet, after all, the Lord gave him to see that in this world a Church-State was impossible, whereinto there enters nothing which defiles."

The theocratic policy, alike in New Haven and in Massachusetts, broke down largely through its inherent weakness. It divided the community, and created among the people a party adverse to its arrogance and exclusiveness. This state of things facilitated the suppression of New Haven by royal edict, and it made possible the victory of Wenlock Christison in Massachusetts. We can now see the fundamental explanation of the deadly hostility with which Endicott and his party regarded the Quakers. The latter aimed a fatal blow at the very root of the idea which had brought the Puritans to New England. Once admit these heretics as citizens, or even as tolerated sojourners, and there was an end of the theocratic state consisting of a united body of believers. It was a life-and-death struggle, in which no quarter was given; and the Quakers, aided by popular discontent with the theocracy, even more than by the intervention of the crown, won a decisive victory.

Breaking down of the theocratic policy.

As the work of planting New England took place chiefly in the eleven years 1629–1640, during which Charles I. contrived to reign without a parliament, so the prosperous period of the New England Confederacy, 1643–1664, covers the time of the Civil War and the Commonwealth, and just laps on to the reign of Charles II. By the summary extinction of the separate existence of one of its members for the benefit of another, its vigour was sadly impaired. But its constitution was revised so as to make it a league of three states instead of four; and the Federal Commissioners kept on holding their meetings, though less frequently, until the revocation of the Massachusetts charter in 1684. During this period a great Indian war occurred, in the course of which this concentration of the military strength of New England, imperfect as it was, proved itself very useful. In the history of New England, from the restoration of the Stuarts until their final expulsion, the two most important facts are the military struggle of the newly founded states with the Indians, and their constitutional struggle against the British government. The troubles and dangers of 1636 were renewed on a much more formidable scale, but the strength of the people had waxed greatly in the mean time, and the new perils were boldly overcome or skilfully warded off; not, however, until the constitution of Massachusetts had been violently wrenched out of shape in the struggle, and seeds of conflict sown which in the following century were to bear fruit in the American Revolution.

Weakening of the Confederacy.

CHAPTER V.

KING PHILIP'S WAR.

For eight-and-thirty years after the destruction of the Pequots, the intercourse between the English and the Indians was to all outward appearance friendly. The policy pursued by the settlers was in the main well considered. While they had shown that they could strike with terrible force when blows were needed, their treatment of the natives in time of peace seems to have been generally just and kind. Except Puritans and Indians. in the single case of the conquered Pequot territory, they scrupulously paid for every rood of ground on which they settled, and so far as possible they extended to the Indians the protection of the law. On these points we have the explicit testimony of Josiah Winslow, governor of Plymouth, in his report to the Federal Commissioners in May, 1676; and what he says about Plymouth seems to have been equally true of the other colonies. Says Winslow, "I think I can clearly say that before these present troubles broke out, the English did not possess one foot of land in this colony but what was fairly obtained by honest purchase of the Indian proprietors. Nay, because some of our people are of a covetous disposition, and the Indians are in their straits easily prevailed with to part with their lands, we first made a law that none should purchase or receive of gift any land of the Indians without the knowledge and allowance of our Court. . . . And if at any time they have brought complaints before us, they have had justice impartial and speedy, so that our own people have frequently complained that we erred on the other hand in showing them overmuch favour." The general laws of Massachusetts and Connecticut as well as of Plymouth bear out what Winslow says, and show us that as a matter of policy the colonial governments were fully sensible of the importance of avoiding all occasions for quarrel with their savage neighbours.

There can, moreover, be little doubt that the material comfort of the Indians was for a time considerably improved by their dealings with the white men. Hitherto their want of foresight and thrift had been wont to involve them during the long winters in a dreadful struggle with famine. Now the settlers were ready to pay liberally for the skin of every fur-covered animal the red men could catch; and where the trade thus arising did not suffice to keep off famine, instances of generous charity were frequent. The Algonquin tribes of New England lived chiefly by hunting, but partly by agriculture. They raised beans and corn, and succotash was a dish which they contributed to the white man's table. They could now raise or buy English vegetables, while from dogs and horses, pigs and poultry, oxen and sheep, little as they could avail themselves of such useful animals, they nevertheless derived some benefit.[1] Better blankets and better knives were brought within their reach; and in spite of all the colonial governments could do to prevent it, they were to some extent enabled to supply themselves with muskets and rum.

Besides all this trade, which, except in the article of liquor, tended to improve the condition of the native tribes, there was on the part of the earlier settlers an earnest and diligent effort to convert them to Christianity and give them the rudiments of a civilized education. Missionary work was begun in 1643 by Thomas Mayhew on the islands of Nantucket and Martha's Vineyard. The savages at first declared they were not so silly as to barter thirty-seven tutelar deities for one, but after much preaching and many pow-wows Mayhew succeeded in persuading them that the Deity of the white man was mightier than all their *manitous*. Whether they ever got much farther than this toward a comprehension of the white man's religion may be doubted; but they were prevailed upon to let their children learn to read and write, and even to set up little courts, in which justice was administered according to some of the simplest rules of English law, and from which there lay an appeal to the court of Plymouth. In 1646 Massachusetts enacted that the elders of the churches should choose two persons each year to go and spread the gospel among the Indians. In 1649 Parliament established the Society for propagating the Gospel in New England, and presently from voluntary con-

Missionary work: Thomas Mayhew.

[1] Palfrey, *History of New England*, iii. 138–140.

tributions the society was able to dispose of an annual income of £2000. Schools were set up in which agriculture was taught as well as religion. It was even intended that Indians should go to Harvard College, and a building was erected for their accommodation, but as none came to occupy it, the college printing-press was presently set to work there. One solitary Indian student afterward succeeded in climbing to the bachelor's degree, — Caleb Cheeshahteaumuck of the class of 1665. It was this one success that was marvellous, not the failure of the scheme, which vividly shows how difficult it was for the white man of that day to understand the limitations of the red man.

<small>John Eliot.</small>
The greatest measure of success in converting the Indians was attained by that famous linguist and preacher, the apostle John Eliot. This remarkable man was a graduate of Jesus College, Cambridge. He had come to Massachusetts in 1631, and in the following year had been settled as teacher in the church at Roxbury of which Thomas Welde was pastor. He had been distinguished at the university for philological scholarship and for linguistic talent — two things not always found in connection — and now during fourteen years he devoted such time as he could to acquiring a complete mastery of the Algonquin dialect spoken by the Indians of Massachusetts bay. To the modern comparative philologist his work is of great value. He published not only an excellent Indian grammar, but a complete translation of the Bible into the Massachusetts language, — a monument of prodigious labour. It

is one of the most instructive documents in existence for the student of Algonquin speech, though the Massachusetts tribe and its language have long been extinct, and there are very few scholars living who can read the book. It has become one of the curiosities of literature and at auction sales of private libraries commands an extremely high price. Yet out of this rare book the American public has somehow or other within the last five or six years contrived to pick up a word which we shall very likely continue to hear for some time to come. In Eliot's Bible, the word which means a great chief — such as Joshua, or Gideon, or Joab — is "mugwump."

It was in 1646 that Eliot began his missionary preaching at a small Indian village near Watertown. President Dunster, of Harvard College, and Mr. Shepard, the minister at Cambridge, felt a warm interest in the undertaking. These worthy men seriously believed that the aborigines of America were the degenerate descendants of the ten lost tribes of Israel, and from this strange backsliding it was hoped that they might now be reclaimed. With rare eloquence and skill did Eliot devote himself to the difficult work of reaching the Indian's scanty intelligence and still scantier moral sense. His ministrations reached from the sands of Cape Cod to the rocky hillsides of Brookfield. But he soon found that single-handed he could achieve but little over so wide an area, and accordingly he adopted the policy of colonizing his converts in village communities near the English towns, where they

<small>Villages of Christian Indians.</small>

might be sequestered from their heathen brethren and subjected to none but Christian influences. In these communities he hoped to train up native missionaries who might thence go and labour among the wild tribes until the whole lump of barbarism should be leavened. In pursuance of this scheme a stockaded village was built at Natick in 1651. Under the direction of an English carpenter the Indians built log-houses for themselves, and most of them adopted the English dress. Their simple government was administered by tithing-men, or "rulers of tens," chosen after methods prescribed in the book of Exodus. Other such communities were formed in the neighbourhoods of Concord and Grafton. By 1674 the number of these "praying Indians," as they were called, was estimated at 4000, of whom about 1500 were in Eliot's villages, as many more in Martha's Vineyard, 300 in Nantucket, and 700 in the Plymouth colony. There seems to be no doubt that these Indians were really benefited both materially and morally by the change in their life. In theology it is not likely that they reached any higher view than that expressed by the Connecticut sachem Wequash who "seeing and beholding the mighty power of God in the English forces, how they fell upon the Pequots, . . . from that time was convinced and persuaded that our God was a most dreadful God;" accordingly, says the author of "New England's First Fruits," "he became thoroughly reformed according to his light." Matters of outward observance, too, the Indians could understand; for we read of one of them rebuking an Englishman "for profaning the Lord's Day by felling of a tree." The Indian's notions of religion were probably confined within this narrow compass; the notions of some people that call themselves civilized perhaps do not extend much further.

From such facts as those above cited we may infer that the early relations of the Puritan settlers to the Algonquin tribes of New England were by no means like the relations between white men and red men in recent times on our western plains. During Philip's War, as we shall see, the Puritan theory of the situation was entirely changed and our forefathers began to act in accordance with the frontiersman's doctrine that the good Indians are dead Indians. But down to that time it is clear that his intention was to deal honourably and gently with his tawny neighbour. We sometimes hear the justice and kindness of the Quakers in Pennsylvania alleged as an adequate reason for the success with which they kept clear of an Indian war. This explanation, however, does not seem to be adequate; it does not appear that, on the whole, the Puritans were less just and kind than the Quakers in their treatment of the red men. The true explanation is rather to be found in the relations between the Indian tribes toward the close of the seventeenth century. Early in that century the Pennsylvania region had been in the hands of the ferocious and powerful Susquehannocks, but in 1672, after a frightful struggle of twenty years, this great tribe was swept from the face of the earth by the resistless league of the Five Na-

Why Pennsylvania was so long unmolested by the Indians.

tions. When the Quakers came to Pennsylvania in 1682, the only Indians in that neighbourhood were the Delawares, who had just been terribly beaten by the Five Nations and forced into a treaty by which they submitted to be called "women," and to surrender their tomahawks. Penn's famous treaty was made with the Delawares as occupants of the land and also with the Iroquois league as overlords.[1] Now the great central fact of early American history, so far as the relations between white men and red men are concerned, is the unshaken friendship of the Iroquois for the English. This was the natural consequence of the deadly hostility between the Iroquois and the French which began with Champlain's defeat of the Mohawks in 1609. During the seventy-three years which intervened between the founding of Pennsylvania and the defeat of Braddock there was never a moment when the Delawares could have attacked the Quakers without incurring the wrath and vengeance of their overlords the Five Nations. This was the reason why Pennsylvania was left so long in quiet. No better proof could be desired than the fact that in Pontiac's war, after the overthrow of the French and when Indian politics had changed, no state suffered so much as Pennsylvania from the horrors of Indian warfare.

In New England at the time of Philip's War, the situation was very different from what it was between the Hudson and the Susquehanna. The settlers were thrown into immediate relations with several tribes whose mutual hostility and rivalry

---

[1] See Parkman, *Conspiracy of Pontiac*, i. 80–85.

was such that it was simply impossible to keep on good terms with all at once. Such complicated questions as that which involved the English in responsibility for the fate of Miantonomo did not arise in Pennsylvania. Since the destruction of the Pequots we have observed the Narragansetts and Mohegans contending for the foremost place among New England tribes. Of the two rivals the Mohegans were the weaker, and therefore courted the friendship of the formidable palefaces. The English had no desire to take part in these barbarous feuds, but they could not treat the Mohegans well without incurring the hostility of the Narragansetts. For thirty years the feeling of the latter tribe toward the English had been very unfriendly and would doubtless have vented itself in murder but for their recollection of the fate of the Pequots. After the loss of their chief Miantonomo their attitude became so sullen and defiant that the Federal Commissioners, in order to be in readiness for an outbreak, collected a force of 300 men. At the first news of these preparations the Narragansetts, overcome with terror, sent a liberal tribute of wampum to Boston, and were fain to conclude a treaty in which they promised to behave themselves well in the future.

Difficulty of the situation in New England.

It was impossible that this sort of English protectorate over the native tribes, which was an inevitable result of the situation, should be other than irksome and irritating to the Indians. They could not but see that the white man stood there as master, and even in the utter absence of provocation, this fact alone must have made them hate him. It is difficult, moreover, for the civilized man and the savage to understand each other. As a rule the one does not know what the other is thinking about. When Mr. Hamilton Cushing a few years ago took some of his Zuñi friends into a hotel in Chicago, they marvelled at his entering such a mighty palace with so little ceremony, and their wonder was heightened at the promptness with which "slaves" came running at his beck and call; but all at once, on seeing an American eagle over one of the doorways, they felt that the mystery was solved. Evidently this palace was the communal dwelling of the Eagle Clan of palefaces, and evidently Mr. Cushing was a great sachem of this clan, and as such entitled to lordly sway there! The Zuñis are not savages, but representatives of a remote and primitive phase of what Mr. Morgan calls the middle status of barbarism. The gulf between their thinking and that of white men is wide because there is a wide gulf between the experience of the two.

It is hard for the savage and the civilized man to understand one another.

This illustration may help us to understand an instance in which the Indians of New England must inevitably have misinterpreted the actions of the white settlers and read them in the light of their uneasy fears and prejudices. I refer to the work of the apostle Eliot. His design in founding his villages of Christian Indians was in the highest degree benevolent and noble; but the heathen Indians could hardly be expected to see anything in it but a cunning scheme for destroying them.

Eliot's converts were for the most part from the Massachusetts tribe, the smallest and weakest of all. The Plymouth converts came chiefly from the tribe next in weakness, the Pokanokets or Wampanoags. The more powerful tribes — Narragansetts, Nipmucks, and Mohegans — furnished very few converts. When they saw the white intruders gathering members of the weakest tribes into villages of English type, and teaching them strange gods while clothing them in strange garments, they probably supposed that the palefaces were simply adopting these Indians into their white tribe as a means of increasing their military strength. At any rate, such a proceeding would be perfectly intelligible to the savage mind, whereas the nature of Eliot's design lay quite beyond its ken. As the Indians recovered from their supernatural dread of the English, and began to regard them as using human means to accomplish their ends, they must of course interpret their conduct in such light as savage experience could afford. It is one of the commonest things in the world for a savage tribe to absorb weak neighbours by adoption, and thus increase its force preparatory to a deadly assault upon other neighbours. When Eliot in 1657 preached to the little tribe of Podunks near Hartford, and asked them if they were willing to accept of Jesus Christ as their saviour, their old men scornfully answered No! they had parted with most of their land, but they were not going to become the white man's servants. A rebuke administered to Eliot by Uncas in 1674 has a similar implication. When the

Eliot's designs misunderstood.

apostle was preaching one evening in a village over which that sachem claimed jurisdiction, an Indian arose and announced himself as a deputy of Uncas. Then he said, "Uncas is not well pleased that the English should pass over Mohegan river to call *his* Indians to pray to God." [1]

Thus, no matter how benevolent the white man's intentions, he could not fail to be dreaded by the Indians as a powerful and ever encroaching enemy. Even in his efforts to keep the peace and prevent tribes from taking the warpath without his permission, he was interfering with the red man's cherished pastime of murder and pillage. The appeals to the court at Plymouth, the frequent summoning of sachems to Boston, to explain their affairs and justify themselves against accusers, must have been maddening in their effects upon the Indian; for there is one sound instinct which the savage has in common with the most progressive races, and that is the love of self-government that resents all outside interference. All things considered, it is remarkable that peace should have been maintained in New England from 1637 to 1675; and probably nothing short of the consuming vengeance wrought upon the Pequots could have done it. But with the lapse of time the wholesome feeling of dread began to fade away, and as the Indians came to use musket instead of bow and arrow, their fear of the English grew less, until at length their ferocious temper broke forth in an

It is remarkable that peace should have been so long preserved.

[1] De Forest, *History of the Indians of Connecticut*, pp. 252, 257.

epidemic of fire and slaughter that laid waste the land.

Massasoit, chief sachem of the Wampanoags and steadfast ally of the Plymouth colonists, died in 1660, leaving two sons, Wamsutta and Metacom, or as the English nicknamed them, Alexander and Philip. Alexander succeeded to his father's position of savage dignity and influence, but his reign was brief. Rumours came to Plymouth that he was plotting mischief, and he was accordingly summoned to appear before the General Court of that colony and explain himself. He seems to have gone reluctantly, but he succeeded in satisfying the magistrates of his innocence of any evil designs. Whether he caught cold at Plymouth or drank rum as only Indians can, we do not know. At any rate, on starting homeward, before he had got clear of English territory, he was seized by a violent fever and died. The savage mind knows nothing of pneumonia or delirium tremens. It knows nothing of what we call natural death. To the savage all death means murder, for like other men he judges of the unknown by the known. In the Indian's experience normal death was by tomahawk or firebrand; abnormal death (such as we call natural) must come either from poison or from witchcraft. So when the honest chronicler Hubbard tells us that Philip suspected the Plymouth people of poisoning his brother, we can easily believe him. It was long, however, before he was ready to taste the sweets of revenge. He schemed and plotted in the dark.

<small>Deaths of Massasoit and Alexander.</small>

In one respect the Indian diplomatist is unlike

his white brethren; he does not leave state-papers behind him to reward the diligence and gratify the curiosity of later generations; and accordingly it is hard to tell how far Philip was personally responsible for the storm which was presently to burst upon New England. Whether his scheme was as comprehensive as that of Pontiac in 1763, whether or not it amounted to a deliberate combination of all red men within reach to exterminate the white men, one can hardly say with confidence. The figure of Philip, in the war which bears his name, does not stand out so prominently as the figure of Pontiac in the later struggle. This may be partly because Pontiac's story has been told by such a magician as Mr. Francis Parkman. But it is partly because the data are too meagre. In all probability, however, the schemes of Sassacus the Pequot, of Philip the Wampanoag, and of Pontiac the Ottawa, were substantially the same. That Philip plotted with the Narragansetts seems certain, and the early events of the war point clearly to a previous understanding with the Nipmucks. The Mohegans, on the other hand, gave him no assistance, but remained faithful to their white allies.

Philip's designs.

For thirteen years had Philip been chief sachem of his tribe before the crisis came. Rumours of his unfriendly disposition had at intervals found their way to the ears of the magistrates at Plymouth, but Philip had succeeded in setting himself right before them. In 1670 the rumours were renewed, and the Plymouth men felt that it was time to strike, but the other colonies held them back, and a meeting was arranged between Philip and three Boston men at Taunton in April, 1671. There the crafty savage expressed humility and contrition for all past offences, and even consented to a treaty in which he promised that his tribe should surrender all their fire-arms. On the part of the English this was an extremely unwise measure, for while it could not possibly be enforced, and while it must have greatly increased the irritation of the Indians, it was at the same time interpretable as a symptom of fear. With ominous scowls and grunts some seventy muskets were given up, but this was all. Through the summer there was much uneasiness, and in September Philip was summoned to Plymouth with five of his under-sachems, and solemnly warned to keep the peace. The savages again behaved with humility and agreed to pay a yearly tribute of five wolves' heads and to do no act of war without express permission.

Meeting at Taunton.

For three years things seemed quiet, until late in 1674 the alarm was again sounded. Sausamon, a convert from the Massachusetts tribe, had studied a little at Harvard College, and could speak and write English with facility. He had at one time been employed by Philip as a sort of private secretary or messenger, and at other times had preached and taught school among the Indian converts at Natick. Sausamon now came to Plymouth and informed Governor Winslow that Philip was certainly engaged in a conspiracy that boded no good to the English. Somehow or other Philip contrived to find out what Sausamon had said, and presently coming to Plymouth loudly asseverated his innocence; but the magistrates warned him that if they heard any more of this sort of thing his arms would surely be seized. A few days after Philip had gone home, Sausamon's hat and gun were seen lying on the frozen surface of Assowamsett Pond, near Middleborough, and on cutting through the ice his body was found with unmistakable marks of beating and strangling. After some months the crime was traced to three Wampanoags, who were forthwith arrested, tried by a mixed jury of Indians and white men, found guilty, and put to death. On the way to the gallows one of them confessed that he had stood by while his two friends had pounded and choked the unfortunate Sausamon.

<small>Murder of Sausamon.</small>

More alarming reports now came from Swanzey, a pretty village of some forty houses not far from Philip's headquarters at Mount Hope. On Sunday June 20, while everybody was at church, a party of Indians had stolen into the town and set fire to two houses. Messengers were hurried from Plymouth and from Boston, to demand the culprits under penalty of instant war. As they approached Swanzey the men from Boston saw a sight that filled them with horror. The road was strewn with corpses of men, women, and children, scorched, dismembered, and mangled with that devilish art of which the American Indian is the most finished master. The savages had sacked the village the day before, burning the houses and slaying the people. Within three days a small force of colonial troops

<small>Massacres at Swanzey and Dartmouth. June, 1675.</small>

had driven Philip from his position at Mount Hope; but while they were doing this a party of savages swooped upon Dartmouth, burning thirty houses and committing fearful atrocities. Some of their victims were flayed alive, or impaled on sharp stakes, or roasted over slow fires. Similar horrors were wrought at Middleborough and Taunton; and now the misery spread to Massachusetts, where on the 14th of July the town of Mendon was attacked by a party of Nipmucks.

At that time the beautiful highlands between Lancaster and the Connecticut river were still an untrodden wilderness. On their southern slope Worcester and Brookfield were tiny hamlets of a dozen houses each. Up the Connecticut valley a line of little villages, from Springfield to Northfield, formed the remotest frontier of the English, and their exposed position offered tempting opportunities to the Indians. Governor Leverett saw how great the danger would be if the other tribes should follow the example set by Philip, and Captain Edward Hutchinson was accordingly sent to Brookfield to negotiate with the Nipmucks. This officer was eldest son of the unfortunate lady whose preaching in Boston nearly forty years before had been the occasion of so much strife. Not only his mother, but all save one or two of his brothers and sisters — and there were not less than twelve of them — had been murdered by Indians on the New Netherland border in 1643; now the same cruel fate overtook the gallant captain. The savages agreed to hold a parley and appointed a time and place for

Murder of Captain Hutchinson.

the purpose, but instead of keeping tryst they lay in ambush and slew Hutchinson with eight of his men on their way to the conference.

Three days afterward Philip, who had found home too hot for him, arrived in the Nipmuck country, and on the night of August 2, took part in a fierce assault on Brookfield. Thirty or forty men, with some fifty women and children — all the inhabitants of the hamlet — took refuge in a large house, where they were besieged by 300 savages whose bullets pierced the wooden walls again and again. Arrows tipped with burning rags were shot into the air in such wise as to fall upon the roof, but they who crouched in the garret were watchful and well supplied with water, while from the overhanging windows the volleys of musketry were so brisk and steady that the screaming savages below could not get near enough to the house to set it on fire. For three days the fight was kept up, while every other house in the village was destroyed. By this time the Indians had contrived to mount some planks on barrels so as to make a kind of rude cart which they loaded with tow and chips. They were just about setting it on fire and preparing to push it against the house with long poles, when they were suddenly foiled by a heavy shower. That noon the gallant Simon Willard, ancestor of two presidents of Harvard College, a man who had done so much toward building up Concord and Lancaster that he was known as the "founder of towns," was on his way from Lancaster to Groton at the head of forty-seven horsemen, when he was overtaken by a

Attack on Brookfield.

courier with the news from Brookfield. The distance was thirty miles, the road scarcely fit to be called a bridle-path, and Willard's years were more than threescore-and-ten; but by an hour after sunset he had gallopped into Brookfield and routed the Indians who fled to a swamp ten miles distant.

The scene is now shifted to the Connecticut valley, where on the 25th of August Captain Lothrop defeated the savages at Hatfield. On the 1st of September simultaneous attacks were made upon Deerfield and Hadley, and among the traditions of the latter place is one of the most interesting of the stories of that early time. The inhabitants were all in church keeping a fast, when the yells of the Indians resounded. Seizing their guns, the men rushed out to meet the foe; but seeing the village green swarming on every side with the horrid savages, for a moment their courage gave way and a panic was imminent; when all at once a stranger of reverend aspect and stately form, with white beard flowing on his bosom, appeared among them and took command with an air of authority which none could gainsay. He bade them charge on the screeching rabble, and after a short sharp skirmish the tawny foe was put to flight. When the pursuers came together again, after the excitement of the rout, their deliverer was not to be found. In their wonder, as they knew not whence he came or whither he had gone, many were heard to say that an angel had been sent from heaven for their deliverance. It was the regicide William Goffe, who from his hiding-place had seen the savages

The mysterious stranger at Hadley.

stealing down the hillside, and sallied forth to win yet one more victory over the hosts of Midian ere death should come to claim him in his woodland retreat. Sir Walter Scott has put this pretty story into the mouth of Major Bridgenorth in "Peveril of the Peak," and Cooper has made use of it in "The Wept of Wish-ton-wish." Like many other romantic stories, it rests upon insufficient authority and its truth has been called in question.[1] But there seems to be nothing intrinsically improbable in the tradition; and a paramount regard for Goffe's personal safety would quite ac-

[1] The story rests chiefly upon the statements of Hutchinson, an extremely careful and judicious writer, and not in the least what the French call a *gobemouche*. Goffe kept a diary which came into Hutchinson's possession, and was one of the priceless manuscripts that perished in the infamous sacking of his house by the Boston mob of August 26, 1765. What light that diary might have thrown upon the matter can never be known. Hutchinson was born in 1711, only thirty-six years after the event, so that his testimony is not so very far removed from that of a contemporary. Whalley seems to have died in Hadley shortly before 1675, and Goffe deemed it prudent to leave that neighbourhood in 1676. His letters to Increase Mather are dated from "Ebenezer," *i. e.*, wherever in his roamings he set up his Ebenezer. One of these letters, dated September 8, 1676, shows that his Ebenezer was then set up in Hartford, where probably he died about 1679. In 1676 the arrival of Edward Randolph (see below, p. 256) renewed the peril of the regicide judge, and his sudden removal from his skilfully contrived hiding-place at Hadley might possibly have been due to his having exposed himself to recognition in the Indian fight. Possibly even the supernatural explanation might have been started, with a touch of Yankee humour, as a blind. The silence of Mather and Hubbard was no more remarkable than some of the other ingenious incidents which had so long served to conceal the existence of this sturdy and crafty man. The reasons for doubting the story are best stated by Mr. George Sheldon of Deerfield, in *Hist.-Genealogical Register*, October, 1874.

count for the studied silence of contemporary writers like Hubbard and Increase Mather.

This repulse did not check for a moment the activity of the Indians, though for a long time we hear nothing more of Philip. On the 2d of September they slew eight men at Northfield and on the 4th they surrounded and butchered Captain Beers and most of his company of thirty-six marching to the relief of that village. The next day but one, as Major Robert Treat came up the road with his 100 Connecticut soldiers, they found long poles planted by the wayside bearing the heads of their unfortunate comrades. They in turn were assaulted, but beat off the enemy, and brought away the people of Northfield. That village was abandoned, and presently Deerfield shared its fate and the people were crowded into Hadley. Yet worse remained to be seen. <small>Ambuscade at Bloody Brook, September 12.</small> A large quantity of wheat had been left partly threshed at Deerfield, and on the 11th of September eighteen wagons were sent up with teamsters and farmers to finish the threshing and bring in the grain. They were escorted by Captain Lothrop, with his train-band of ninety picked men, known as the "Flower of Essex," perhaps the best drilled company in the colony. The threshing was done, the wagons were loaded, and the party made a night march southward. At seven in the morning, as they were fording a shallow stream in the shade of overarching woods, they were suddenly overwhelmed by the deadly fire of 700 ambushed Nipmucks, and only eight of them escaped to tell the tale. A "black and fatal" day was this, says the chronicler, "the saddest that ever befell New England." To this day the memory of the slaughter at Bloody Brook survives, and the visitor to South Deerfield may read the inscription over the grave in which Major Treat's men next day buried all the victims together. The Indians now began to feel their power, and on the 5th of October they attacked Springfield and burned thirty houses there.

Things were becoming desperate. For ten weeks, from September 9 to November 19, the Federal Commissioners were in session daily in Boston. The most eminent of their number, for ability and character, was the younger John Winthrop, who was still governor of Connecticut. Plymouth was represented by its governor, Josiah Winslow, with the younger William Bradford; Massachusetts by William Stoughton, Simon Bradstreet, and Thomas Danforth. These strong men were confronted with a difficult problem. From Batten's journal, kept during that disastrous summer, we learn the state of feeling in Boston. The Puritans had by no means got rid of that sense of corporate responsibility which civilized man has inherited from prehistoric ages, and which has been one of the principal causes of religious persecution. This sombre feeling has prompted men to believe that to spare the heretic is to bring down the wrath of God upon the whole community; and now in Boston many people stoutly maintained that God had let loose the savages, with firebrand and tomahawk, to punish the people of New England for ceasing

Popular excitement in Boston.

to persecute "false worshippers and especially idolatrous Quakers." Quaker meetings were accordingly forbidden under penalty of fine and imprisonment. Some harmless Indians were murdered. At Marblehead two were assaulted and killed by a crowd of women. There was a bitter feeling toward the Christian Indians, many of whom had joined their heathen kinsmen in burning and slaying. Daniel Gookin, superintendent of the "praying Indians," a gentleman of the highest character, was told that it would not be safe to show himself in the streets of Boston. Mrs. Mary Pray, of Providence, wrote a letter recommending the total extermination of the red men.

The measures adopted by the Commissioners certainly went far toward carrying out Mrs. Pray's suggestion. The demeanour of the Narragansetts had become very threatening, and their capacity for mischief exceeded that of all the other tribes together. In July the Commissioners had made a treaty with them, but in October it became known in Boston that they were harbouring some of Philip's hostile Indians. When the Commissioners sharply called them to account for this, their sachem Canonchet, son of Miantonomo, promised to surrender the fugitives within ten days. But the ten days passed and nothing was heard from the Narragansetts. The victory of their brethren at Bloody Brook had worked upon their minds, so that they no longer thought it worth while to keep faith with the white men. They had overcome their timidity and were now ready to take part in the work of massacre.¹ The Commissioners soon learned of their warlike preparations and lost no time in forestalling them. The Narragansetts were fairly warned that if they did not at once fulfil their promises they must expect the utmost severities of war. A thousand men were enlisted for this service and put under command of Governor Winslow, and in December they marched against the enemy. The redoubtable fighter and lively chronicler Benjamin Church accompanied the expedition.

The Indians had fortified themselves on a piece of rising ground, six acres in extent, in the middle of a hideous swamp impassable at most seasons but now in some places frozen hard enough to afford a precarious footing. They were surrounded by rows of tall palisades which formed a wall twelve feet in thickness; and the only approach to the single door of this stronghold was over the trunk of a felled tree some two feet in diameter and slippery with snow and ice. A stout block-house filled with sharpshooters guarded this rude bridge, which was raised some five feet from the ground. Within the palisadoed fortress perhaps not less than 2000 war-

Expedition against the Narragansetts.

---

[1] If Philip was half the diplomatist that he is represented in tradition, he never would have gone into such a war without assurance of Narragansett help. Canonchet was a far more powerful sachem than Philip, and played a more conspicuous part in the war. May we not suppose that Canonchet's desire to avenge his father's death was one of the principal incentives to the war; that Philip's attack upon Swanzey was a premature explosion; and that Canonchet then watched the course of events for a while before making up his mind whether to abandon Philip or support him?

riors, with many women and children, awaited the onset of the white men, for here had Canonchet gathered together nearly the whole of his available force. This was a military mistake. It was cooping up his men for slaughter. They would have been much safer if scattered about in the wilderness, and could have given the English much more trouble. But readily as they acknowledged the power of the white man, they did not yet understand it. One man's courage is not another's, and the Indian knew little or nothing of that Gothic fury of self-abandonment which rushes straight ahead and snatches victory from the jaws of death. His fortress was a strong one, and it was no longer, as in the time of the Pequots, a strife in which firearms were pitted against bow and arrow. Many of the Narragansetts were equipped with muskets and skilled in their use, and under such circumstances victory for the English was not to be lightly won.

On the night of December 18 their little army slept in an open field at Pettyquamscott without other blanket than a "moist fleece of snow." Thence to the Indian fortress, situated in what is now South Kingston, the march was eighteen miles. The morrow was a Sunday, but Winslow deemed it imprudent to wait, as food had wellnigh given out. Getting up at five o'clock, they toiled through deep snow till they came within sight of the Narragansett stronghold early in the afternoon. First came the 527 men from Massachusetts, led by Major Appleton, of Ipswich, and next the 158 from Plymouth, under Major Bradford; while Major Robert Treat, with the 300 from Connecticut, brought up the rear. There were 985 men in all. As the Massachusetts men rushed upon the slippery bridge a deadly volley from the block-house slew six of their captains, while of the rank and file there were many killed or wounded. Nothing daunted they pressed on with great spirit till they forced their way into the enclosure, but then the head of their column, overcome by sheer weight of numbers in the hand-to-hand fight, was pushed and tumbled out into the swamp. Meanwhile some of the Connecticut men had discovered a path across the partly frozen swamp leading to a weak spot in the rear, where the palisades were thin and few, as undue reliance had been placed upon the steep bank crowned with a thick rampart of bushes that had been reinforced with clods of turf. In this direction Treat swept along with his men in a spirited charge. Before they had reached the spot a heavy fire began mowing them down, but with a furious rush they came up, and climbing on each other's shoulders, some fought their way over the rampart, while others hacked sturdily with axes till such a breach was made that all might enter. This was effected just as the Massachusetts men had recovered themselves and crossed the treacherous log in a second charge that was successful and soon brought the entire English force within the enclosure. In the slaughter which filled the rest of that Sunday afternoon till the sun went down behind a dull gray cloud, the grim and wrathful Puritan, as he swung his heavy cutlass, thought of Saul and Agag, and spared not. The Lord had

Storming of the great swamp fortress, December 19.

delivered up to him the heathen as stubble to his sword. As usual the number of the slain is variously estimated. Of the Indians probably not less than 1000 perished. Some hundreds, however, with Canonchet their leader, saved themselves in flight, well screened by the blinding snow-flakes that began to fall just after sunset. Within the fortified area had been stored the greater part of the Indians' winter supply of corn, and the loss of this food was a further deadly blow. Captain Church advised sparing the wigwams and using them for shelter, but Winslow seems to have doubted the ability of his men to maintain themselves in a position so remote from all support. The wigwams with their tubs of corn were burned, and a retreat was ordered. Through snowdrifts that deepened every moment the weary soldiers dragged themselves along until two hours after midnight, when they reached the tiny village of Wickford. Nearly one-fourth of their number had been killed or wounded, and many of the latter perished before shelter was reached. Forty of these were buried at Wickford in the course of the next three days. Of the Connecticut men eighty were left upon the swamp and in the breach at the rear of the stronghold. Among the spoils which the victors brought away were a number of good muskets that had been captured by the Nipmucks in their assault upon Deerfield.

This headlong overthrow of the Narragansett power completely changed the face of things. The question was no longer whether the red men could possibly succeed in making New England too hot for the white men, but simply how long it would take for the white men to exterminate the red men. The shiftless Indian was abandoning his squalid agriculture and subsisting on the pillage of English farms; but the resources of the colonies, though severely taxed, were by no means exhausted. The dusky warriors slaughtered in the great swamp fight could not be replaced; but, as Roger Williams told the Indians, there were still ten thousand white men who could carry muskets, and should all these be slain, he added, with a touch of hyperbole, the Great Father in England could send ten thousand more. For the moment Williams seems to have cherished a hope that his great influence with the savages might induce them to submit to terms of peace while there was yet a remnant to be saved; but they were now as little inclined to parley as tigers brought to bay, nor was the temper of the colonists a whit less deadly, though it did not vent itself in inflicting torture or in merely wanton orgies of cruelty.

<small>Effect of the blow.</small>

To the modern these scenes of carnage are painful to contemplate. In the wholesale destruction of the Pequots, and to a less degree in that of the Narragansetts, the death-dealing power of the white man stands forth so terrible and relentless that our sympathy is for a moment called out for his victim. The feeling of tenderness toward the weak, almost unknown among savages, is one of the finest products of civilization. Where murderous emotions are frequently excited, it cannot thrive. Such advance in humanity as we have made within recent times is chiefly due to the fact that the horrors of war are seldom brought home to everybody's door. Either war is conducted on some remote frontier, or if armies march through a densely peopled country the conditions of modern warfare have made it essential to their efficiency as military instruments that depredation and riot should be as far as possible checked. Murder and pillage are comparatively infrequent, massacre is seldom heard of, and torture is almost or quite as extinct as cannibalism. The mass of citizens escape physical suffering, the angry emotions are so directed upon impersonal objects as to acquire a strong ethical value, and the intervals of strife may find individual soldiers of hostile armies exchanging kindly services. Members of a complex industrial society, without direct experience of warfare save in this mitigated form, have their characters wrought upon in a way that is distinctively modern, as they become more and more disinclined to violence and cruelty. European historians have noticed, with words of praise, the freedom from bloodthirstiness which characterizes the American people. Mr. Lecky has more than once remarked upon this humane temperament which is so characteristic of our peaceful civilization, and which sometimes, indeed, shows the defects of its excellence and tends to weaken society by making it difficult to inflict due punishment upon the vilest criminals. In respect of this humanity the American of the nineteenth century has without doubt improved very considerably upon his forefathers of the seven-

Growth of humane sentiment in recent times.

teenth. The England of Cromwell and Milton was not, indeed, a land of hard-hearted people as compared with their contemporaries. The long experience of internal peace since the War of the Roses had not been without its effect; and while the Tudor and Stuart periods had atrocities enough, we need only remember what was going on at the same time in France and Germany in order to realize how much worse it might have been. In England, as elsewhere, however, it was, when looked at with our eyes, a rough and brutal time. It was a day of dungeons, whipping-posts, and thumbscrews, when slight offenders were maimed and bruised and great offenders cut into pieces by sentence of court. The pioneers of New England had grown up familiar with such things; and among the townspeople of Boston and Hartford in 1675 were still many who in youth had listened to the awful news from Magdeburg or turned pale over the horrors in Piedmont upon which Milton invoked the wrath of Heaven.

When civilized men are removed from the safeguards of civilization and placed in the wilderness amid the hideous dangers that beset human existence in a savage state of society, whatever barbarism lies latent in them is likely to find many opportunities for showing itself. The feelings that stir the meekest of men, as he stands among the smouldering embers of his homestead and gazes <small>Warfare with savages likely to be truculent in character.</small> upon the mangled bodies of wife and children, are feelings that he shares with the most bloodthirsty savage, and the primary effect of his higher intelligence and greater sensitiveness is only to increase their bitterness. The neighbour who hears the dreadful story is quick to feel likewise, for the same thing may happen to him, and there is nothing so pitiless as fear. With the Puritan such gloomy and savage passions seemed to find justification in the sacred text from which he drew his rules of life. To suppose that one part of the Bible could be less authoritative than another would have been to him an incomprehensible heresy; and bound between the same covers that included the Sermon on the Mount were tales of wholesale massacre perpetrated by God's command. Evidently the red men were not stray children of Israel, after all, but rather Philistines, Canaanites, heathen, sons of Belial, firebrands of hell, demons whom it was no more than right to sweep from the face of the earth. Writing in this spirit, the chroniclers of the time were completely callous in their accounts of suffering and ruin inflicted upon Indians, and, as has elsewhere been known to happen, those who did not risk their own persons were more truculent in tone than the professional fighters. Of the narrators of the war, perhaps the fairest toward the Indian is the doughty Captain Church, while none is more bitter and cynical than the Ipswich pastor William Hubbard.

While the overthrow of the Narragansetts changed the face of things, it was far from putting an end to the war. It showed that when the white man could find his enemy he could deal crushing blows, but the Indian was not always so easy to find. Before the end of January Winslow's little army was partially disbanded for want of food, and its three contingents fell back upon Stonington, Boston, and Plymouth. Early in February the Federal Commissioners called for a new levy of 600 men to assemble at Brookfield, for the Nipmucks were beginning to renew their incursions, and after an interval of six months the figure of Philip again appears for a moment upon the scene. What he had been doing, or where he had been, since the Brookfield fight in August, was never known. When in February, 1676, he re-appeared it was still in company with his allies the Nipmucks, in their bloody assault upon Lancaster. On the 10th of that month at sunrise the Indians came swarming into the lovely village. Danger had already been apprehended, the pastor, Joseph Rowlandson, the only Harvard graduate of 1652, had gone to Boston to solicit aid, and Captain Wadsworth's company was slowly making its way over the difficult roads from Marlborough, but the Indians were beforehand. Several houses were at once surrounded and set on fire, and men, women, and children began falling under the tomahawk. The minister's house was large and strongly built, and more than forty people found shelter there until at length it took fire and they were driven out by the flames. Only one escaped, a dozen or more were slain, and the rest, chiefly women and children, taken captive. The Indians aimed at plunder as well as destruction; for they were in sore need of food and blankets, as well as of powder and ball. Presently, as they saw Wadsworth's armed men approaching,

Attack upon Lancaster, February 10, 1676.

they took to flight and got away, with many prisoners and a goodly store of provisions.

Among the captives was Mary Rowlandson, the minister's wife, who afterward wrote the story of her sad experiences. The treatment of the prisoners varied with the caprice or the cupidity of the captors. Those for whom a substantial ransom might be expected fared comparatively well; to others death came as a welcome relief. One poor woman with a child in her arms was too weak to endure the arduous tramp over the icy hillsides, and begged to be left behind, till presently the savages lost their patience. They built a fire, and after a kind of demon dance killed mother and child with a club and threw the bodies into the flames. Such treatment may seem exceptionally merciful, but those modern observers who best know the Indian's habits say that he seldom indulges in torture except when he has abundance of leisure and a mind quite undisturbed. He is an epicure in human agony and likes to enjoy it in long slow sips. It is for the end of the march that the accumulation of horrors is reserved; the victims by the way are usually despatched quickly; and in the case of Mrs. Rowlandson's captors their irregular and circuitous march indicates that they were on the alert. Their movements seem to have covered much of the ground between Wachusett mountain and the Connecticut river. They knew that the white squaw of the great medicine man of an English village was worth a heavy ransom, and so they treated Mrs. Rowlandson unusually well. She had

Mrs. Rowlandson's narrative.

been captured when escaping from the burning house, carrying in her arms her little six-year-old daughter. She was stopped by a bullet that grazed her side and struck the child. The Indian who seized them placed the little girl upon a horse, and as the dreary march began she kept moaning "I shall die, mamma." "I went on foot after it," says the mother, "with sorrow that cannot be expressed. At length I took it off the horse, and carried it in my arms till my strength failed me, and I fell down with it. . . . After this it quickly began to snow, and when night came on they stopped. And now down I must sit in the snow, by a little fire, and a few boughs behind me, with my sick child in my lap, and calling much for water, being now, through the wound, fallen into a violent fever. . . . Oh, may I see the wonderful power of God that my spirit did not utterly sink under my affliction; still the Lord upheld me with his gracious and merciful spirit." The little girl soon died. For three months the weary and heart-broken mother was led about the country by these loathsome savages, of whose habits and manners she gives a vivid description. At first their omnivorousness astonished her. "Skunks and rattlesnakes, yea the very bark of trees" they esteemed as delicacies. "They would pick up old bones and cut them in pieces at the joints, . . . then boil them and drink up the liquor, and then beat the great ends of them in a mortar and so eat them." After some weeks of starvation Mrs. Rowlandson herself was fain to partake of such viands. One day, having made a cap for one of Philip's boys, she was invited to dine with the great sachem. "I went," she says, "and he gave me a pancake about as big as two fingers. It was made of parched wheat, beaten, and fried in bear's grease; but I thought I never tasted pleasanter meat in my life." Early in May she was redeemed for £20, and went to find her husband in Boston, where the Old South Church society hired a house for them.

Such was the experience of a captive whose treatment was, according to Indian notions, hospitable. There were few who came off so well. Almost every week while she was led hither and thither by the savages, Mrs. Rowlandson heard ghastly tales of fire and slaughter. It was a busy winter and spring for these Nipmucks. Before February was over, their exploit at Lancaster was followed by a shocking massacre at Medfield. They sacked and destroyed the towns of Worcester, Marlborough, Mendon, and Groton, and even burned some houses in Weymouth, within a dozen miles of Boston. Murderous attacks were made upon Sudbury, Chelmsford, Springfield, Hatfield, Hadley, Northampton, Wrentham, Andover, Bridgewater, Scituate, and Middleborough. On the 18th of April Captain Wadsworth, with 70 men, was drawn into an ambush near Sudbury, surrounded by 500 Nipmucks, and killed with 50 of his men; six unfortunate captives were burned alive over slow fires. But Wadsworth's party made the enemy pay dearly for his victory; that afternoon 120 Nipmucks bit the dust. In such wise, by

Virtual extermination of the Indians, February — August, 1676.

killing two or three for one, did the English wear out and annihilate their adversaries. Just one month from that day Captain Turner surprised and slaughtered 300 of these warriors near the falls of the Connecticut river which have since borne his name, and this blow at last broke the strength of the Nipmucks.

Meanwhile the Narragansetts and Wampanoags had burned the towns of Warwick and Providence. After the wholesale ruin of the great "swamp fight," Canonchet had still some 600 or 700 warriors left, and with these, on the 26th of March, in the neighbourhood of Pawtuxet, he surprised a company of 50 Plymouth men under Captain Pierce and slew them all, but not until he had lost 140 of his best warriors. Ten days later Captain Denison, with his Connecticut company, defeated and captured Canonchet, and the proud son of Miantonomo met the same fate as his father.

Death of Canonchet. He was handed over to the Mohegans and tomahawked. The Narragansett sachem had shown such bravery that it seemed, says the chronicler Hubbard, as if "some old Roman ghost had possessed the body of this western pagan." But next moment this pious clergyman, as if ashamed of the classical eulogy just bestowed upon the hated redskin, alludes to him as a "damned wretch."

The fall of Canonchet marked the beginning of the end. In four sharp fights in the last week of June, Major Talcott, of Hartford, slew from 300 to 400 warriors, being nearly all that were left of the Narragansetts; and during the month of July Captain Church patrolled the country about Taunton, making prisoners of the Wampanoags. Once more King Philip, shorn of his prestige, comes upon the scene. We have seen that his agency in these cruel events had been at the outset a potent one. Whatever else it may have been, it was at least the agency of the match that explodes the powder-cask. Under the conditions of that savage society, organized leadership was not to be looked for. In the irregular and disorderly series of murdering raids Philip may have been often present, but except for Mrs. Rowlandson's narrative we should have known nothing of him since the Brookfield fight.

At length in July, 1676, having seen the last of his Nipmuck friends overwhelmed, the tattered chieftain showed himself near Bridgewater, with a handful of followers. In these his own hunting-grounds some of his former friends had become disaffected. The daring and diplomatic Church had made his way into the wigwam of Ashawonks, the squaw sachem of Saconet, near Little Compton, and having first convinced her that a flask of brandy might be tasted without fatal results, followed up his advantage and persuaded her to make an alliance with the English. Many Indians came in and voluntarily surrendered themselves, in order to obtain favourable terms, and some lent their aid in destroying their old sachem. Defeated at Taunton, the son of Massasoit was hunted by Church to his ancient lair at Bristol Neck and there besieged. His only escape was over the narrow isthmus of which the pursuers now took possession, and in this dire extremity one of Philip's men presumed to advise his chief that the hour for surrender had come. For his unwelcome counsel the sachem forthwith lifted his tomahawk and struck him dead at his feet. Then the brother of the slain man crept away through the bushes to Church's little camp, and offered to guide the white men to the morass where Philip lay concealed. At daybreak of August 12 the English stealthily advancing beat up their prey. The savages in sudden panic rushed from under cover, and as the sachem showed himself running at the top of his speed, a ball from an Indian musket pierced his heart, and "he fell upon his face in the mud and water, with his gun under him." His severed head was sent to Plymouth, where it was mounted on a pole and exposed aloft upon the village green, while the meeting-house bell summoned the townspeople to a special service of thanksgiving..

<small>Death of Philip, August 12.</small>

It may be supposed that in such services at this time a Christian feeling of charity and forgiveness was not uppermost. Among the captives was a son of Philip, the little swarthy lad of nine years for whom Mrs. Rowlandson had made a cap, and the question as to what was to be done with him occasioned as much debate as if he had been a Jesse Pomeroy[1] or a Chicago anarchist. The

---

[1] A wretched little werewolf who some few years ago, being then a lad of fourteen or fifteen years, most cruelly murdered two or three young children, just to amuse himself with their dying agonies. The misdirected "humanitarianism," which in our country makes every murderer an object of popular sympathy, prevailed to save this creature from the gallows. Massachusetts has

opinions of the clergy were, of course, eagerly sought and freely vouchsafed. One minister somewhat doubtfully urged that "although a precept in Deuteronomy explicitly forbids killing the child for the father's sin," yet after all "the children of Saul and Achan perished with their parents, though too young to have shared their guilt." Thus curiously did this English reverence for precedent, with a sort of grim conscientiousness colouring its gloomy wrath, search for guidance among the ancient records of the children of Israel. Commenting upon the truculent suggestion, Increase Mather, soon to be president of Harvard, observed that, "though David had spared the infant Hadad, yet it might have been better for his people if he had been less merciful." These bloodthirsty counsels did not prevail, but the course that was adopted did not lack in harshness. Among the sachems a dozen leading spirits were hanged or shot, and hundreds of captives were shipped off to the West Indies to be sold into slavery; among these was Philip's little son. The rough soldier Church and the apostle Eliot were among the few who disapproved of this

<small>Indians sold into slavery.</small>

---

lately witnessed a similar instance of misplaced clemency in the case of a vile woman who had poisoned eight or ten persons, including some of her own children, in order to profit by their life insurance. Such instances help to explain the prolonged vitality of "Judge Lynch," and sometimes almost make one regret the days in old England when William Probert, after escaping in 1824 as "king's evidence," from the Thurtell affair, got caught and hanged within a twelvemonth for horse-stealing. Any one who wishes to study the results of allowing criminality to survive and propagate itself should read Dugdale's *The Jukes; Hereditary Crime*, New York, 1877.

policy. Church feared it might goad such Indians as were still at large to acts of desperation. Eliot, in an earnest letter to the Federal Commissioners, observed: "To sell souls for money seemeth to me dangerous merchandise." But the plan of exporting the captives was adhered to. As slaves they were understood to be of little or no value, and sometimes for want of purchasers they were set ashore on strange coasts and abandoned. A few were even carried to one of the foulest of mediæval slave-marts, Morocco, where their fate was doubtless wretched enough.

In spite of Church's doubts as to the wisdom of this harsh treatment, it did not prevent the beaten and starving savages from surrendering themselves in considerable numbers. To some the Federal Commissioners offered amnesty, and the promise was faithfully fulfilled. Among those who laid down arms in reliance upon it were 140 Christian Indians, with their leader known as James the Printer, because he had been employed at Cambridge in setting up the type for Eliot's Bible. Quite early in the war it had been discovered that these converted savages still felt the ties of blood to be stronger than those of creed. At the attack on Mendon, only three weeks after the horrors at Swanzey that ushered in the war, it was known that Christian Indians had behaved themselves quite as cruelly as their unregenerate brethren. Afterwards they made such a record that the jokers and punsters of the day — for such there were, even among those sombre Puritans — in writing about the "Praying

Indians," spelled *praying* with an *e*. The moral scruples of these savages, under the influence of their evangelical training, betrayed queer freaks. One of them, says Mrs. Rowlandson, would rather die than eat horseflesh, so narrow and scrupulous was his conscience, although it was as wide as the whole infernal abyss, when it came to torturing white Christians. The student of history may have observed similar inconsistencies in the theories and conduct of people more enlightened than these poor red men. "There was another Praying Indian," continues Mrs. Rowlandson, "who, when he had done all the mischief he could, betrayed his own father into the English's hands, thereby to purchase his own life; . . . and there was another . . . so wicked . . . as to wear a string about his neck, strung with Christian fingers."

Such incidents help us to comprehend the exasperation of our forefathers in the days of King Philip. The month which witnessed his death saw also the end of the war in the southern parts of New England; but, almost before people had time to offer thanks for the victory, there came news of bloodshed on the northeastern frontier. The Tarratines in Maine had for some time been infected with the war fever. How far they may have been comprehended in the schemes of Philip and Canonchet, it would be hard to say. They had attacked settlers on the site of Brunswick as early as September, 1675. About the time of Philip's death, Major Waldron of Dover had entrapped a party of them by an unworthy stratagem, and after satisfying

<small>War with the Tarratines, 1676–78.</small>

himself that they were accomplices in that chieftain's scheme, sent them to Boston to be sold into slavery. A terrible retribution was in store for Major Waldron thirteen years later. For the present the hideous strife, just ended in southern New England, was continued on the northeastern frontier, and there was scarcely a village between the Kennebec and the Piscataqua but was laid in ashes.

By midsummer of 1678 the Indians had been everywhere suppressed, and there was peace in the land. For three years, since Philip's massacre at Swanzey, there had been a reign of terror in New England. Within the boundaries of Connecticut, indeed, little or no damage had been inflicted, and the troops of that colony, not needed on their own soil, did noble service in the common cause.

In Massachusetts and Plymouth, on the other hand, the destruction of life and property had been simply frightful. Of ninety towns, twelve had been utterly destroyed, while more than forty others had been the scene of fire and slaughter. Out of this little society nearly a thousand staunch men, including not few of broad culture and strong promise, had lost their lives, while of the scores of fair women and poor little children that had perished under the ruthless tomahawk, one can hardly give an accurate account. Hardly a family throughout the land but was in mourning. The war-debt of Plymouth was reckoned to exceed the total amount of personal property in the colony; yet although it pinched every household for many a year, it was

Destructiveness of the war.

paid to the uttermost farthing; nor in this respect were Massachusetts and Connecticut at all behindhand.

But while King Philip's War wrought such fearful damage to the English, it was for the Indians themselves utter destruction. Most of the warriors were slain, and to the survivors, as we have seen, the conquerors showed but scant mercy. The Puritan, who conned his Bible so earnestly, had taken his hint from the wars of the Jews, and swept his New English Canaan with a broom that was pitiless and searching. Henceforth the red man figures no more in the history of New England, except as an ally of the French in bloody raids upon the frontier. In that capacity he does mischief enough for yet a half-century more, but from central and southern New England, as an element of disturbance or a power to be reckoned with, he disappears forever.

CHAPTER VI.

THE TYRANNY OF ANDROS.

THE beginnings of New England were made in the full daylight of modern history. It was an age of town records, of registered deeds, of contemporary memoirs, of diplomatic correspondence, of controversial pamphlets, funeral sermons, political diatribes, specific instructions, official reports, and private letters. It was not a time in which mythical personages or incredible legends could flourish, and such things we do not find in the history of New England. There was nevertheless a romantic side to this history, enough to envelop some of its characters and incidents in a glamour that may mislead the modern reader. This wholesale migration from the smiling fields of merry England to an unexplored wilderness beyond a thousand leagues of sea was of itself a most romantic and thrilling event, and when viewed in the light of its historic results it becomes clothed with sublimity. The men who undertook this work were not at all free from self-consciousness. They believed that they were doing a wonderful thing. They felt themselves to be instruments in accomplishing a kind of "manifest destiny." Their exodus was that of a chosen people who were at

<small>Romantic features in the early history of New England.</small>

length to lay the everlasting foundations of God's kingdom upon earth. Such opinions, which took a strong colour from their assiduous study of the Old Testament, reacted and disposed them all the more to search its pages for illustrations and precedents, and to regard it as an oracle, almost as a talisman. In every propitious event they saw a special providence, an act of divine intervention to deliver them from the snares of an ever watchful Satan. This steadfast faith in an unseen ruler and guide was to them a pillar of cloud by day and of fire by night. It was of great moral value. It gave them clearness of purpose and concentration of strength, and contributed toward making them, like the children of Israel, a people of indestructible vitality and aggressive energy. At the same time, in the hands of the Puritan writers, this feeling was apt to warp their estimates of events and throw such a romantic haze about things as seriously to interfere with a true historical perspective.

Among such writings that which perhaps best epitomizes the Puritan philosophy is "The Wonder-working Providence of Zion's Saviour in New England," by Captain Edward Johnson, one of the principal founders of Woburn. *Edward Johnson.* It is an extremely valuable history of New England from 1628 to 1651, and every page is alive with the virile energy of that stirring time. With narrative, argument, and apologue, abounding in honesty of purpose, sublimity of trust, and grotesqueness of fancy, wherein touching tenderness is often alternated with sternness most grim and merciless, yet now and then relieved by a sudden gleam of humour, — and all in a style that is usually uncouth and harsh, but sometimes bursts forth in eloquence worthy of Bunyan, — we are told how the founders of New England are soldiers of Christ enlisted in a holy war, and how they must "march manfully on till all opposers of Christ's kingly power be abolished." "And as for you who are called to sound forth his silver trumpets, blow loud and shrill to this chiefest treble tune — for the armies of the great Jehovah are at hand." "He standeth not as an idle spectator beholding his people's ruth and their enemies' rage, but as an actor in all actions, to bring to naught the desires of the wicked, . . . having also the ordering of every weapon in its first produce, guiding every shaft that flies, leading each bullet to his place of settling, and weapon to the wound it makes." To men engaged in such a crusade against the powers of evil, nothing could seem insignificant or trivial; for, as Johnson continues, in truly prophetic phrase, "the Lord Christ intends to achieve greater matters by this little handful than the world is aware of."

The general sentiment of the early New England writers was like that of the "Wonder-working Providence," though it did not always find such rhapsodic expression. It has left its impress upon the minds of their children's children down to our own time, and has affected the opinions held about them by other people. It has had something to do with a certain tacit assumption of superiority on the part of New Englanders, upon which the men and women of other communities have been heard to comment in resentful and carping tones. There has probably never existed, in any age or at any spot on the earth's surface, a group of people that did not take for granted its own preëminent excellence. Upon some such assumption, as upon an incontrovertible axiom, all historical narratives, from the chronicles of a parish to the annals of an empire, alike proceed. But in New England it assumed a form especially apt to provoke challenge. One of its unintentional effects was the setting up of an unreal and impossible standard by which to judge the acts and motives of the Puritans of the seventeenth century. We come upon instances of harshness and cruelty, of narrow-minded bigotry, and superstitious frenzy; and feel, perhaps, a little surprised that these men had so much in common with their contemporaries. Hence the interminable discussion which has been called forth by the history of the Puritans, in which the conclusions of the writer have generally been determined by circumstances of birth or creed, or perhaps of reaction against creed. One critic points to the Boston of 1659 or the Salem of 1692 with such gleeful satisfaction as used to stir the heart of Thomas Paine when he alighted upon an inconsistency in some text of the Bible; while another, in the firm conviction that Puritans could do no wrong, plays fast and loose with arguments that might be made to justify the deeds of a Torquemada.

Acts of the Puritans often judged by a wrong standard.

From such methods of criticism it is the duty of

historians as far as possible to free themselves.
If we consider the Puritans in the light of their
surroundings as Englishmen of the seventeenth
century and inaugurators of a political movement
that was gradually to change for the better the
aspect of things all over the earth, we cannot fail
to discern the value of that sacred enthusiasm
which led them to regard themselves as chosen
soldiers of Christ. It was the spirit of
the "Wonder-working Providence" that
hurled the tyrant from his throne at
Whitehall and prepared the way for the emancipation of modern Europe. No spirit less intense, no spirit nurtured in the contemplation of things terrestrial, could ever have done it. The political philosophy of a Vane or a Sidney could never have done it. The passion for liberty as felt by a Jefferson or an Adams, abstracted and generalized from the love of particular liberties, was something scarcely intelligible to the seventeenth century. The ideas of absolute freedom of thought and speech, which we breathe in from childhood, were to the men of that age strange and questionable. They groped and floundered among them, very much as modern wool growers in Ohio or iron-smelters in Pennsylvania flounder and grope among the elementary truths of political economy. But the spirit in which the Hebrew prophet rebuked and humbled an idolatrous king was a spirit they could comprehend. Such a spirit was sure to manifest itself in narrow cramping measures and in ugly acts of persecution; but it is none the less to the fortunate alliance of that

Spirit of the "Wonder-working Providence."

fervid religious enthusiasm with the Englishman's love of self-government that our modern freedom owes its existence.

The history of New England under Charles II. yields abundant proof that political liberty is no less indebted in the New World than in the Old to the spirit of the "Wonder-working Providence." The theocratic ideal which the Puritan sought to put into practice in Massachusetts and Connecticut was a sacred institution in defence of which all his faculties were kept perpetually alert. Much as he loved self-government, he would never have been so swift to detect and so stubborn to resist every slightest encroachment on the part of the crown had not the loss of self-government involved the imminent danger that the ark of the Lord might be abandoned to the worshippers of Dagon. It was in Massachusetts, where the theocracy was strongest, that the resistance to Charles II. was most dogged and did most to prepare the way for the work of achieving political independence a century later. Naturally it was in Massachusetts at the same time that the faults of the theocracy were most conspicuous. It was there that priestly authority most clearly asserted itself in such oppressive acts as are always witnessed when too much power is left in the hands of men whose primary allegiance is to a kingdom not of this world. Much as we owe to the theocracy for warding off the encroachments of the crown, we cannot be sorry that it was itself crushed in the process. It was well that it did not survive its day of usefulness, and that the outcome

<small>Merits and faults of the theocracy.</small>

of the struggle was what has been aptly termed "the emancipation of Massachusetts."

The basis of the theocratic constitution of this commonwealth was the provision by which the exercise of the franchise was made an incident of church-membership. Unless a man could take part in the Lord's Supper, as administered in the churches of the colony, he could not vote or hold office. Church and state, parish and town, were thus virtually identified. Here, as in some other aspects of early New England, one is reminded of the ancient Greek cities, where the freeman who could vote in the market-place or serve his turn as magistrate was the man qualified to perform sacrifices to the tutelar deities of the tribe; other men might dwell in the city but had no share in making or executing its laws. The limitation of civil rights by religious tests is indeed one of those common inheritances from the old Aryan world that we find again and again cropping out, even down to the exclusion of Catholics from the House of Commons from 1562 to 1829. The obvious purpose of this policy in England was self-protection; and in like manner the restriction of the suffrage in Massachusetts was designed to protect the colony against aggressive episcopacy and to maintain unimpaired the uniformity of purpose which had brought the settlers across the ocean. Under the circumstances there was something to be said in behalf of such a measure of self-protection, and the principle required but slight extension to cover such cases as the banishment of Roger Williams

Restriction of the suffrage to church members.

and the Antinomians. There was another side to the case, however. From the very outset this exclusive policy was in some ways a source of weakness to Massachusetts, though we have seen that the indirect effect was to diversify and enrich the political life of New England as a whole.

At first it led to the departure of the men who founded Connecticut, and thereafter the way was certainly open for those who preferred the Connecticut policy to go where it prevailed. Some such segregation was no doubt effected, but it could not be complete and thorough. Men who preferred Boston without the franchise to Hartford with it would remain in Massachusetts; and thus the elder colony soon came to possess a discontented class of people, always ready to join hand in glove with dissenters or mischief-makers, or even with emissaries of the crown. *It was a source of political discontent.* It afforded a suggestive commentary upon all attempts to suppress human nature by depriving it of a share in political life; instead of keeping it inside where you can try conclusions with it fairly, you thrust it out to plot mischief in the dark. Within twenty years from the founding of Boston the disfranchisement of such citizens as could not participate in church-communion had begun to be regarded as a serious political grievance. These men were obliged to pay taxes and were liable to be called upon for military service against the Indians; and they naturally felt that they ought to have a voice in the management of public affairs.

Besides this fundamental ground of complaint,

there were derivative grievances. Under the influence of the clergy justice was administered in somewhat inquisitorial fashion, there was an uncertainty as to just what the law was, a strong disposition to confuse questions of law with questions of ethics, and great laxity in the admission and estimation of evidence. As early as 1639 people had begun to complain that too much power was rested in the discretion of the magistrate, and they clamoured for a code of laws; but as Winthrop says, the magistrates and ministers were "not very forward in this matter," for they preferred to supplement the common law of England by decisions based on the Old Testament rather than by a body of statutes. It was not until 1649, after a persistent struggle, that the deputies won a decisive victory over the assistants and secured for Massachusetts a definite code of laws. In the New Haven colony similar theocratic notions led the settlers to dispense with trial by jury because they could find no precedent for it in the laws of Moses. Here, as in Massachusetts, the inquisitorial administration of justice combined with partial disfranchisement to awaken discontent, and it was partly for this reason that New Haven fell so easily under the sway of Connecticut.

Inquisitorial administration of justice.

In Massachusetts after 1650 the opinion rapidly gained ground that all baptized persons of upright and decorous lives ought to be considered, for practical purposes, as members of the church, and therefore entitled to the exercise of political rights, even though unqualified for participation in the Lord's Supper. This theory

The "Halfway Covenant."

of church-membership, based on what was at that time stigmatized as the "Halfway Covenant," aroused intense opposition. It was the great question of the day. In 1657 a council was held in Boston, which approved the principle of the Half way Covenant; and as this decision was far from satisfying the churches, a synod of all the clergy men in Massachusetts was held five years later, to reconsider the great question. The decision of the synod substantially confirmed the decision of the council, but there were some dissenting voices. Foremost among the dissenters, who wished to retain the old theocratic régime in all its strictness, was Charles Chauncey, the president of Harvard College, and Increase Mather agreed with him at the time, though he afterward saw reason to change his opinion, and published two tracts in favour of the Halfway Covenant. Most bitter of all toward the new theory of church-membership was, naturally enough, Mr. Davenport of New Haven.

This burning question was the source of angry contentions in the First Church of Boston. Its teacher, the learned and melancholy Norton, died in 1663, and four years later the aged pastor, John Wilson, followed him. In choosing a successor to Wilson the church decided to declare itself in opposition to the liberal decision of the synod, and in token thereof invited Davenport to come from New Haven to take charge of it. Davenport, who was then seventy years old, was disgusted at the recent annexation of his colony to Connecticut. He accepted the invitation and came to Boston, against the wishes of nearly half of the Boston congregation who did not like the illiberal principle which he represented. In little more than a year his ministry at Boston was ended by death; but the opposition to his call had already proceeded so far that a secession from the old church had become inevitable. In 1669 the advocates of the Halfway Covenant organized themselves into a new society under the title of the "Third Church in Boston." A wooden meeting-house was built on a lot which had once belonged to the late governor Winthrop, in what was then the south part of the town, so that the society and its meeting-house became known as the South Church; and after a new church founded in Summer Street in 1717 took the name of the New South, the church of 1669 came to be further distinguished as the Old South. As this church represented a liberal idea which was growing in favour with the people, it soon became the most flourishing church in America. After sixty years its numbers had increased so that the old meeting-house could not contain them; and in 1729 the famous building which still stands was erected on the same spot, — a building with a grander history than any other on the American continent, unless it be that other plain brick building in Philadelphia where the Declaration of Independence was adopted and the Federal Constitution framed.

Founding of the Old South Church, 1669.

The wrath of the First Church at this secession from its ranks was deep and bitter, and for thirteen years it refused to entertain ecclesiastical intercourse with the South Church. But by 1682 it had become apparent that the king and his friends were meditating an attack upon the Puritan theocracy in New England. It had even been suggested, in the council for the colonies, that the Church of England should be established in Massachusetts, and that none but duly ordained Episcopal clergymen should be allowed to solemnize marriages. Such alarming suggestions began to impress the various Puritan churches with the importance of uniting their forces against the common enemy; and accordingly in 1682 the quarrel between the two Boston societies came to an end. There was urgent need of all the sympathy and good feeling that the community could muster, whereby to cheer itself in the crisis that was coming. The four years from 1684 to 1688 were the darkest years in the history of New England. Massachusetts, though not lacking in the spirit, had not the power to beard the tyrant as she did eighty years later. Her attitude toward the Stuarts — as we have seen — had been sometimes openly haughty and defiant, sometimes silent and sullen, but always independent. At the accession of Charles II. the colonists had thought it worth while to send commissioners to England to confer with the king and avoid a quarrel. Charles promised to respect their charter, but insisted that in return they must take an oath of allegiance to the crown, must administer justice in Demands of Charles II. the king's name, and must repeal their laws restricting the right of suffrage to church members and prohibiting the Episcopal form of worship. When the people of Massachusetts received this message they consented to administer justice in the king's name, but all the other matters were referred for consideration to a committee, and so they dropped out of sight. When the royal commissioners came to Boston in 1664, they were especially instructed to ascertain whether Massachusetts had complied with the king's demands; but upon this point the legislature stubbornly withheld any definite answer, while it frittered away the time in trivial altercations with the royal commissioners. The war with Holland and the turbulent state of English politics operated for several years in favour of this independent attitude of the colonists, though during all this time their enemies at court were busy with intrigues and accusations. Apart from mere slanders the real grounds of complaint were the restriction of the suffrage, whereby members of the Church of England were shut out; the claims of the eastern proprietors, heirs of Mason and Gorges, whose territory Massachusetts had absorbed; the infraction of the navigation laws; and the coinage of pine-tree shillings. The last named measure had been forced upon the colonists by the scarcity of a circulating medium. Until 1661 Indian wampum had been a legal tender, and far into the eighteenth century it remained current in small transactions. "In 1693 the ferriage from New York to Brooklyn was eight stivers in wampum or a silver twopence."[1] As early as 1652 Massachusetts had sought to supply the defi-

Complaints against Massachusetts.

---

[1] Weeden, *Indian Money as a Factor in New England Civilization*, Johns Hopkins University Studies, II. viii., ix. p. 30.

ciency by the issue of shillings and sixpences. It was an affair of convenience and probably had no political purpose. The infraction of the navigation laws was a more serious matter. "Ships from France, Spain, and the Canaries traded directly with Boston, and brought in goods which had never paid duty in any English port."[1] The effect of this was to excite the jealousy of the merchants in London and other English cities and to deprive Massachusetts of the sympathy of that already numerous and powerful class of people.

In 1675, the first year of King Philip's War, the British government made up its mind to attend more closely to the affairs of its American colonies. It had got the Dutch war off its hands, and could give heed to other things. The general supervision of the colonies was assigned to a standing committee of the privy council, styled the "Lords of the Committee of Trade and Plantations," and henceforth familiarly known as the "Lords of Trade." Next year the Lords of Trade sent an agent to Boston, with a letter to Governor Leverett about the Mason and Gorges claims. Under cover of this errand the messenger was to go about and ascertain the sentiments which people in the Kennebec and Piscataqua towns, as well as in Boston, entertained for the government of Massachusetts. The person to whom this work was entrusted was Edward Randolph, a cousin of Robert Mason who inherited the proprietary claim to the Piscataqua country. To these men had old John

The Lords of Trade.

Edward Randolph.

[1] Doyle, ii. 253.

Mason bequeathed his deadly feud with Massachusetts, and the fourteen years which Randolph now spent in New England were busily devoted to sowing the seeds of strife. In 1678 the king appointed him collector and surveyor of customs at the port of Boston, with instructions to enforce the navigation laws. Randolph was not the man to do unpopular things in such a way as to dull the edge of the infliction; he took delight in adding insult to injury. He was at once harsh and treacherous. His one virtue was pecuniary integrity; he was inaccessible to bribes and did not pick and steal from the receipts at the custom-house. In the other relations of life he was disencumbered of scruples. His abilities were not great, but his industry was untiring, and he pursued his enemies with the tenacity of a sleuth-hound. As an excellent British historian observes, " he was one of those men who, once enlisted as partisans, lose every other feeling in the passion which is engendered of strife." [1]

The arrival of such a man boded no good to Massachusetts. His reception at the town-house was a cold one. Leverett liked neither his looks nor his message, and kept his peaked hat on while he read the letter; when he came to the signature of the king's chief secretary of state, he asked, with careless contempt, " Who is this Henry Coventry ? " Randolph's choking rage found vent in a letter to the king, taking pains to remind him that the governor of Massachusetts had once been an officer in Cromwell's army. As we read this and think with what ghoulish glee the writer would

[1] Doyle, *Puritan Colonies*, ii. 254.

have betrayed Colonel Goffe into the hands of the headsman, had any clue been given him, we can quite understand why Hubbard and Mather had nothing to say about the mysterious stranger at Hadley. Everything that Randolph could think of that would goad and irritate the king, he reported in full to London; his letters were specimens of that worst sort of lie that is based upon distorted half-truths; and his malicious pen but seldom lay idle.

While waiting for the effects of these reports to ripen, Randolph was busily intriguing with some of the leading men in Boston who were dissatisfied with the policy of the dominant party, and under his careful handling a party was soon brought into existence which was ready to counsel submission to the royal will. Such was the birth of Toryism in New England. The leader of this party was Joseph Dudley, son of the grim verse-maker who had come over as lieutenant to Winthrop. *Joseph Dudley.* The younger Dudley was graduated at Harvard in 1665, and proceeded to study theology, but soon turned his attention entirely to politics. In 1673 he was a deputy from Roxbury in the General Court; in 1675 he took part in the storming of the Narragansett fort; in 1677 and the three following years he was one of the Federal Commissioners. In character and temper he differed greatly from his father. Like the proverbial minister's son whose feet are swift toward folly, Joseph Dudley seems to have learned in stern bleak years of childhood to rebel against the Puritan theory of life. Much of the abuse that has been heaped upon him, as a renegade and traitor, is probably undeserved. It does not appear that he ever made any pretence of love for the Puritan commonwealth, and there were many like him who had as lief be ruled by king as by clergy. But it cannot be denied that his suppleness and sagacity went along with a moral nature that was weak and vulgar. Joseph Dudley was essentially a self-seeking politician and courtier, like his famous kinsman of the previous century, Robert, Earl of Leicester. His party in Massachusetts was largely made up of men who had come to the colony for commercial reasons, and had little or no sympathy with the objects for which it was founded. Among them were Episcopalians, Presbyterians, and Baptists, who were allowed no chance for public worship, as well as many others who, like Gallio, cared for none of these things. Their numbers, moreover, must have been large, for Boston had grown to be a town of 5000 inhabitants, the population of Massachusetts was approaching 30,000, and, according to Hutchinson, scarcely one grown man in five was a church-member qualified to vote or hold office. Such a fact speaks volumes as to the change which was coming over the Puritan world. No wonder that the clergy had begun to preach about the weeds and tares that were overrunning Christ's pleasant garden. No wonder that the spirit of revolt against the disfranchising policy of the theocracy was ripe.

It was in 1679, when this weakness of the body politic had been duly studied and reported by Randolph, and when all New England was groaning under the bereavements and burdens entailed by Philip's war, that the Stuart government began its final series of assaults upon Massachusetts. The claims of the eastern proprietors, the heirs of Mason and Gorges, furnished the occasion. Since 1643 the four Piscataqua towns — Hampton, Exeter, Dover, and Portsmouth — had remained under the jurisdiction of Massachusetts. *Royal province of New Hampshire.* After the Restoration the Mason claim had been revived, and in 1677 was referred to the chief-justices North and Rainsford. Their decision was that Mason's claim had always been worthless as based on a grant in which the old Plymouth Company had exceeded its powers. They also decided that Massachusetts had no valid claim since the charter assigned her a boundary just north of the Merrimack. This decision left the four towns subject to none but the king, who forthwith in 1679 proceeded to erect them into the royal province of New Hampshire, with president and council appointed by the crown, and an assembly chosen by the people, but endowed with little authority, — a tricksome counterfeit of popular government. Within three years an arrogant and thieving ruler, Edward Cranfield, had goaded New Hampshire to acts of insurrection.

To the decisions of the chief-justices Massachusetts must needs submit. The Gorges claim led to more serious results. Under Cromwell's rule in 1652 — the same year in which she began coining money — Massachusetts had extended her sway over Maine. In 1665 Colonel Nichols and his commissioners, acting upon the express instructions of Charles II., took it away from her. In 1668, after the commissioners had gone home, Massachusetts coolly took possession again. In 1677 the chief-justices decided that the claim of the Gorges family, being based on a grant from James I., was valid. Then the young Ferdinando Gorges, grandson of the first proprietor, offered to sell the province to the king, who had now taken it into his head that he would like to bestow it upon the Duke of Monmouth, his favourite son by Lucy Walters. Before Charles had responded, Governor Leverett had struck a bargain with Gorges, who ceded to Massachusetts all his rights over Maine for £1250 in hard cash. When the king heard of this transaction he was furious. He sent a letter to Boston, commanding the General Court to surrender the province again on repayment of this sum of £1250, and expressing his indignation that the people should thus dare to dispose of an important claim off-hand without consulting his wishes. In the same letter the colony was enjoined to put in force the royal orders of seventeen years before, concerning the oath of allegiance, the restriction of the suffrage, and the prohibition of the Episcopal form of worship.

<small>The Gorges claim.</small>

This peremptory message reached Boston about Christmas, 1679. Leverett, the sturdy Ironsides, had died six months before, and his place was filled by Simon Bradstreet, a man of moderate powers but great integrity, and held in peculiar reverence as the last survivor of those that had been chosen to office before leaving England by the leaders of the great Puritan exodus. Born in a Lincolnshire village in 1603, he was now seventy-six years old. He had taken his degree at Emmanuel College, Cambridge, had served as secretary to the Earl of Warwick, and in 1629 had been appointed member of the board of assistants for the colony about to be established on Massachusetts bay. In this position he had remained with honour for half a century, while he had also served as Federal Commissioner and as agent for the colony in London. His wife, who died in 1672, was a woman of quaint learning and quainter verses, which her contemporaries admired beyond measure. One of her books was republished in London, with the title: "The Tenth Muse, lately sprung up in America." John Norton once said that if Virgil could only have heard the seraphic poems of Anne Bradstreet, he would have thrown his heathen doggerel into the fire. She was sister of Joseph Dudley, and evidently inherited this rhyming talent, such as it was, from her father. Governor Bradstreet belonged to the moderate party who would have been glad to extend the franchise, but he did not go with his brother-in-law in subservience to the king.

Simon Bradstreet and his wife.

When the General Court assembled, in May, 1680, the full number of eighteen assistants appeared, for the first time in the history of the colony, and in accordance with an expressed wish of the king. They were ready to yield in trifles, but not in essentials. After wearisome discussion, the answer to the royal letter was decided on. It stated in vague and unsatisfactory terms that the royal orders of 1662 either had been carried out already or would be in good time, while to the demand for the surrender of Maine no reply whatever was made, save that "they were heartily sorry that any actings of theirs should be displeasing to his Majesty." After this, when Randolph wrote home that the king's letters were of no more account in Massachusetts than an old London Gazette, he can hardly be accused of stretching the truth. Randolph kept busily at work, and seems to have persuaded the Bishop of London that if the charter could be annulled, episcopacy might be established in Massachusetts as in England. In February, 1682, a letter came from the king demanding submission and threatening legal proceedings against the charter. Dudley was then sent as agent to London, and with him was sent a Mr. Richards, of the extreme clerical party, to watch him.

Massachusetts answers the king.

Meanwhile the king's position at home had been changing. He had made up his mind to follow his father's example and try the experiment of setting his people at defiance and governing without a parliament. This could not be done without a great supply of money. Louis XIV. had plenty of money, for there was no constitution in France to prevent his squeezing what he wanted out of the pockets of an oppressed people. France was thriving greatly now, for Colbert had introduced a comparatively free system of trade between the provinces and inaugurated an era of prosperity soon to be cut short by the expulsion of the

Huguenots. Louis could get money enough for the asking, and would be delighted to foment civil disturbances in England, so as to tie the hands of the only power which at that moment could interfere with his seizing Alsace and Lorraine and invading Flanders. The pretty Louise de Keroualle, Duchess of Portsmouth, with her innocent baby face and heart as cold as any reptile's, was the French Delilah chosen to shear the locks of the British Samson. By such means and from such motives a secret treaty was made in February, 1681, by which Louis agreed to pay Charles 2,000,000 livres down, and 500,000 more in each of the next two years, on condition that he should summon no more parliaments within that time. This bargain for securing the means of overthrowing the laws and liberties of England was, on the part of Charles II., an act no less reprehensible than some of those for which his father had gone to the block. But Charles could now afford for a while to wreak his evil will. He had already summoned a parliament for the 21st of March, to meet at Oxford within the precincts of the subservient university, and out of reach of the high-spirited freemen of London. He now forced a quarrel with the new parliament and dissolved it within a week. A joiner named Stephen College, who had spoken his mind too freely in the taverns at Oxford with regard to these proceedings, was drawn and quartered. The Whig leader Lord Shaftesbury was obliged to flee to Holland. In the absence of a parliament the only power of organized resistance

Secret treaty between Charles II. and Louis XIV.

to the king's tyranny resided in the corporate governments of the chartered towns. The charter of London was accordingly attacked by a writ of *quo warranto*, and in June, 1683, the time-serving judges declared it confiscated. George Jeffreys, a low drunken fellow whom Charles had made Lord Chief Justice, went on a circuit through the country; and, as Roger North says, "made all the charters, like the walls of Jericho, fall down before him, and returned laden with surrenders, the spoils of towns." At the same time a terrible blow was dealt at two of the greatest Whig families in England. Lord William Russell, son of the Earl of Bedford, and Algernon Sidney, younger son of the Earl of Leicester, two of the purest patriots and ablest liberal leaders of the day, were tried on a false charge of treason and beheaded.

<small>Shameful proceedings in England.</small>

By this quick succession of high-handed measures, the friends of law and liberty were for a moment disconcerted and paralyzed. In the frightful abasement of the courts of justice which these events so clearly showed, the freedom of Englishmen seemed threatened in its last stronghold. The doctrine of passive obedience to monarchs was preached in the pulpits and inculcated by the university of Oxford, which ordered the works of John Milton to be publicly burned. Sir Robert Filmer wrote that "not only in human laws, but even in divine, a thing may by the king be commanded contrary to law, and yet obedience to such a command is necessary." Charles felt so strong that in 1684 he flatly refused to summon a parliament.

It was not long before the effects of all this were felt in New England. The mission of Dudley and his colleague was fruitless. They returned to Boston, and Randolph, who had followed them to London, now followed them back, armed with a writ of *quo warranto* which he was instructed not to serve until he should have given Massachusetts one more chance to humble herself in the dust. Should she modify her constitution to please a tyrant or see it trampled under foot? Recent events in England served for a solemn warning; for the moment the Tories were silenced; perhaps after all, the absolute rule of a king was hardly to be preferred to the sway of the Puritan clergy; the day when the House of Commons sat still and wept seemed to have returned. A great town-meeting was held in the Old South Meeting-House, and the moderator requested all who were for surrendering the charter to hold up their hands. Not a hand was lifted, and out from the throng a solitary voice exclaimed, with deep-drawn breath, "The Lord be praised!" Then arose Increase Mather, president of Harvard College, and reminded them how their fathers did win this charter, and should they deliver it up unto the spoiler who demanded it "even as Ahab required Naboth's vineyard, Oh! their children would be bound to curse them." Such was the attitude of Massachusetts, and when it was known in London, the blow was struck. For technical reasons Randolph's writ was not served; but on the 21st of June a decree in chancery annulled the charter of Massachusetts.

Massachusetts refuses to surrender her charter.

It is annulled by decree of chancery, June 21, 1684.

To appreciate the force of this blow we must pause for a moment and consider what it involved. The right to the soil of North America had been hitherto regarded in England, on the strength of the discoveries of the Cabots, as an appurtenance to the crown of Henry VII., — as something which descended from father to son like the palace at Hampton Court or the castle at Windsor, but which the sovereign might alienate by his voluntary act just as he might sell or give away a piece of his royal domain in England. Over this vast territory it was doubtful how far Parliament was entitled to exercise authority, and the rights of Englishmen settled there had theoretically no security save in the provisions of the various charters by which the crown had delegated its authority to individual proprietors or to private companies. It was thus on the charter granted by Charles I. to the Company of Massachusetts Bay that not only the cherished political and ecclesiastical institutions of the colony, but even the titles of individuals to their lands and houses, were supposed to be founded. By the abrogation of the charter, all rights and immunities that had been based upon it were at once swept away, and every rood of the soil of Massachusetts became the personal property of the Stuart king, who might, if he should possess the will and the power, turn out all the present occupants or otherwise deal with them as trespassers. Such at least was the theory of Charles II., and to show that he meant to wreak his vengeance with no gentle hand, he appointed as his viceroy the brutal

Effect of annulling the charter.

Percy Kirke, — a man who would have no scruples about hanging a few citizens without trial, should occasion require it.

But in February, 1685, just as Charles seemed to be getting everything arranged to his mind, a stroke of apoplexy carried him off the scene, and his brother ascended the throne. Monmouth's rebellion, and the horrible cruelties that followed, kept Colonel Kirke busy in England through the summer, and left the new king scant leisure to think about America. Late in the autumn, having made up his mind that he could not spare such an exemplary knave as Kirke, James II. sent over Sir Edmund Andros. In the mean time the government of Massachusetts had been administered by Dudley, who showed himself willing to profit by the misfortunes of his country. Andros had long been one of James's favourites. He was the dull and dogged English officer such as one often meets, honest enough and faithful to his master, neither cruel nor rapacious, but coarse in fibre and wanting in tact. Some years before, when governor of New York, he had a territorial dispute with Connecticut, and now cherished a grudge against the people of New England, so that, from James's point of view, he was well fitted to be their governor. James wished to abolish all the local governments in America, and unite them, as far as possible, under a single administration. With Plymouth there could be no trouble; she had never had a charter, but had existed on sufferance from the outset. In 1687 the charters of Rhode Island and Connecticut were re-

Sir Edmund Andros.

scinded, but the decrees were not executed in due form. In October of that year Andros went to Hartford, to seize the Connecticut charter, but it was not surrendered. While Sir Edmund was bandying threats with stout Robert Treat, the queller of Indians and now governor of Connecticut, in the course of their evening conference the candles were suddenly blown out, and when after some scraping of tinder they were lighted again the document was nowhere to be found, for Captain Wadsworth had carried it away and hidden it in the hollow trunk of a mighty oak tree. Nevertheless for the moment the colony was obliged to submit to the tyrant. Next day the secretary John Allyn wrote "Finis" on the colonial records and shut up the book. Within another twelvemonth New York and New Jersey were added to the viceroyalty of Andros; so that all the northern colonies from the forests of Maine to the Delaware river were thus brought under the arbitrary rule of one man, who was responsible to no one but the king for whatever he might take it into his head to do.

The Charter Oak.

The vexatious character of the new government was most strongly felt at Boston where Andros had his headquarters. Measures were at once taken for the erection of an Episcopal church, and meantime the royal order was that one of the principal meeting-houses should be seized for the use of the Church of England. This was an ominous beginning. In the eyes of the people it was much more than a mere question of disturbing Puritan prejudices. They

Episcopal services in Boston.

had before them the experience of Scotland during the past ten years, the savage times of "Old Mortality," the times which had seen the tyrannical prelate, on the lonely moor, begging in vain for his life, the times of Drumclog and Bothwell Brigg, of Claverhouse and his flinty-hearted troopers, of helpless women tied to stakes on the Solway shore and drowned by inches in the rising tide. What had happened in one part of the world might happen in another, for the Stuart policy was the same. It aimed not at securing toleration but at asserting unchecked supremacy. Its demand for an inch was the prelude to its seizing an ell, and so our forefathers understood it. Sir Edmund's formal demand for the Old South Meeting-House was flatly refused, but on Good Friday, 1687, the sexton was frightened into opening it, and thenceforward Episcopal services were held there alternately with the regular services until the overthrow of Andros. The pastor, Samuel Willard, was son of the gallant veteran who had rescued the beleaguered people of Brookfield in King Philip's war. Amusing passages occurred between him and Sir Edmund, who relished the pleasantry of keeping minister and congregation waiting an hour or two in the street on Sundays before yielding to them the use of their meeting-house. More kindly memories of the unpopular governor are associated with the building of the first King's Chapel on the spot where its venerable successor now stands. The church was not finished until after Sir Edmund had taken his departure, but Lady Andros, who died in February,

Founding of the King's Chapel, 1689.

1688, lies in the burying-ground hard by. Her gentle manners had won all hearts. For the moment, we are told, one touch of nature made enemies kin, and as Sir Edmund walked to the town-house "many a head was bared to the bereaved husband that before had remained stubbornly covered to the exalted governor." [1]

The despotic rule of Andros was felt in more serious ways than in the seizing upon a meeting-house. Arbitrary taxes were imposed, encroachments were made upon common lands as in older manorial times, and the writ of *habeas corpus* was suspended. Dudley was appointed censor of the press, and nothing was allowed to be printed without his permission. All the public records of the late New England governments were ordered to be brought to Boston, whither it thus became necessary to make a tedious journey in order to consult them. All deeds and wills were required to be registered in Boston, and excessive fees were charged for the registry. It was proclaimed that all private titles to land were to be ransacked, and that whoever wished to have his title confirmed must pay a heavy quit-rent, which under the circumstances amounted to blackmail. The General Court was abolished. The power of taxation was taken from the town-meetings and lodged with the governor. Against this crowning iniquity the town of Ipswich, led by its sturdy pastor, John Wise, made protest. In re-

Tyranny.

---

[1] The quotation is from an unpublished letter of Rev. Robert Ratcliffe to the Bishop of London, cited in an able article in the *Boston Herald*, January 4, 1888. I have not seen the letter.

sponse Mr. Wise was thrown into prison, fined £50, and suspended from the ministry. A notable and powerful character was this John Wise. One of the broadest thinkers and most lucid writers of his time, he seems like a forerunner of the liberal Unitarian divines of the nineteenth century. His "Vindication of the Government of the New England Churches," published in 1717, was a masterly exposition of the principles of civil government, and became "a text book of liberty for our Revolutionary fathers, containing some of the notable expressions that are used in the Declaration of Independence." *John Wise of Ipswich.*

It was on the trial of Mr. Wise in October, 1687, that Dudley openly declared that the people of New England had now no further privileges left them than not to be sold for slaves. Such a state of things in the valley of the Euphrates would not have attracted comment; the peasantry of central Europe would have endured it until better instructed; but in an English community it could not last long. If James II. had remained upon the throne, New England would surely have soon risen in rebellion against Andros. But the mother country had by this time come to repent the fresh lease of life which she had granted to the Stuart dynasty after Cromwell's death. Tired of the disgraceful subservience of her Court to the schemes of Louis XIV., tired of fictitious plots and judicial murders, tired of bloody assizes and declarations of indulgence and all the strange devices of Stuart tyranny, England endured the arrogance of James but three years, *Fall of James II.*

and then drove him across the Channel, to get such consolation as he might from his French paymaster and patron. On the 4th of April, 1689, the youthful John Winslow brought to Boston the news of the landing of the Prince of Orange in England. For the space of two weeks there was quiet and earnest deliberation among the citizens, as the success of the Prince's enterprise was not yet regarded as assured. But all at once, on the morning of the 18th, the drums beat to arms, the signal-fire was lighted on Beacon Hill, a meeting was held at the Town-House, militia began to pour in from the country, and Andros, summoned to surrender, was fain to beseech Mr. Willard and the other ministers to intercede for him. But the ministers refused. Next day the Castle was surrendered, the Rose frigate riding in the harbour was seized and dismantled, and Andros was arrested as he was trying to effect his escape disguised in woman's clothes. Dudley and the other agents of tyranny were also imprisoned, and thus the revolution was accomplished. It marks the importance which the New England colonies were beginning to attain, that, before the Prince of Orange had fully secured the throne, he issued a letter instructing the people of Boston to preserve decorum and acquiesce yet a little longer in the government of Andros, until more satisfactory arrangements could be made. But Increase Mather, who was then in London on a mission in behalf of New England, judiciously prevented this letter of instructions from being sent. The zeal of the people outstripped the cautious policy of the

Insurrection in Boston, and overthrow of Andros, April 18, 1689.

new sovereign, and provisional governments, in accordance with the old charters, were at once set up in the colonies lately ruled by Andros. Bradstreet now in his eighty-seventh year was reinstated as governor of Massachusetts. Five weeks after this revolution in Boston the order to proclaim King William and Queen Mary was received, amid such rejoicings as had never before been seen in that quiet town, for it was believed that self-government would now be guaranteed to New England.

This hope was at least so far realized that from the most formidable dangers which had threatened it, New England was henceforth secured. The struggle with the Stuarts was ended, and by this second revolution within half a century the crown had received a check from which it never recovered. There were *Effects of the Revolution of 1689.* troubles yet in store for England, but no more such outrages as the judicial murders of Russell and Sidney. New England had still a stern ordeal to go through, but never again was she to be so trodden down and insulted as in the days of Andros. The efforts of George III. to rule Englishmen despotically were weak as compared with those of the Stuarts. In his time England had waxed strong enough to curb the tyrant, America had waxed strong enough to defy and disown him. After 1689 the Puritan no longer felt that his religion was in danger, and there was a reasonable prospect that charters solemnly granted him would be held sacred. William III. was a sovereign of modern type, from whom freedom of thought and worship had nothing to fear. In his theology he agreed, as a Dutch Calvinist, more nearly with the Puritans than with the Church of England. At the same time he had no great liking for so much independence of thought and action as New England had exhibited. In the negotiations which now definitely settled the affairs of this part of the world, the intractable behaviour of Massachusetts was borne in mind and contrasted with the somewhat less irritating attitude of the smaller colonies. It happened that the decree which annulled the charters of Rhode Island and Connecticut had not yet been formally enrolled. It was accordingly treated as void, and the old charters were allowed to remain in force. They were so liberal that no change in them was needed at the time of the Revolution, so that Connecticut was governed under its old charter until 1818, and Rhode Island until 1842.

There was at this time a disposition on the part of the British government to unite all the northern colonies under a single administration. The French in Canada were fast becoming rivals to be feared; and the wonderful explorations of La Salle, bringing the St. Lawrence into political connection with the Mississippi, had at length foreshadowed a New France in the rear of all the English colonies, aiming at the control of the centre of the continent and eager to confine the English to the sea-board. Already the relations of position which led to the great Seven Years' War were beginning to shape themselves; and the conflict between France and England actually broke out in 1689, as soon as Louis

Need for union among all the northern colonies.

XIV.'s hired servant, James II., was superseded by William III. as king of England and head of a Protestant league.

In view of this new state of affairs, it was thought desirable to unite the northern English colonies under one head, so far as possible, in order to secure unity of military action. But natural prejudices had to be considered. The policy of James II. had aroused such bitter feeling in America that William must needs move with caution. Accordingly he did not seek to unite New York with New England, and he did not think it worth while to carry out the attack which James had only begun upon Connecticut and Rhode Island. As for New Hampshire, he seems to have been restrained by what in the language of modern politics would be called "pressure," brought to bear by certain local interests.[1] But in the case of the little colony founded by the Pilgrims of the Mayflower there was no obstacle. She was now annexed to Massachusetts, which also received not only Maine but even Acadia, just won from the French; so that, save for the short break at Portsmouth, the coast of Massachusetts now reached all the way from Martha's Vineyard to the Gulf of St. Lawrence.

_{Plymouth, Maine, and Acadia annexed to Massachusetts.}

But along with this great territorial extension there went some curtailment of the political privileges of the colony. By the new charter of 1692 the right of the people to be governed by a legislature of their own choosing was expressly confirmed.

[1] Doyle, *Puritan Colonies*, ii. 379, 380.

The exclusive right of this legislature to impose taxes was also confirmed. But henceforth no qualification of church-membership, but only a property qualification, was to be required of voters; the governor was to be appointed by the crown instead of being elected by the people; and all laws passed by the legislature were to be sent to England for royal approval. These features of the new charter, — the extension, or if I may so call it, the *secularization* of the franchise, the appointment of the governor by the crown, and the power of veto which the crown expressly reserved, — were grave restrictions upon the independence which Massachusetts had hitherto enjoyed. Henceforth her position was to be like that of the other colonies with royal governors. But her history did not thereby lose its interest or significance, though it became, like the history of most of the colonies, a dismal record of irrepressible bickerings between the governor appointed by the crown and the legislature elected by the people. In the period that began in 1692 and ended in 1776, the movements of Massachusetts, while restricted and hampered, were at the same time forced into a wider orbit. She was brought into political sympathy with Virginia. While two generations of men were passing across the scene, the political problems of Massachusetts were assimilated to those of Virginia. In spite of all the other differences, great as they were, there was a likeness in the struggles between the popular legislature and the royal governor which subordinated them all. It was this similarity of experi-

<small>Massachusetts becomes a royal province.</small>

ence, during the eighteenth century, that brought these two foremost colonies into cordial alliance during the struggle against George III., and thus made it possible to cement all the colonies together in the mighty nation whose very name is fraught with so high and earnest a lesson to mankind, — the UNITED STATES!

For such a far-reaching result, the temporary humiliation of Massachusetts was a small price to pay. But it was not until long after the accession of William III. that things could be seen in these grand outlines. With his coronation began the struggle of seventy years between France and England, far grander than the struggle between Rome and Carthage, two thousand years earlier, for primacy in the world, for the prerogative of determining the future career of mankind. That warfare, so fraught with meaning, was waged as much upon American as upon European ground; and while it continued, it was plainly for the interest of the British government to pursue a conciliatory policy toward its American colonies, for without their whole-hearted assistance it could have no hope of success. As soon as the struggle was ended, and the French power in the colonial world finally overthrown, the perpetual quarrels between the popular legislatures and the royal governors led immediately to the Stamp Act and the other measures of the British government that brought about the American revolution. People sometimes argue about that revolution as if it had no past behind it and was simply the result of a discussion over abstract principles.

Seeds of the American Revolution already sown.

We can now see that while the dispute involved an abstract principle of fundamental importance to mankind, it was at the same time for Americans illustrated by memories sufficiently concrete and real. James Otis in his prime was no further distant from the tyranny of Andros than middle-aged men of to-day are distant from the Missouri Compromise. The sons of men cast into jail along with John Wise may have stood silent in the moonlight on Griffin's Wharf and looked on while the contents of the tea-chests were hurled into Boston harbour. In the events we have here passed in review, it may be seen, so plainly that he who runs may read, how the spirit of 1776 was foreshadowed in 1689.

BIBLIOGRAPHICAL NOTE.

AN interesting account of the Barons' War and the meeting of the first House of Commons is given in Prothero's *Simon de Montfort*, London, 1877. For Wyclif and the Lollards, see Milman's *Latin Christianity*, vol. vii.

The ecclesiastical history of the Tudor period may best be studied in the works of John Strype, to wit, *Historical Memorials*, 6 vols.; *Annals of the Reformation*, 7 vols.; *Lives of Cranmer, Parker, Whitgift*, etc., Oxford, 1812–28. See also Burnet's *History of the Reformation of the Church of England*, 3 vols., London, 1679–1715; Neal's *History of the Puritans*, London, 1793; Tulloch, *Leaders of the Reformation*, Boston, 1859. A vast mass of interesting information is to be found in *The Zurich Letters, comprising the Correspondence of Several English Bishops, and Others, with some of the Helvetian Reformers*, published by the Parker Society, 4 vols., Cambridge, Eng., 1845–46. Hooker's *Ecclesiastical Polity* was published in London, 1594; a new edition, containing two additional books, the first complete edition, was published in 1622.

For the general history of England in the seventeenth century, there are two modern works which stand far above all others, — Gardiner's *History of England*, 10 vols., London, 1883–84; and Masson's *Life of Milton, narrated in connection with the Political, Ecclesiastical, and Literary History of his Time*, 6 vols., Cambridge, Eng., 1859–80. These are books of truly colossal erudition, and written in a spirit of judicial fairness. Mr. Gardiner's ten volumes cover the forty years from the accession of James I. to the beginning of the Civil War, 1603–1643. Mr. Gardiner has lately published the first two volumes of his history of the Civil War, and it is to be hoped that he will not stop until he reaches the accession of William and Mary. Indeed, such books as his ought never to stop. My friend and colleague, Prof. Hosmer, tells me that Mr. Gardiner is a lineal descendant of Cromwell and Ireton. His little book, *The Puritan Revolution*, in the "Epochs of History" series, is extremely useful, and along with it one should read Airy's *The English Restoration and Louis XIV.*, in the same series, New York, 1889. The best biography of Cromwell is by Mr. Allanson Picton, London, 1882; see also Frederic Harrison's *Cromwell*, London, 1888, an excellent little book. Hosmer's *Young Sir Henry Vane*, Boston, 1888, should be read in the same connection; and one should not forget Carlyle's *Cromwell*. See also Tulloch, *English Puritanism and its Leaders*, 1861, and *Rational Theology and Christian Philosophy in England in the Seventeenth Century*, 1872; Skeats, *History of the Free Churches of England*, London, 1868; Mountfield, *The Church and Puritans*, London, 1881. Dexter's *Congregationalism of the Last Three Hundred Years*, New York, 1880, is a work of monumental importance.

On the history of New England the best general works are Palfrey, *History of New England*, 4 vols., Boston, 1858-75; and Doyle, *The English in America — The Puritan Colonies*, 2 vols., London, 1887. In point of scholarship Dr. Palfrey's work is of the highest order, and it is written in an interesting style. Its only shortcoming is that it deals somewhat too leniently with the faults of the Puritan theocracy, and looks at things too exclusively from a Massachusetts point of view. It is one of the best histories yet written in America. Mr. Doyle's work is admirably fair and impartial, and is based throughout upon a careful study of original documents. The author is a Fellow of All Souls College, Oxford, and has apparently made American history his specialty. His work on the Puritan colonies is one of a series which when completed will cover the whole story of English colonization in America. I have looked in vain in his pages for any remark or allusion indicating that he has ever visited America, and am therefore inclined to think that he has not done so. He now and then makes a slight error such as would not be likely to be made by a native of New England, but this is very seldom The accuracy and thoroughness of its research, its judicial temper, and its philosophical spirit make Mr. Doyle's book in some respects the best that has been written about New England.

Among original authorities we may begin by citing John Smith's *Description of New England*, 1616, and *New England's Trial*, 1622, contained in Arber's new edition of Smith's works, London, 1884. Bradford's narrative of the founding of Plymouth was for a long time supposed to be lost. Nathaniel Morton's *New England's Memorial*, published in 1669, was little more than an abridgment of it. After two centuries Bradford's manuscript was discovered, and an excellent edition by Mr. Charles Deane was published in the *Massachusetts Historical Collections*, 4th series, vol. iii., 1856. Edward Winslow's *Journal of the Proceedings of the English Plantation settled at Plymouth*, 1622, and *Good News from New England*, 1624, are contained, with other valuable materials, in Young's *Chronicles of the Pilgrim Fathers*, Boston, 1844. See also Shurtleff and Pulsifer, *Records of Plymouth*, 12 vols., ending with the annexation of the colony to Massachusetts in 1692; Prince's *Chronological History of New England*, ed. Drake, 1852; and in this connection Hunter's *Founders of New Plymouth*, London, 1854; Steele's *Life of Brewster*, Philadelphia, 1857; Goodwin's *Pilgrim Republic*, Boston, 1887; Bacon's *Genesis of the New England Churches*, New York, 1874; Baylies's *Historical Memoir*, 1830; Thacher's *History of the Town of Plymouth*, 1832.

Sir Ferdinando Gorges wrote a *Briefe Narration of the Originall Undertakings of the advancement of plantations into the parts of America, especially showing the beginning, progress, and continuance of that of New England*, London, 1658, contained in his grandson's collection entitled *America Painted to the Life*. Thomas Morton, of Merrymount, gave his own view of the situation in his *New English Canaan*, which has been edited for the Prince Society, with great learning, by C. F. Adams. Samuel Maverick also had his say in a valuable pamphlet entitled *A Description of New England*, which has only come to light since 1875 and has been edited by

Mr. Deane. Maverick is, of course, hostile to the Puritans. See also Lechford's *Plain Dealing in New England*, ed. J. H. Trumbull, 1867.

The earliest history of Massachusetts is by Winthrop himself, a work of priceless value. In 1790, nearly a century and a half after the author's death, it was published at Hartford. The best edition is that of 1853. In 1869 a valuable life of Winthrop was published by his descendant Robert Winthrop. Hubbard's *History of New England* (*Mass. Hist. Coll.*, 2d series, vols. v., vi.) is drawn largely from Winthrop and from Nathaniel Morton. There is much that is suggestive in William Wood's *New England's Prospect*, 1634, and Edward Johnson's *Wonder-working Providence of Zion's Saviour in New England*, 1654; the latter has been ably edited by W. F. Poole, Andover, 1867. The records of the Massachusetts government, from its founding in 1629 down to the overthrow of the charter in 1684, were edited by Dr. Shurtleff in 6 vols. quarto, 1853-54; and among the documents in the British Record Office, published since 1855, three volumes — *Calendar of State Papers, Colonial America*, vol. i., 1574-1660; vol. v., 1661-1668; vol. vii., 1669 — are especially useful. Of the later authorities the best is Hutchinson's *History of Massachusetts Bay*, the first volume of which, coming down to 1689, was published in Boston in 1764. The second volume, continuing the narrative to 1749, was published in 1767. The third volume, coming down to 1774, was found among the illustrious author's MSS. after his death, and was published in London in 1828. Hutchinson had access to many valuable documents since lost, and his sound judgment and critical acumen deserve the highest praise. In 1769 he published a volume of *Original Papers*, illustrating the period covered by the first volume of his history. Many priceless documents perished in the shameful sacking of his house by the Boston rioters, Aug. 26, 1765. The second volume of Hutchinson's *History* was continued to 1764 by G. R. Minot, 2 vols., 1798, and to 1820 by Alden Bradford, 3 vols., 1822-29. Of recent works, the best is Barry's *History of Massachusetts*, 3 vols., 1855-57. Many original authorities are collected in Young's *Chronicles of*

Massachusetts, Boston, 1846. Cotton Mather's *Magnalia Christi Americana,* London, 1702 (reprinted in 1820 and 1853), though crude and uncritical, is full of interest.

Many of the early Massachusetts documents relate to Maine. Of later books, especial mention should be made of Folsom's *History of Saco and Biddeford,* Saco, 1830; Willis's *History of Portland,* 2 vols., 1831-33 (2d ed. 1865); *Memorial Volume of the Popham Celebration,* Portland, 1862; Chamberlain's *Maine, Her Place in History,* Augusta, 1877. On New Hampshire the best general work is Belknap's *History of New Hampshire,* 3 vols., Phila., 1784-92; the appendix contains many original documents, and others are to be found in the *New Hampshire Historical Collections,* 8 vols., 1824-66.

The *Connecticut Colonial Records* are edited by Dr. J. H. Trumbull, 12 vols., 1850-82. The *Connecticut Historical Society's Collections,* 1860-70, are of much value. The best general work is Trumbull's *History of Connecticut,* 2 vols., Hartford, 1797. See also Stiles's *Ancient Windsor,* 2 vols., 1859-63; Cothren's *Ancient Woodbury,* 3 vols., 1854-79. Of the Pequot War we have accounts by three of the principal actors. Mason's *History of the Pequod War* is in the *Mass. Hist. Coll.,* 2d series, vol. viii.; Underhill's *News from America* is in the 3d series, vol. vi.; and Lyon Gardiner's narrative is in the 3d series, vol. iii. In the same volume with Underhill is contained *A True Relation of the late Battle fought in New England between the English and the Pequod Savages,* by Philip Vincent, London, 1638. The *New Haven Colony Records* are edited by C. J. Hoadly, 2 vols., Hartford, 1857-58. See also the *New Haven Historical Society's Papers,* 3 vols., 1865-80; Lambert's *History of New Haven,* 1838; Atwater's *History of New Haven,* 1881; Levermore's *Republic of New Haven,* Baltimore, 1886; Johnston's *Connecticut,* Boston, 1887. The best account of the Blue Laws is by J. H. Trumbull, *The True Blue Laws of Connecticut and New Haven, and the False Blue Laws invented by the Rev. Samuel Peters,* etc., Hartford, 1876. See also Hinman's *Blue Laws of New Haven Colony,* Hartford, 1838; Barber's *History and Antiquities of New Haven,* 1831; Peters's *His-*

tory of Connecticut, London, 1781. The story of the regicides is set forth in Stiles's *History of the Three Judges* [the third being Colonel Dixwell], Hartford, 1794; see also the *Mather Papers* in *Mass. Hist. Coll.*, 4th series, vol. viii.

The *Rhode Island Colonial Records* are edited by J. R. Bartlett, 7 vols., 1856–62. One of the best state histories ever written is that of S. G. Arnold, *History of the State of Rhode Island and Providence Plantations*, 2 vols., New York, 1859–60. Many valuable documents are reprinted in the *Rhode Island Historical Society's Collections*. The *History of New England, with particular reference to the denomination called Baptists*, by Rev. Isaac Backus, 3 vols., 1777–96, has much that is valuable relating to Rhode Island. The series of *Rhode Island Historical Tracts*, issued since 1878 by Mr. S. S. Rider, is of great merit. Biographies of Roger Williams have been written by J. D. Knowles, 1834; by William Gammell, 1845; and by Romeo Elton, 1852. Williams's works have been republished by the Narragansett Club in 6 vols., 1866. The first volume contains the valuable *Key to the Indian Languages of America*, edited by Dr. Trumbull. Williams's views of religious liberty are set forth in his *Bloudy Tenent of Persecution*, London, 1644; to which John Cotton replied in *The Bloudy Tenent washed and made White in the Blood of the Lamb*, London, 1647; Williams's rejoinder was entitled *The Bloudy Tenent made yet more Bloudy through Mr. Cotton's attempt to Wash it White*, London, 1652. The controversy was conducted on both sides with a candour and courtesy rare in that age. The titles of Williams's other principal works, *George Fox digged out of his Burrowes*, Boston, 1676; *Hireling Ministry none of Christ's*, London, 1652; and *Christenings make not Christians*, 1645; sufficiently indicate their character. The last-named tract was discovered in the British Museum by Dr. Dexter and edited by him in Rider's *Tracts*, No. xiv., 1881. The treatment of Roger Williams by the government of Massachusetts is thoroughly discussed in Dexter's *As to Roger Williams*, Boston, 1876. See also G. E. Ellis on "The Treatment of Intruders and Dissentients by the Founders of Massachusetts," in *Lowell Lectures*, Boston, 1869.

The case of Mrs. Hutchinson is treated, from a hostile and somewhat truculent point of view, in Thomas Welde's pamphlet entitled *A Short Story of the Rise, Reign, and Ruin of Antinomians, Familists, and Libertines that infected the Churches of New England*, London, 1644. It was answered in an anonymous pamphlet entitled *Mercurius Americanus*, republished for the Prince Society, Boston, 1876, with prefatory notice by C. H. Bell. Cotton's view of the theocracy may be seen in his *Milk for Babes, drawn out of the Breasts of both Testaments*, London, 1646; *Keyes of the Kingdom of Heaven;* and *Way of the Congregational Churches Cleared*, London, 1648. See also Thomas Hooker's *Survey of the Summe of Church Discipline*, London, 1648. The intolerant spirit of the time finds quaint and forcible expression in Nathaniel Ward's satirical book, *The Simple Cobbler of Aggawam*, 1647.

For the Gorton controversy the best original authorities are his own book entitled *Simplicitie's Defence against Seven-headed Polity*, London, 1646; and Winslow's answer entitled *Hypocracie Unmasked*, London, 1646. See also Mackie's *Life of Samuel Gorton*, Boston, 1845, and Brayton's *Defence of Samuel Gorton*, in Rider's *Tracts*, No. xvii.

For the early history of the Quakers, see Robert Barclay's *Inner Life of the Religious Societies of the Commonwealth*, London, 1876, — an admirable book. See also *New England a Degenerate Plant*, 1659; Bishop's *New England judged by the Spirit of the Lord*, 1661; Sewel's *History of the Quakers*, 1722; Besse's *Sufferings of the Quakers*, 1753; *The Popish Inquisition newly erected in New England*, London, 1659; *The Secret Works of a Cruel People made Manifest*, 1659; and the pamphlet of the martyrs Stevenson and Robinson, entitled *A Call from Death to Life*, 1660. John Norton's view of the case was presented in his book, *The Heart of New England Rent at the Blasphemies of the Present Generation*, London, 1660. See also J. S. Pike's *New Puritan*, New York, 1879; Hallowell's *Pioneer Quakers*, Boston, 1887; and his *Quaker Invasion of Massachusetts*, Boston, 1883; Brooks Adams, *The Emancipation of Massachusetts*, Boston, 1887; Ellis, *The Puritan Age and Rule*, Boston, 1888.

Some additional light upon the theocratic idea may be found in a treatise by the apostle Eliot, *The Christian Commonwealth; or, the Civil Polity of the Rising Kingdom of Jesus Christ*, London, 1659. An account of Eliot's missionary work is given in *The Day breaking, if not the Sun rising, of the Gospel with the Indians in New England*, London, 1647; and *The Glorious Progress of the Gospel amongst the Indians in New England*, 1649. See also Shepard's *Clear Sunshine of the Gospel breaking forth upon the Indians*, 1648; and Whitfield's *Light appearing more and more towards the Perfect Day*, 1651.

The principal authority for Philip's war is Hubbard's *Present State of New England, being a Narrative of the Troubles with the Indians*, 1677. Church's *Entertaining Passages relating to Philip's War*, published in 1716, and republished in 1865, with notes by Mr. Dexter, is a charming book. See also Mrs. Rowlandson's *True History*, Cambridge, Mass., 1682; Mather's *Brief History of the War*, 1676; Drake's *Old Indian Chronicle*, Boston, 1836; Gookin's *Historical Collections of the Indians in New England*, 1674; and *Account of the Doings and Sufferings of the Christian Indians*, in *Archæologia Americana*, vol. ii. Batten's *Journal* is the diary of a citizen of Boston, sent to England, and is now in MS. among the *Colonial Papers*. Mrs. Mary Pray's letter (Oct. 20, 1675) is in *Mass. Hist. Coll.*, 5th series, vol. i. p. 105.

The great storehouse of information for the Andros period is the *Andros Tracts*, 3 vols., edited for the Prince Society by W. H. Whitmore. See also Sewall's *Diary, Mass. Hist. Coll.*, 5th series, vols. v.–viii. Sewall has been appropriately called the Puritan Pepys. His book is a mirror of the state of society in Massachusetts at the time when it was beginning to be felt that the old theocratic idea had been tried in the balance and found wanting. There is a wonderful charm in such a book. It makes one feel as if one had really "been there" and taken part in the homely scenes, full of human interest, which it so naively portrays. Anne Bradstreet's works have been edited by J. H. Ellis, Charlestown, 1867.

For further references and elaborate bibliographical discussions, see Winsor's *Narrative and Critical History of America*, vol. iii. ; and his *Memorial History of Boston*, 4 vols., Boston, 1880. There is a good account of the principal New England writers of the seventeenth century, with illustrative extracts, in Tyler's *History of American Literature*, 2 vols., New York, 1878. For extracts see also the first two volumes of Stedman and Hutchinson's *Library of American Literature*, New York, 1888.

In conclusion I would observe that town histories, though seldom written in a philosophical spirit and apt to be quite amorphous in structure, are a mine of wealth for the philosophic student of history.

INDEX.

Abolitionists and Republicans, 67.
Acadia, 275.
Achaian league, 22.
Adams, C. F., 113 note.
Adams, Samuel, 105, 117, 175, 246.
Adoption, absorption of savage tribes by, 209.
Altolian league, 22.
Albigenses, 40-42, 46.
Alexander (Wamsutta), 211.
Alexandria, 6.
Alfred, 18.
Allyn, John, 268.
Alsace, 263.
Anabaptists, 182.
Andover, 233.
Andros, Sir E., 267-273 ; Lady, 269.
Antinomians, 117-120, 135, 154, 163, 167, 248.
Appleton, Major Samuel, 223.
Aquedneck, 120, 166.
Aquinas, 19.
Architecture, Gothic, 19.
Armada, the Invincible, 61, 70, 102.
Armagnacs, 35.
Arminius, 24.
Arnold, Benedict, governor of Rhode Island, 167.
Arnold, Matthew, 147.
Arnold, William, 167.
Artaxerxes, 14.
Arundel, Earl of, 114.
Ashawonks, squaw sachem, 235.
Assistants, Board of, 96, 105, 124 ; disagreement with deputies, 106-108, 173, 187, 188.
Assowamsett Pond, 214.
Assyria, 10, 12, 21.
Atheism, charges of, 91.
Attika, 12.
Augustine, Bp. of Hippo, 5.
Augustine, missionary to Britain, 27.
Austerfield, 64.
Austin, Anne, 183.
Avignon, exile of popes at, 4, 34.

Bacon, Sir Nicholas, 61.
Bacon, Roger, 20.
Barons' War, 31.
Batten's journal, 220.
Baxter, Richard, 115.

Beers, Captain, 219.
Bellingham, Richard, 183.
Benedict, St., 18.
Bermudas, 161.
Bible, Eliot's, 203.
Bible, English version of, 53-55.
Black, Joseph, 152.
Blackstone, William, 92, 104.
Blair education bill, 14.
Blake, Robert, 116.
Bloody Brook, 219, 220, 221.
Blue Laws, 136.
Bogomilians, 39.
Bohemia, 42.
Boniface, St., 18.
Bosnia, 42.
Boston, Lincolnshire, 63, 110.
Boston, Mass., 63, 104, 117, 168, 172; population in 1680, 258.
Bosworth, battle of, 99.
Botolph's, St., 110.
Braddock's defeat, 206.
Bradford, William, 72, 73, 80, 83, 85, 90, 91.
Bradford, William, the younger, 220, 223.
Bradstreet, Anne, 261.
Bradstreet, Simon, 220, 260, 261, 273.
Branford, 136.
Brewster, William, 68, 71, 73, 80, 82.
Bridgewater, 233.
Britain, English conquest of, 26, 28.
Brookfield, 215-217, 230.
Brown, Robert, 66-68.
Bryce, James, 3.
Buckingham, Duke of, 89, 97, 98.
Buckle, H. T., 152.
Bunyan, John, 51, 115, 244.
Burgundians, French party, 35.
Burgundians, tribe, 26.
Burleigh, Lord, 61, 66, 68.
Burns, Robert, 152.
Byzantine empire, 2.

Cæsar, C. J., 5, 8, 19, 28.
Calverts in Maryland, 155.
Calvin, John, 57-59, 61.
Cambridge, Eng., 62, 110 ; meeting of Puritans at, 101.
Cambridge, Mass. (Newtown, 104, 105, 124, 125,) 126 ; name changed, 110.

290 INDEX.

Cambridge Platform, 177.
Canonchet, 221-225, 234.
Canonicus, 85.
Cape Ann, 78, 92.
Cape Cod, 76, 78, 81.
Cape Elizabeth, 78.
Carlisle, Earl of, 113.
Castle Island. 113, 272.
Cathari, 39-42, 43.
Catholics excluded from House of Commons, 248; relations with Quakers, 191.
Cavendish, Thomas, 61.
Century, fifth, 27; sixth, 27; thirteenth, 19, 20, 30, 33, 38-40; fourteenth, 35; fifteenth, 35; seventeenth, 7, 36.
Champlain's defeat of the Mohawks, 206.
Charles the Great, 4, 18, 29.
Charles I., 50, 95, 97-100, 111-113, 137, 160, 161, 197, 246, 266.
Charles II., 120, 191, 194, 195, 196, 198, 247, 253, 260, 262, 263, 264, 266, 267.
Charles river, 78, 94.
Charlestown, 104, 113.
Charter granted to Company of Massachusetts Bay, 96, 100; transferred to New England, 102; threatened by Charles I., 113; by Long Parliament, 161; by the royal commissioners, 196; annulled by Charles II., 265; effects of annulling it, 266; new one granted by William and Mary, 267.
Charter Oak, 268.
Charters of English towns attacked by Charles II., 264.
Chaucer, Geoffrey, 20.
Chauncey, Charles, 251.
Cheeshahteaumuck, Caleb, 202.
Chelmsford, 233.
Chicago, 208.
Child, Robert, 175-177, 192.
Chlodwig, King of the Franks, 3.
Christendom, 13.
Christianity destroyed in Britain, 27.
Christison, Wenlock, 189, 190, 197.
Church, Benjamin, 222, 225, 229, 235, 237.
Cicero, M. T., 5.
Civil War in America, 22, 100, *note*.
Civilis, 24.
Clarke, John, 162.
Claverhouse, John, 269.
Cleveland, Grover, 24, 31.
Climate of New England, 77.
Coke, Sir E., 99, 114.
Coligny, Gaspard, 58.
College, Stephen, 263.
Commons, first House of, 31; extraordinary scenes in, 98, 99.
Conant, Roger, 92, 93, 95.
Concord, Indian village near, 204.
Confederacy, the New England, 153-198; its constitution, 158; its weakness, 159; its formation involved a tacit assumption of sovereignty, 160, 192; weakened by suppression of New Haven, 198.
Congregationalism and self-government, 59.
Congress, 28.
Connecticut, founding of, 122-128, 249; its place in American history, 128; obtains a charter, 195; partly rescinded, 268; hidden, 268; restored, 274.
Cooper, J. F., 218.
Corporate responsibility, 173, 220.
Cortes, Spanish, 33.
Cotton, John, 110, 117, 118, 124, 135, 136, 151, 178, 179.
Council for New England, 89, 112.
County meetings, 28.
Covenant of grace and of works, 118.
Coventry, Henry, 256.
Coverdale, Miles, 55.
Cranfield, Edward, 259.
Cromwell, Oliver, 8, 45, 47, 51, 55, 58, 62, 117, 137, 139, 160, 162, 185, 186, 193, 228, 256, 259, 271.
Cross of St. George cut out of the flag by Endicott, 116.
Cushing, F. H., 208.
Cuttyhunk, 76.

Danforth, Thomas, 220.
Danish invasions of England, 29.
Dante, 5, 20.
Dark Ages, 18.
Dartmouth, Eng., 81.
Dartmouth, Mass., massacre at, 215.
Davenport, John, 135, 136, 194, 196, 197, 251.
Davison, Sir W., 68.
Death, savage's idea of, 211.
Death penalty, 187.
Deerfield, 217, 219.
De Forest's *History of the Indians in Connecticut*, 171, 210, *notes*.
Delaware Indians, 206.
Delegated power, 16, 22.
Delft haven, 80.
Democracy discussed between Winthrop and Hooker, 124.
Denison, George, defeats and captures Canonchet, 234.
Deputies, chamber of, 106; disagreements with Board of Assistants, 106-108, 173, 187, 188.
Descartes, René, 151.
Despotism the weakest form of government, 23.
Devonshire, 63.
Digges, Sir Dudley, 99.
Diocletian, 17.
Dorchester, Eng., 93.
Dorchester, Mass., 104, 113, 124, 125, 126.
Dorchester adventurers, 92.
Dorset, 63, 92.
Dover, N. H., 119, 259.

INDEX. 291

Doyle, J. A., 172, 185, 255, 256, *notes*.
Drake, Sir F., 61.
Dudley, Lord Guilford, 103.
Dudley, Joseph, 257, 258, 261, 262, 265, 267, 270, 271, 272.
Dudley, Robert, Earl of Leicester, 103, 258.
Dudley, Thomas, 102, 103, 257.
Dunbar, battle of, 140, 193.
Dunster, Henry, 203.
Dutch, 60, 70, 122, 123, 155, 162, 196.
Dyer, Mary, 188, 189, 191.

East Anglia, heresy in, 62; contributions to the Puritan exodus, 63, 141; familiar look to a New Englander, 64.
East Greenwich, manor of, 174.
Eaton, Theophilus, 134.
Ecclesiastical beginnings of Massachusetts, 108, 109.
"Ecclesiastical Polity," by Richard Hooker, 65.
Edinburgh, 153.
Education, popular, 151.
Edward I., 19, 44.
Edward II., 40.
Edward III., 44.
Edward IV., 64.
Eliot, Sir John, 99, 100.
Eliot, John, apostle, 202-205, 208-210, 237.
Elizabeth, 44, 57, 59-61, 65-68, 70; conversation with a lady of the court, 60.
Elizabeth Islands, 76.
Emmanuel College, 110, 261.
Empire, Holy Roman, 2-5, 19, 34.
Endicott, John, 94, 95, 97, 104, 108, 115, 116, 151, 179, 183, 184, 187, 188, 190, 191, 197.
England, importance of part played by her in seventeenth century, 37, 50-51; union with Scotland, 21; church of, 44.
English method of nation-making, 20-46; nature of Puritan exodus, 140.
Episcopal worship forbidden in Massachusetts, 108, 260; introduced by Andros, 268, 269.
Episcopius, 73.
Erasmus, 65.
Essex, county of, 63.
Essex, Earl of, 88.
Ethical nature of the Puritan ideal, 147.
Exeter, N. H., 119, 259.

Fairfax, Sir T., 131.
Fairfield, 133.
Familists, 164.
Federal Convention of 1788, 128.
Federalism, pacific tendency of, 21, 22.
Ferdinand of Aragon, 5, 57.
Feudalism, its destruction, 35.
Filmer, Sir R., 264.
Fisher, Mary, 183, 184.

Fleet street, tumult in, 67.
Florida, Huguenots massacred in, 61, 79.
Fortune, ship, 83.
Fox, George, 179.
France, 36; damaged by persecution of Albigenses and Huguenots, 40, 42, 46, 47; failure of Reformation in, 47.
Francis of Assisi, 20-38.
Francis II., last Roman emperor, 5.
Franklin, Benjamin, 24.
Franks, 26.
Frederick II. of Prussia, 48.
Frederick II., Roman emperor, 19, 34.
Freeman, E. A., 19.
French in America, 154, 274, 277.
French Revolution, 48, 51.

Gardiner, Sir Christopher, 104, 109.
Gardiner, S. R., 60, 97, 100, *notes*.
Gauls, 21.
Geneva, 57.
George III., 273, 277.
Germanic invasions of Roman empire, 17-28.
Gettysburg, battle of, 51.
Gilbert, Sir H., 61.
Gladstone, W. E., 31.
Goffe, William, 193, 217, 218, 257.
Gookin, Daniel, 221.
Gorges, Sir Ferdinando, 88, 89, 90, 92, 94, 95, 104, 109, 112, 113, 119, 154, 155, 156, 254, 255, 259.
Gorges, Ferdinando, the younger, 260.
Gorges, John, 95, 104.
Gorges, Robert, 95.
Gorton, Samuel, 162-174, 192.
Gortonoges, 170.
Gosnold, Bartholomew, 76.
Goths, 26.
Grafton, Indian village near, 204.
Grants of territory, conflicting, 90, 92, 94, 95, 104.
Greek cities, 12, 22, 248.
Green, J. R., 69, *note*.
Gregory of Tours, 19.
Gregory the Great, 18.
Gregory VII., 38.
Gregory XI., 43.
Grey, Lady Jane, 103.
Grindal, Edmund, 61.
Groton, 233.
Guiana, 79.
Guises, 46, 56, 61.
Gustavus, Adolphus, 101.

Hadley, 193, 233; mysterious stranger at, 217, 218.
Halfway covenant, 250, 252.
Hamilton, Alexander, 124.
Hamilton, Marquis of, 112.
Hampden, John, 51, 105, 193.
Hampton, N. H., 119, 259.
Hampton Court, conference at, 70-71.
Hardscrabble, 123.
Hartford, 122, 126-128, 170, 209.
Harvard, John, 110.

292　INDEX.

Harvard College, 110, 117, 130, 175.
Hatfield, 217, 233.
Hawkins, Sir John, 61.
Hell-huddle, 123.
Hengest, 27.
Henry IV. (*England*), 41.
Henry VII., 35, 266.
Henry VIII., 43, 44, 56.
Henry III. (*France*), 46.
Henry IV., 46.
Hertfordshire, 135.
Higginson, Francis, 96, 108.
High Commission, court of, 109.
Hildebrand, 38.
History, changes in the study of, 2, 9.
Hobbes, Thomas, 151.
Holmes, William, 122.
Holland, English exiles in, 68, 73, 74, 135; toleration in, 74.
Hooker, Richard, 65.
Hooker, Thomas, 110, 124, 126, 127, 128, 136.
Hubbard, William, 211, 218, 229, 234, 257.
Hudson river, 94.
Huguenots, 47, 60, 70, 74, 80, 93, 101, 139; in Florida, 61, 79; in Massachusetts, 141.
Hull, 63.
Humane feelings allowed to develop through decline of war, 100, *note*, 227.
Hume, David, 152.
Hunter, John, 152.
Hutchinson, Anne, 117-129, 166, 188.
Hutchinson, Edward, 215.
Hutchinson, Thomas, 120, 218, 258.
Hutton, James, 152.

"Incorruptible Key," Gorton's, 165, *note*.
Indians, 26, 155; their dealings with the settlers, 199-210; missionary work, 201-204, 208-210; sold into slavery, 237
Innocent III., 19, 34, 40, 42.
Inquisition, 40-42, 153.
Inquisitorial administration of justice, 250.
Ipswich, 63, 270.
Iroquois league, 121, 206.
Isabella the Catholic, 57.
Italy consolidated under Rome, 12.

Jabberwok, 137.
James I., 41, 52, 68-71, 80, 87, 89, 97, 161.
James II., 191, 267, 271, 272, 275.
James the Printer, 238.
Jamestown, 77, 105.
Jefferson, Thomas, 24, 117, 124, 246.
Jeffreys, George, 264.
Jesus College, 202.
Jinghis Khan, 50.
John, King of England, 31.
Johnson, Edward, 172, 243.
Johnston, Alexander, 128, *note*.

Jury trial abandoned in the New Haven colony, 136, 250.
Justinian, 2.

Keayne, Robert, and his pig, 106-108.
Kennebec river, 76, 77, 94.
Kent, 135.
Keroualle, Louise de, 263.
Kings have become harmless, 32.
King's Chapel founded, 269.
"King's Missive," the, 191.
Kingdoms, modern growth of, 34-36.
Kirk, the Scotch, 153.
Kirke, Percy, 266, 267.
Knighton, Henry, 42.
Knox, John, 55.
Kynaxa, battle of, 10.

Lancaster, 215, 216, 230.
La Salle, 274.
Latimer, Hugh, 44, 45, 51, 55.
Laud, William, 109, 114, 115, 135.
Leddra, William, 189.
Lenox, Earl of, 89.
Leo III., 4.
Leverett, John, 215, 255, 256, 260.
Levermore, C. H., 187, *note*.
Lewes, battle of, 31.
Leyden, home of the Pilgrims, 73.
Liberty, religious, not the object of the Puritan exodus, 144-146.
Light, supernatural or inward, 118, 180.
Locke, John, 48, 51.
Lollards, 42-46, 52-56.
London Company, 75, 79, 81, 89.
Londonderry, N. H., 141.
Long Parliament, 137.
Longland, John, 62.
Lords of Trade, 255.
Lorraine, 263.
Lothrop, Captain, 217, 219.
Louis IX., 19.
Louis XII., 5.
Louis XIII., 98.
Louis XIV., 36, 47, 80, 262, 263, 271, 275.
Lucullus's villa, 1.
Luther, Martin, 44, 58, 65.
Lydians, 21.
Lyell, Sir C., 152.

Magna Charta, 12, 127, *note*.
Mahomet II., 48.
Mahomet III., 184.
Manichæans, 39.
Map of New England, Smith's, 78
Marathon, 139.
Marblehead, 221.
Marlborough, 233.
Marston Moor, 51.
Martha's Vineyard, 76, 201, 204, 275.
Mary Stuart, 61.
Mary Tudor, 41, 57.
Mason, John, captain in Pequot war, 131-133.
Mason, John, grantee of lands in the

Piscataqua country, 94, 112, 113, 119, 154, 254, 255, 259.
Mason, Robert, 255.
Massachusetts annexes New Hampshire towns, 154, 259, and Maine, 259; population in 1643, 159; and in 1680, 258; brought into sympathy with Virginia, 276.
Massachusetts Bay, Company of, 96.
Massa-wachusetts, or "At-the-great Hill" tribe, 120.
Massasoit, 84, 116, 120, 211.
Mather, Cotton, charges against the Quakers, 181; remark about the theocratic idea, 197.
Mather, Increase, 218, 219, 237, 251, 257, 265, 272.
Maverick, Samuel, 90, 92, 104, 175, 176, 192, 196.
Mayflower, ship, 49, 61, 81, 90; the compact drawn up in her cabin, 127, *note*.
Mayhew, Thomas, 201.
Mazzini, 51.
Medfield, 233.
Media, 12.
Melanchthon, 58.
Melville, Andrew, 69.
Mendon, 215, 233, 238.
Merrimack river, 94, 259.
Merrymount, 90, 91, 104, 112.
Miantonomo, 68-72, 207, 221.
Middle class in England, 30.
Middleborough, 214, 215, 233.
Milford, 135, 136.
Milman, H. H., 43, 181, *notes*.
Milton, John, 48, 51, 55, 185, 228, 264.
Mohawks, 121, 122, 133, 206.
Mohegans, 121, 122, 131, 133, 169-172, 207, 209, 212, 234.
Monadnock, 121.
Monmouth, Duke of, 100, 260, 267.
Montesquieu, 51.
Montfort, Simon de, 31-33.
Moors in Spain, 11, 37.
Morton, Thomas, 90, 91, 104, 109, 174.
Mount Hope, 214, 215.
Münster, 182.
"Mugwump" in Eliot's Bible, 203.

Nantes, Edict of, 47, 141.
Nantasket, 91.
Nantucket, 201, 204.
Napoleon, 48.
Narragansetts, 85, 121, 131, 133, 168-172, 207, 209, 212, 221-226, 234.
Naseby, battle of, 31, 51, 193.
Natick, Indian village, 204, 213.
Nation-making, 7, 37.
Naumkeag, 93, 95.
Navigation laws, 254, 256.
Netherlands, 33.
New Amsterdam, 123, 196.
Newark founded, 196.
"New England's Jonas cast up at London," 177.

"New England's Salamander discovered," 177.
New Hampshire, beginnings of, 120, 154, 259, 275.
New Haven colony, 134-137; annexed to Connecticut, 192-196.
Newhouse, Thomas, 182.
New Netherlands, 122.
Newport, R. I., 120, 157, 166.
New South Church, 252.
Newtown, *see* Cambridge, Mass.
Nichewaug, 121.
Nichols, Richard, 193, 196, 259.
Nipmucks, 121, 209, 212, 215, 219, 225, 230, 233.
Noddle's Island, 92, 176.
Norfolk, 63.
Norman conquest of England, 30.
North, Roger, 264.
North Virginia, 75-78.
Northampton, 233.
Norton, John, 179, 180, 251, 261.
Norwich, scene of Miantonomo's defeat 169.
Nyantics, 121, 131.

Odovakar, 1, 3, 48.
Oldham, John, 104, 125, 129.
"Old Mortality," 269.
Old South Church, 182, 231, 252, 265, 269.
Orestes, 1.
Oriental method of nation-making, 9-11, 14, 21.
Otis, James, 278.
Oxford university, 62, 110, 264; parliament, 263.

Paine, Thomas, 245.
Palfrey, J. G., 140, 201, *note*.
Papacy, 3, 34.
Parkman, F., 206, *note*, 212.
Parliament turned out of doors by Charles I.; creates a board of commissioners for superintending colonial affairs, 157; question as to its authority over the colonies, 160-162, 174, 175.
Paulicians, 39.
Pawtuxet, 166, 167, 168, 234.
Pembroke, Earl of, 89.
Penn, William, 191, 206.
Pennsylvania, why so long unmolested by Indians, 205-206.
Penobscot river, 78.
Pension jobbery, 14.
Pequots, 121, 122, 128-133, 168, 199, 204, 207, 210.
Persecuting spirit, origin of, 163.
Persecution, mildness of, in England, 40-43.
Persia, 10, 12, 21,
Petition of Right, 98, 99.
Peters, Rev. Samuel, 136, 137.
"Peveril of the Peak," 218.
Philip Augustus, 40.
Philip II., of Spain, 36, 57, 61.

294 INDEX.

Philip (Metacom), 211-216, 230-233, 235-237, 239, 240; his son, 232, 236.
Picton, J. A., 100, *note*.
Pierce, Captain, 234.
Pierson, Abraham, 196.
Pig, Keayne's, 106-108.
Pilgrims at Leyden, 73, 79.
Pine-tree shillings, 192, 254.
Piscataqua river, 91, 94, 121, 259.
Pitt, William, 48.
Plymouth Company, 75, 77, 82, 86, 89.
Plymouth colony, 78, 82, 105; population of, 86; annexed to Massachusetts, 275.
Podunks, 209.
Point Judith, 121.
Pokanokets, *see* Wampanoags.
Pontiac's war, 206, 212.
Popham colony, 77, 81.
Portsmouth, N. H., 119, 259.
Portsmouth, R. I., 120, 157, 166.
Portland, Oregon, 140.
Præmunire, 43.
Pray, Mary, 221.
Praying Indians, 204, 221, 238.
Presbyterian cabal, 162, 175-177.
Presbyterianism, 66, 69, 71.
Pride's Purge, 177.
Primitive society, 8.
Protective tariffs, 14, 32.
Protestantism, beginnings of, 37-42.
Providence, R. I., 116, 158, 166, 167, 169, 172.
Puritanism as a militant force, 7, 45, 46, 51, 59, 243-247.
Pym, John, 51.

Quakers, 162, 173; their opinions, 179-181; persecuted in Boston, 182-190, 221; they win the victory, 190, 197; why Charles II. defended them, 191; their relations to the Indians, 205, 206.
Quincy, Josiah, 111, *note*.
Quinnipiack, 135.
Quinsigamond, 121.

Raleigh, Sir W., 76, 103.
Randolph, Edward, 218, 255-258, 262, 265.
Ratcliffe, Robert, 270, *note*.
Rationalistic spirit among the Puritans of New England and Scotland, 150-153.
Redemptioners, 142.
Reformation in England, 42-57.
Regicide judges, 192-194, 218, 257.
Religious liberty not the motive of the Puritan exodus, 144-146.
Representation, no taxation without, 31, 105.
Representative assemblies unknown to the ancients, 16, 22; found generally among the Teutonic tribes, 25; die out on the continent of Europe, 33.
Republicans and abolitionists, 67.

Republics, fallacy of the notion that they must be small, 23.
Respectable character of the migration to New England, 141.
Restitution, edict of, 101.
Rhode Island, toleration in, 154, 156; asks for a charter, 157; noble attitude with reference to Quakers, 184-186; obtains a charter, 196; it is partly rescinded, 268; restored, 274.
Ribault, Jean, 61.
Rich, Sir N., 99.
Richard II., 42, 71.
Roanoke island, 111.
Robinson, John, 72, 73, 81, 108.
Robinson, William, 188.
Robsart, Amy, 103.
Rochelle, fall of, 93, 101.
Roman church, 18-20, 38.
Roman empire, when did it come to an end, 1-5, 48, 49.
Roman method of nation-making, 12-21.
Romulus Augustus, 1.
Roses, war of the, 35, 55, 99.
Rousseau, J. J., 51.
Rowlandson, Joseph, 230.
Rowlandson, Mary, 231-233, 239.
Royal Society founded, 195.
Rumford, Count, 5.
Russell, Lord William, 264, 273.

Sachem's Plain, 171.
St. Giles's Church, Edinburgh, 113.
Salem, Mass., 93, 95, 104, 108, 112, 115, 116, 245.
Salem, Oregon, 140.
Sandys, Sir E., 79.
Sassacus, 128-130, 132, 133, 212.
Sausamon, 213, 214.
Savoy, 42, 47.
Say and Sele, Lord, 123.
Saybrook, 123, 125.
Scituate, 176, 233.
Scotland, great achievements of, 152.
Scott, Sir W., 123, 152, 218, 269.
Scottish prisoners sent to Boston, 140.
Scrooby, 64, 71.
Sedgmoor, battle of, 99.
Separatists, 66-68, 72, 108.
Servetus, Michael, 58.
Shaftesbury, Lord, 263.
Shakespeare, William, 89.
Shawmut peninsula, 92.
Shawomet, 168-174.
Sheldon, George, 218, *note*.
Shepard, Thomas, 203.
Sherman, Mrs., and the stray pig, 106-108.
Shillings, pine-tree, 192, 254.
Shipmoney, 113.
Sidney, Algernon, 48, 51, 246, 264, 273.
Sigismund, Roman emperor, 38.
Skelton, Samuel, 108.
Slavery, 14.
Smith, Adam, 152.
Smith, John, 77-79, 82, 88.

INDEX.   295

Solemn League and Covenant, 113.
Somerset, 63.
Southampton, 81.
Southampton, Earl of, 89.
Southold, L. I., 136.
Spain, 11, 36, 37.
Speedwell, ship, 80, 81.
Spoils system, 14.
Springfield, 126, 215, 220, 233.
Stagnation of the stream of human life, 17.
Stamford, 120, 136.
Stamp Act congress, 32.
Standish, Miles, 80, 82, 84.
States General, 33.
Steele, A., 74, *note*.
Stein, 51.
Stevenson, Marmaduke, 188.
Stiles, Ezra, 174, *note*.
Stirling, Earl of, 113.
Stoughton, William, 143, 220.
Strafford, Earl of, 109, 116, 119.
Stubbs, William, 25.
Sudbury, 233.
Suevi, 26.
Suffolk, 63.
Suffrage restricted to church members, in Massachusetts, 109, 123, 175, 194, 195, 248–252, 254, 258, 276 ; in New Haven, 136, 196, 250.
Susquehannocks, 86, 205.
Swanzey, massacre at, 214, 238.
Switzerland, 21, 33.

Talcott, Major, completes the overthrow of the Narragansetts, 234.
Tamerlane, 50.
Tarratines, 121, 239.
Taunton, 213, 215, 235.
Tel-el-Kebir, 11.
Templars, 40.
Teutonic institutions less modified in England than in Germany, 29.
Texas seed-bill, 24.
Thames river, Conn., 121, 130.
Thanksgiving, 83.
Theocratic ideal of the Puritans, 146 ; broken down, 197 ; its services to political liberty, 247.
Thirty Years War, 101.
Thompson, Benjamin, 5.
Tilly, Count, 133.
Toleration, Dudley's verses on, 103 ; Roger Williams's theory of, 115 ; views of Cotton and Winthrop, 178 ; true theory expressed by Vane, 185.
Torquemada, 38, 245.
Torture, how the Indian likes to enjoy it, 231.
Toryism in New England, birth of, 257.
Toulouse, Counts of, 40.
Tours, battle of, 139.
Town-meetings, 27.
Trajan, 19.
Trastamare, feuds of the, 35.
Treat, Robert, 219, 223, 224, 265.

Turgot, 51.
Turks, 11, 14.
Turner, Captain, defeats the Nipmucks, 234.
Tyndall, William, 55.
Tyranny and insurrection in Boston, 270–273.

Uncas, 131, 169–172, 209, 210.
Underhill, John, 118, 131–133.
Union among colonies needed for military reasons, 274.
United States, 21, 277.
Universities, Puritanism in the, 62.

Vandals, 26.
Vane, Sir Henry, 48, 116, 118, 119, 129, 185, 246.
Van Twiller, Wouter, 122.
Vassall, William, 175–177, 192.
Verres, Caius, 13.
Virginia, 30, 75, 79, 93, 141, 142.
Virginia Company, 75 ; suppressed by James I., 161.
Voltaire, 5, 51.
Vulgate, 54.

Wadsworth, Capt. Samuel, 230, 233.
Wadsworth, Capt. (Charter Oak), 268.
Waldron, Major, 239.
Walford, Thomas, 104.
Walsingham, Sir F., 61.
Wallenstein, 103.
Walters, Lucy, 260.
Wampanoags, 84, 120, 209, 234.
Wampum as a legal tender, 254.
Wardwell, Lydia, 182.
Warfare not an essential part of the English method of nation-making, 21–22 ; with savages sure to be truculent, 228–229.
Warwick, 174, 234.
Warwick, Earl of, 157, 173, 261.
Washington, George, 31, 102, 139, 193.
Washington, Sir Henry, 193.
Watertown, 104, 105, 106, 124, 125, 126.
Wattaconoges, 170.
Welde, Thomas, 202.
"Wept of Wish-ton-Wish," 218.
Wequash, 204.
Wessagusset, 90, 93.
Weston, Thomas, 90.
Wethersfield, 125, 126.
Weymouth, attack on, 233.
Weymouth, George, 76, 77, 88.
Whalley, Edward, 192, 193, 218.
White, John, 93, 95, 97.
White trash, 142.
Willard, Samuel, 269, 272.
Willard, Simon, 216, 217, 272.
William the Silent, 58, 68.
William III., 272–274.
Williams, Roger, 114–116, 151, 154, 157, 158, 166, 167, 170, 178, 184–186, 226, 248.
Wilson, Deborah, 182.

Wilson, John, 118. 188, 251.
Windsor, Conn., 122, 123, 125, 126.
Winslow, Edward, 85, 160, 177.
Winslow, John, 272.
Winslow, Josiah, 199, 200, 213, 220, 222, 225, 229.
Winthrop, John, 102, 103, 106, 113, 116, 117, 118, 119, 123, 124, 136, 141, 146, 151, 174, 175, 178, 179, 250, 252.
Winthrop, John, the younger, 123, 186, 195, 220.
Wise, John, 271, 278.
Wollaston, Captain, 91.

"Wonder-working Providence," 243-247
Worcester, battle of, 140, 192; capture of, 193.
Worcester, Mass., 215, 233.
Wrentham, 233.
Wyclif, John, 42, 43, 52, 55, 59, 181.

Yorkshire, 135.
Yorktown, 31.

Zeno, Roman emperor, 3.
Zuñis, 208.

www.ingramcontent.com/pod-product-compliance
Lightning Source LLC
Chambersburg PA
CBHW022023240426
43667CB00042B/1070